FIRE IN HIS BONES

Oswald J. Smith.

Fire in His Bones

◆◆◆

The official biography of
OSWALD · J · SMITH
by Lois Neely

Tyndale House
Publishers, Inc.
Wheaton, Illinois

All Scripture references are taken from
the *King James Version* of the Bible
unless otherwise noted.

First printing, December 1982

Library of Congress Catalog Card Number 82-50693
ISBN 0-8423-0869-5

Printed in the United States of America

Then I recalled the dreams that cannot die,
The fires that burn forever in the soul
Like some volcanic force that must erupt
And pour its passion in *one living flame*
Of holiness and sanctified desire.

Oswald Jeffrey Smith

His Word in my heart
is like
fire that burns in my bones
and I cannot
hold it any longer.

Jeremiah 20:9, *The Living Bible*

CONTENTS

FOREWORD
by Billy Graham

The name, Oswald J. Smith, symbolizes worldwide evangelization. Some men of God are called to minister the gospel to a city, others to a nation; and a few in each century to the whole world. Oswald J. Smith is a prophet to the nations of the whole world.

His evangelistic campaigns at home and abroad have been among the greatest and most successful in the history of the Christian Church. His missionary zeal and vision have had no equal or even parallel in the twentieth century.

On repeated and protracted itineraries, he has himself gone to the ends of the earth with the gospel. Where he has not been personally able to go, his words on radio and television and his pamphlets, books, and hymns have communicated the gospel of Jesus Christ, whom he so deeply loves.

No other man has influenced so many people in so many diverse ways. His life is a shining example to young and old throughout Asia, Europe, Africa, South America, and the islands of the sea, as well as across the British Isles and North America.

He is the most remarkable man I have ever met. His books have been used of the Holy Spirit to sear into the very depths of my soul and have had a tremendous influence on my personal life and ministry. I have counted it one of the greatest privileges the Lord ever gave me to know this man, to call him "friend." All of us who know him and love him are amazed at his vitality, zeal, and continued strength for the Master whom he has served so faithfully for over seventy years.

Dr. Smith will go down in history as the greatest combination pastor, hymn writer, missionary statesman, and evangelist of our time.

FOREWORD
by Paul Brainerd Smith

To say the least, it is very difficult to find someone who you believe can be trusted to write a biography of your own father. Years ago Dr. J. Edwin Orr wrote a very short one called *Always Abounding.* Then in 1969 Doug Hall wrote a much more definitive story, *Not Made for Defeat.* Orr, of course, has written thousands of pages about worldwide revival while Hall has become a prolific writer of secular detective stories.

Who could do an adequate job after these two authors — one that would bring the story to its conclusion and also give some sort of feeling about the "real man"? Who would take the time to wade through the enormous amount of material that my father had collected and kept? Mother used to say that he lived and kept records right from the beginning as if he expected someone to write his story someday.

Lois Neely is a godly person whose heart beat with Father's. She is a professional writer and agreed to write the book the moment I asked her — almost as if the Holy Spirit had been leading her in this direction even before I opened my mouth. I think she has done a superb job. I really believe she has portrayed not only the man and his deeds, but also his heart and his feelings.

Father has been the most "one-track" man I have ever

known. He lived for his work and spent nearly all his time on it. Our family basked in this kind of service and love that blessed us, gave us confidence, stabilized us, and enriched our lives without his having to "climb down from building the wall" in order to play ball with us and take us to the country fair.

I shudder to think how inferior our lives would have been had he taken the advice of most psychologists and stayed home with his family when God had called him to minister to the world.

Because of the slow forms of transportation in the early days — trains and ships — it was not unusual for my father to be gone four to six months at a time. But we never suffered or resented his lifestyle. He was never a stranger to us. We loved and respected him and were extremely proud that God had given us a father whom He was using to such an extent.

Maybe part of this was because we all knew that my father lived where he preached. The day's battle was fought in his "prayer closet," so the rest of the work was no real problem. I would sum his philosophy: "Wage the war before you face the world; then the world will not be all that difficult." And his world was not that difficult. He worked hard, but never seemed to be in a hurry. He never procrastinated. He didn't try to look busy. He just worked — often months ahead of the deadlines.

To my father, whatever he did was the most important thing in the world, and somehow the rest of the family was continually caught up in the excitement that he always exuded.

My brother, Glen, and my sister, Hope, went to Sunday school more faithfully than I, but perhaps I attended the church services — and there were many of them — more often than they. I can still preach many of my father's sermons almost verbatim. Now that he is inactive, I actually use a great deal of his material. It's far too important to let die. I've been using his missionary message about the feeding of the 5,000, using his actual words: " 'Those people in the front rows have had helping after helping, and we haven't had the first helping of bread and fish.' And they would have been justified in their complaint."

Then I quote his most famous line, the question around which he built his entire life and my life: "Why should anybody hear the gospel twice before everybody has heard it once?"

INTRODUCTION

Oswald Jeffrey Smith: spanning two eras and three worlds with an evangelistic fervor that burned as brightly in his ninety-second year as it did when he preached his first sermon seventy-four years earlier. In the style of the old-time, itinerant evangelist, a young Oswald carried the gospel of Jesus Christ on horse and muleback across the Canadian prairies and over the Kentucky mountains, moving to repentance the crowds that gathered even then in response to his rousing, revival-type preaching. Traveling to over seventy countries by boat, train, and jet plane, he preached the simple Christian gospel to sophisticated city masses and primitive jungle throngs. In addition he made scores of evangelistic trips crisscrossing this continent. All the while he kept firing up a congregation at homebase that filled the 2,500 seats night after night and sometimes had to move into Toronto's larger Massey Hall, and even to the 18,000-seat Maple Leaf Gardens.

Still, in the contemporary, more comprehensive sense of *evangelist,* one who spreads the good news of Jesus Christ, Oswald J. Smith used every modern tool, every means available to multiply his evangelistic efforts ten thousand fold. "There is no better way to evangelize than with the *printed page,"* he said as his Peoples Press turned out millions of mini-sermons in tracts and pamphlets and at least six-million books in 128 languages. Bibles, as well as his books, were provided for the national church in many languages. "I expect the printed page to accomplish more than the spoken message," he said. "The gospel is 'the dynamite,' the 'power of God unto salvation' and I want to leave it wherever I go so that every now and again there will be an explosion and some-one will be saved."

In addition, Oswald J. Smith utilized the media to extend evangelism beyond the four walls of his church. His was one of the first churches in Canada to use radio with *hymns* to sing the message into hurting hearts, *TV, movies,* and *cassette tapes.* He believed as did Saint Paul: "By every means let Christ be preached."

"Yet why should anyone hear the gospel twice before everyone has heard it once?" he would ask. "I must go, or send a substitute." Always striving, always reaching for the "unreached," he relentlessly drove his frail body, never knowing what it was to feel well for the space of a week, but compelled by the same surging force that had driven the Apostle Paul: "Woe is me if I preach not the gospel. . . ." So much to do and so little time.

Said publisher Fleming Revell:

> There's a fire in his bones. Those who have heard him have seen the fire in his heart, his eyes, his speech, the fire which has leaped out and set them afire. He has started in our world a great blaze of hope.

ONE

♦♦♦

RABBITS AND WHIPPINGS

I want adventure. . . OJS

The wind off the Pacific lashed through the tall pines, whipping wet snow against the log cabin, whistling through the chinks, and gusting down the chimney. Inside, lying on a makeshift bunk, the scrawny nineteen-year-old Oswald shivered uncontrollably as the fire burned lower. Was it just from the cold or from fear and apprehension? That afternoon he had arrived in the Indian village and had seen the children he planned to teach by day and their parents whom he'd preach to each evening. But how alone he felt as the only white person. How far from home!

Home and his snug bed above the train station 3,000 miles away, warmed by the heat from the big potbellied stove in the waiting room below. The trains lumbering by with their mournful whistles crying down the tunnel of light. His brother Ernie close behind him; father snoring contentedly in the next room; his sisters giggling under their feather tick. What a secure world Oswald Jeffrey Smith had been born into.

Maud Laidley had met Benny Smith when he came to pick up his mail in Erneston, a little village near Kingston, Ontario.

Benny fell in love almost immediately with the tiny, businesslike postmistress. He had gone to work at twelve years of age to help support the family after his father's death. Like his father, he had become a telegrapher and station agent for the railway.

Maud was thin, ruddy-cheeked, and twenty-five when they moved to Embro Station, a hamlet near London, Ontario, in 1893. Oswald was just four, with Ernest Gilmour toddling two years behind. Soon baby Hazel was lying in a basket by the stove, and another baby was on the way. There would be ten children in all. A long trestle table covered with flowered oilcloth sat on the rough kitchen floor. Saturday was bath night, with everyone scrubbing in turn in the big washtub filled with water heated on the cookstove.

Theirs was a frugal life, but the children didn't know it. Father would put Maud on the train bound for the nearest town with fifteen dollars to buy groceries for the month. In summer the children would be up at 5:00 A.M. to help pick raspberries. Quarts of preserves lined the cellar. Sometimes Oswald was sent to the neighbor's farm with a quarter for a chicken; while still young he became adept at chopping off the head. His mother would then pluck the body for boiling or frying.

Oswald's father, Benny, was about 5′11″ and of average build. He was a courteous, gentlemanly sort, with shoes always shined and a neat crease in his trousers. His days were taken up attending to station business so that the chores fell mostly to Oswald and Ernie. Often they helped unload freight cars, dropping the heavy bags of feed onto the station platform. The floors of the waiting room had to be swept, and enough hardwood crosscut and split to fill the ever-hungry woodbox in the kitchen. The lawns had to be cut and the garden weeded.

Then the livestock had to be attended to. Grandfather had started it all by giving the boys a pair of pigeons on one of their frequent two-week vacations at the Laidley farm. Oswald and Ernie hatched the pigeon eggs and soon had money to buy two settings of eggs which a neighbor obligingly put under a brood hen. Soon these enterprising youngsters had thirty or forty hens laying ten-cents-a-dozen eggs and roosters to fatten the family table.

Then they bought a jersey calf for twenty-five dollars to provide cream and butter, often with milk left over to sell for five cents a quart. Oswald bought a sickly bronco for three dollars, nursed it to health, and sold it for forty dollars. The two rabbits the boys bought for pets quickly became a ravenous zoo, with their rapidly multiplying progeny overflowing the big rabbit house which Oswald and Ernie had built for them. Finally the boys let them loose to fend for themselves. The animals burrowed tunnels under the station and raised even more young, much to the chagrin of neighboring farmers who resented the hordes raiding their vegetable patches.

At one point, Oswald had a snake in a box under his bed and a pet squirrel that loved to play on the wooden treadmill he had fashioned. But "Tommy" was his favorite pet, a crow that Oswald had swiped as a baby from a nest in the tallest pine tree. He taught the crow to say a few words, and as soon as it was daylight, Tommy would wake up the household by calling out, "Hello, hello, good morning, Oswald." Tommy was a fine worm-hunter; Oswald would dig and Tommy would grab and hold onto the succulent fishing bait. Tommy went to school with the boys, flitting from pole to pole always just a little behind Oswald. All day he would hang around the school in the trees, then with the final bell dart for home, scolding the boys when they dawdled to play barefoot in the icy water which rushed along the ditches in the first thaw of spring. He would join them when they raced around the frozen pond on skates tied to shoes or when they swam in summer in the swimming hole where the creek widened under a big willow.

But always, the boys had to be home punctually to light the semaphore signal lamps about a half mile east and west of the train station. Oswald would go one way, and Ernie the other, sometimes hopping on the railroad jigger, but more often hiking along the ties. The coal-oil lamps would be lit at the bottom of the pole, then hoisted up by a pulley. But if the pulley stuck, as it often did in the wind and rain, snow and sleet, the boys would have to climb up the high ladder to the little platform and do their best to fix it.

One evening, Oswald lost all track of time while playing cops and robbers in his friend Andy's barn and was not home in time to light the lamps. His father, usually a gentle man, was furious, and in a blind rage lashed Oswald's bare body with a razor strap while his mother frantically tried to stop the savage blows. She knew that when Oswald's father lost his temper, he could not control himself and seemed not to know what he was doing. One day Oswald had watched, sick with loathing and terrible fright, as his father senselessly and viciously whipped their faithful watchdog, a Great Dane who could easily have turned on the man.

Oswald must have forgotten about his father's temper when he and his friend Andy decided to set fire to the grass alongside the tracks extending around the bend and out of sight of the station. The younger Ernie kept stamping out the fires, but the bigger boys became angry and held him until the flames got going. Then to their horror, the fire raced along the tracks to a large pile of railway ties where creosote quickly flared up into a blaze the boys could not extinguish. Of course their father, seeing the smoke, raced to the site, then dragged Oswald home and locked him in his room to await suitable punishment for destroying company property. But this time Oswald got off scot-free because Grandmother Smith was visiting and was able to persuade the headstrong Benny that a thrashing was not necessary — only the promise that the boy would not do it again.

He was not so lucky the next time, when Oswald, bored and looking for some amusement, harnessed the Great Dane to the baby's sleigh and put little Hazel in it. The Dane, who had never been harnessed before, bolted, racing down the road at high speed with Hazel screaming in terror. The sleigh tipped and little Hazel tumbled out onto the snow and toddled off unhurt and crying to the house, while Oswald chased after the dog. Finally, he caught up with it, and after unharnessing the Dane, discovered to his dismay that one of the wooden runners had been torn from the sleigh.

He was bending over trying to repair the damage when his father strode up, grabbed the broken runner and Oswald, and marched off to the waiting room. Laying Oswald across his knee and taking the iron-edged runner, he began to beat the boy with blow upon heavy blow. Oswald's cries brought his mother running. She pleaded with her husband to stop, afraid that he would break bones. But again she was powerless; only when his arm tired did Benny Smith let the terrified boy go.

Oswald does not recall the other children getting punished; he seemed to be the worst behaved, the one most often wilful and disobedient and thus often thrashed. In turn, he discovered that he had his father's same ugly temper that would flare up suddenly at the slightest provocation, and more often than his father's. As he grew older, Oswald would take his temper out on his younger brothers and sisters, hitting and slapping them around roughly when his mother, whom he worshiped, was not looking. He became the bully of the school yard, picking only on those who couldn't defend themselves and avoiding any scraps where he might get the worst of it.

But he had not always been a bully. Because he had been such a sickly child and because it was a long, two-mile walk to school, Oswald had not started classes until he was seven. During these years, it seemed he spent as much time in bed as in school, with recurring throat-and-ear infections and an undiagnosed prolonged fever that kept him out for months, probably due to tuberculosis as later tests revealed.

Oswald had begun to think of himself as delicate, sickly, and weak. He'd let even the smaller boys bully him, hiding his face in his hands and crying when they hit him. Also, he was a very poor scholar. He could barely tolerate geography and history, was bored with the intricacies of grammar, and simply could not spell or do arithmetic. He failed tests repeatedly until finally the teacher in the one-room school would just push him into the next grade. He did not pass his high school entrance exams until he was going on seventeen. (Oswald wrote his first poem to a favorite teacher who had joined in their games and who had been especially kind to him as a slow student.) He enjoyed these later years when he was the oldest and biggest in the school, and able to shove everyone else around.

When he was twelve, his mother gave him a one-dollar box camera with which he roamed the countryside for hours, taking snapshots. Then he would develop, print, and enlarge them in his bedroom closet. When he was well enough and his mother could find the fifty cents a week, he began taking piano lessons from a farmer's wife two miles away, learning to play simple hymns. Both parents shared an enjoyment of music and when someone came by who could play the Heintzman upright in the parlor, his father would dust off his violin and fiddle along.

Particularly during his days in bed, Oswald developed a love for reading, nurtured by Grandmother Smith who introduced him to Henty's books, often reading away the long hours for him. For months after devouring *True to the Flag,* he and his friends played "Army Scout" with Oswald always "The General" giving orders and conducting drill maneuvers. The title stuck for years. He followed the adventures of Jack Archer in *Five Weeks in a Balloon* and *Trapped in the Ice,* then through the Crimea and Russia, the Coral Islands and the South Seas. "Someday I want to travel all over the world; I want adventure, and to see all these countries," young Oswald decided.

TWO
♦♦♦
THY GRACE DISCOVERED ME

Long ago thy grace discovered me, and made me thine. OJS

Oswald was almost fifteen when his sister Hazel, just ten years old, became terminally ill with an enlarged heart. Oswald was smitten with remorse for how badly he had treated her. "So often in a fit of violent temper I had struck her and made her cry with my meanness."

In an outburst of agony he knelt beside her bed and asked, "Hazel, can you forgive me for the times I have been ugly to you?" His "little angel sister" reached a frail arm around his neck, and kissed him. "I can only stay until Sunday," she told her family. "I want to be where Jesus is." And on Sunday she folded her hands, closed her eyes, and with a sweet smile said, "Blessed Jesus, take me now." And He did.

Oswald's father sobbed aloud, scarcely able to bear the anguish. With his mother, it was months before her heartbreak showed any signs of healing. Oswald was deeply affected; night after night he sobbed out his grief and guilt. "Thank God He took her from me that I might no longer abuse her," he finally concluded.

A new gentleness and a deep concern about heaven began to invade the mean disposition. *How did Hazel know she was going to be with Jesus?* Oswald wondered. He developed a terror of dying; often he'd waken in the night in a cold sweat and shake his brother from his sleep: "Ernie, Ernie, we must prepare for heaven." "But, how?" Oswald asked his mother, and even though she had made a commitment in a tent meeting when a girl at home, she did not seem to know how to share her experience with the children. Oswald became afraid to swear or to lie, fearful of offending God and being lost. He began saying his prayers religiously every night.

Actually, the Smith children had seen little of the inside of a church over the years; the nearest place of worship was three-and-a-half miles away, and the family had no means of transportation. However, Oswald did attend the Sunday school organized in the school house each summer by the local farmers. One afternoon, his teacher challenged the class, "Any one of you boys might become a minister." And something in young Oswald's heart responded, "I will be that one!" From that moment on, he had the assurance that someday he would be a preacher.

The first time he was asked, "Are you saved?" was during special children's meetings in Toronto's St. Mark's Presbyterian Church where his Aunt Phoebe (his father's sister) and Uncle Tom Findley attended. What did it mean, this "being saved"? At Embro Station, the neighborhood drunk got converted and was so totally transformed that all he wanted to do was talk about the Lord. He organized cottage meetings in homes throughout the community, and young Oswald was strangely drawn to attend, walking alone across the starlit countryside. When his father permitted the meetings to be moved into the station waiting room, Oswald drank up the singing of the gospel hymns and the unvarnished preaching. Still, his heart was searching.

Finally in January 1906, Toronto newspapers carried the story of the Torrey-and-Alexander evangelistic campaign packing the 3,400-seat Massey Hall with two services each day. Sometimes they ran the full sermon, along with the words and music of the new "Glory Song" that had sung its way into the hearts of listeners all across America and now was being introduced to Canada.

As the men lounged about the Embro station waiting room and discussed these news reports, Oswald, just turned sixteen, was seized by an impulse that he and Ernie should attend these evangelistic meetings. Then his father came home from a business trip to Toronto with a firsthand report: he had attended the services and they were splendid. Of course the boys could go. Skipping school, Ernie and Oswald arrived in Toronto in time for the last nine days of the campaign. After checking in at Aunt Phoebe's, they headed straight downtown where they pushed their way through the crowds to a front seat.

These youngsters from the "country corners" were spellbound by the glittering concert hall with galleries rising up to the lofty ceiling and Charles M. Alexander's wonderful smile as he led the great throng in singing the spirited new gospel songs. As they sang, "When by His grace I shall look on His face, that will be glory for me," Oswald thought he would burst with the thrill of such rapturous music.

Dr. Reuben A. Torrey was a serious preacher, a scholarly and highly educated man whose sermons pierced the hearts of his listeners. Oswald went to the special for-men-and-boys-only session at 4:00 P.M. on the final day, determined that he would go forward "to accept Christ." Torrey spoke from Isaiah fifty-three, reading it with a personal emphasis: ". . . he was wounded for *my* transgressions, he was bruised for *my* iniquities; the chastisement of *my* peace was upon him, and with his stripes *I am* healed" (v.5). Oswald did not hear a word of the sermon — only the Scripture that kept repeating over and over in his mind, ringing into the depths of his being. He was aware that the evangelist had started the appeal: "All those men over twenty who want to be saved, come forward." Then he asked, "All those between seventeen and twenty." Almost in a trance, Oswald heard Torrey calling, "those younger, between twelve and sixteen, now is your opportunity."

"Let's go," Ernie nudged him. At the front, they shook hands with Dr. Torrey and were directed to an "Inquiry Room." There the boys were separated, and Oswald sat alone. A counselor approached him, asking, "What do you want to know?" The sixteen-year-old country boy hardly knew, so they chatted awhile and the counselor left. Oswald fell to his knees, and burying his head in his hands, cried out to God for forgiveness. As he prayed, tears came, a rare thing for this young man. Oswald later related, "As I opened my heart to the Saviour, asking Him to be my sin-bearer, my substitute, I felt no great change, no wonderful experience; but I trusted Christ Jesus and from then on I experienced sweet peace."

When Ernie blurted out to Aunt Phoebe that both boys had gone forward, Oswald was upset. "Someone has been praying for you at home—your mother," Aunt Phoebe reassured. Still Oswald was not sure he wanted anyone to know about his conversion experience.

THREE

♦♦♦

WHAT WILL YOU HAVE ME DO?

Here is a man I can follow, . . . whose preaching inspires me. . . . OJS

At school, Oswald talked to three or four boys about their need of salvation, and soon the word got around, "Gout's got religion. Hey, Gout's carrying his Bible." ("Gout" was the nickname for the goats Oswald was always talking about but never had owned.)

The recently converted brothers had no church, no mature Christian to nurture and guide them. Even so, they began to look for some work to do for the Lord, and with their mother's help, started a Sunday school for the neighboring children in the station waiting room.

Oswald began studying his Bible, underlining with pencil and ruler as he read. He started praying as he walked down the tracks to light the lamps. Sometimes he would race along the ties singing the Torrey-and-Alexander campaign songs — "That will be glory for me" and "I am so glad that Jesus loves me." His childhood decision to become a minister was now translated into a burning desire to be a great evangelist preaching to massed thousands. He also began putting together sermons that he would preach to the birds perched along the fence posts and telegraph poles.

Finally, the visionary young man finished his schooling at Embro, and Uncle Tom Findley got him a job as messenger in the plant where he was an executive. One evening after work, attracted by the hymn singing, Oswald dropped into a tent that had been set up on a vacant downtown lot. His heart was hungering for Bible teaching; however, this teaching of the "Hornerites" disturbed him greatly because they said that salvation does not come through faith, only through an experience of feelings.

The sixteen-year-old Oswald was plunged into black despair, a period of excruciating, heart-rending agony. "Am I saved or still bound for hell?" was the question that tortured him all day as he went about his work. Evening after evening in the tent he knelt in the straw in view of hundreds while members gathered round to pray aloud, pleading with God to save his soul. He became afraid to go to bed for fear he would fall asleep and wake up in hell.

One day he came across the little booklet "Safety, Certainty and Enjoyment" by George Cutting which was distributed widely by the godly Queen Mary. As he read, the light went on in his confused soul. Once and for all he saw clearly what is required for salvation: stop struggling to perform good works or to be religious and simply trust, giving oneself up to Jesus Christ, handing oneself over into His keeping.

Once more Oswald had glorious peace. But the terrible pleadings to God night and day, the weeks of sleeplessness, had taken their toll, and he collapsed at work with a severe throat infection. Aunt Phoebe, with whom he was staying, did her best to nurse him back to health, but after two weeks packed him back home to his family now living in Mount Albert, a hamlet some thirty-five miles north of Toronto. There Benny Smith was opening a station for a new railway line.

"Poor lad is in consumption and hasn't long to live," the neighbors decided. But slowly Oswald recovered his strength. He took a job as janitor of a Presbyterian church and enrolled for courses in the high school. But again he was bored and restless. His desire to preach the gospel was growing stronger day by day, but no one had told him how much schooling was necessary to enter the ministry. He fancied that one day he simply would go into a village and ask a minister to let him take over his services. Oswald was perfectly sure that he could preach without notes and no one would dream it was his first sermon. So shortly after his seventeenth birthday, Oswald dropped out of high school and left home for good, moving to Toronto where a cousin had gotten him an office-boy job.

A new young minister J.D. Morrow, who was also a Canadian champion runner, had just taken over St. Mark's Presbyterian Church and was packing it to capacity. This was the church Aunt Phoebe and Uncle Tom attended, and Oswald too, was quickly captivated by Morrow's brilliant evangelistic preaching and the cheerful gospel songs which Morrow himself led. He preached "as a dying man to dying men, pleading, entreating, beseeching, laying bare the souls of those before him."

"Here is a man I can follow, a man whose preaching inspires me and who can lead me as I want to be led," young Oswald decided. He immediately asked for a Sunday school class and was given five- and six-year-old girls. He threw himself into helping Morrow build up his workingman's church.

Oswald shared a small downtown apartment with his brother Ernie. One day when leafing through an old copy of *The Presbyterian,* Oswald noticed an advertisement for the Toronto Bible Training School (which later became the Toronto Bible College, then Ontario Bible College), offering a thorough knowledge of the Bible for foreign and home-mission work. The two-dollar registration was the only fee. This excited Oswald, who eagerly signed up for lectures two evenings each week. How he reveled in the lectures and the fellowship of other eager Christian young people. As they went out in teams to speak and sing in the jails and missions, a whole new world opened up for young Oswald.

At the same time, along with his desire to preach, he was becoming concerned for foreign mission work. He attended the Friday night prayer meetings for the China Inland Mission, and was among the crowd at the station waving farewell to Jonathan and Rosalind Goforth as they set out from Knox Presbyterian Church as missionaries to the Orient. Thus it was not surprising that as the term drew to a close, Oswald applied to the Presbyterian Church for a posting with the foreign missions board. He wrote home to his father:

> Constantly, daily I have prayed for you, and oh, father! I do pray that I may have the consolation of knowing that my father is saved and sure to be in heaven when I am far away in China.

The Presbyterian Missions Board had different ideas about sending this 6-foot, 119-pound, eighteen-year-old as its representative. He was simply not qualified, and besides, he could not pass the medical examination required for the strenuous missionary life. J.D. Morrow pleaded the cause for his young Sunday school teacher, but in vain. Yet, "Lord, what will You have have me to do?" had been Oswald's increasingly passionate plea since his conversion. So packing away his disappointment and determined to get on with God's work, Oswald persuaded the Upper Canada Bible Society to let him sell Bibles (colportage) in the Muskoka region, some ninety miles north of Toronto.

Going from door to door, Oswald very quickly learned what it was to have one slammed in his face. Usually he could find lodgings with a minister. On the nights no one would take in the lanky youth, he would crawl into a barley stook or whatever for a little protection from the cold. At the first streak of daylight, he would shake off the thistles, tidy himself up and set off for the nearest town, perhaps five or six miles away. "Colportage work is the most discouraging and at the same time the most useful for a good experience that I know of," Oswald concluded. "A few months of this work and a man will never find a mission field which can discourage him."

And quite wonderfully for Oswald, it was also this colportage work that opened the door to begin the realization of the dream that had become the motivating force in his life. "Would you preach for me this Sunday?" the Methodist minister asked as they walked from the train station to the parsonage in the little town of Severn. Oswald's heart leaped for joy. Would he preach? What else had he been living for these past two years since he had come to know the Lord? What else had he been crying out to God for as he knelt long hours in prayer? Night after night, he had lain awake composing sermons and imagining he was preaching to vast throngs. He knew in his bones he could preach; all he needed was the chance to prove it.

"I suppose you have spoken before? . . ." The dreaded question hung like a sword threatening to sever this golden opportunity. Oswald struggled, reaching for a reply. Yes, of course he had "spoken"; what if for only a few minutes at young people's gatherings?

"Fine, you'll preach at my three circuit churches."

"Gladly," Oswald agreed with a great show of confidence. But his heart was sinking. That night he threw himself on the floor before God: whatever would he preach? Every word of those carefully composed sermons had flown from his mind. Then he remembered a splendid address he had heard recently, given by one of the editors of the *Scofield Reference Bible,* and Oswald was able to recall it in detail. For thirty minutes the next morning, Oswald stood behind the pulpit, mouthing this borrowed sermon, without a note, without a pause. Oswald was elated. But then his heart sank again: "I can't preach the same sermon or he'll think that is all I have. Please God, can you give me another?" The "Serpent in the Wilderness" of John three was the text, and somehow he made it through in spite of a lumbering freight train that drowned out his middle points.

"One more to go, Lord," and that night Oswald spoke for

forty minutes on the "Parable of the Ten Virgins." To his immense surprise, the minister told the congregation: "I have received great blessing from the preaching of our young brother today."

Oswald now knew for sure that God had called him to preach. The next morning, Oswald purchased a notebook to be his "Record of Sermons Preached." The date, the place, and the topic were carefully noted. At last he was in business for his King.

"Oswald Smith is one of our best colporteurs," the Upper Canada Bible Society reported at the end of the summer. Word of his success reached British Columbia, and the Bible Society there wired Oswald: "Will you come west to open up work in the logging camps and Indian settlements of this province?" His brother Ernie saw him off the night of September 10, 1908. Oswald had an upper berth for the six-day trip and cooked his meals on the little stoves set up in some of the cars. Food supplies such as bread, tea, and tinned beans could be purchased in train stations along the way, and often there was time at stops to dash to a nearby café.

Oswald reveled in the prairies, "the gardens of the desert," but he was eager for the first sight of the mountains, and kept dashing to the front of the car to ask the conductor, "How far is it now?" Finally he settled down with a book, then chanced to look up, seeing a shadow on the horizon. He rushed to the platform to feast on the approaching panorama. An excited Oswald described the scene:

> Within an hour and a half the train was among hundreds of snow-covered peaks rising above trees and walls of bare rock, with glaciers spilling down, and mountain streams flowing into angry rivers, rushing in torrents among gigantic rocks.

FOUR

♦♦♦

BIBLES FOR THE COAST

The work of God never before has been so vividly impressed on me. OJS

After spending seven days in Vancouver selecting and assembling his Bibles and Bible portions in several different languages, Oswald boarded a steamship for the 500-mile trip up the coast, traveling the spectacular Inside Passage. He wrote as follows:

> The work of God never before has been so vividly impressed on me. The scenery is magnificent beyond description. The mountains rose up on either side of the channel with their snowy peaks shining brightly in the sunlight. The vessel cut the waves at a rapid rate, leaving a foaming wake behind as we sped along, winding in and out among the islands. A whale surfaced off our stern and blew two spouts of water some fourteen feet into the air before diving down again.

When their ship encountered open sea, Oswald noted

> The great swells rising some fifteen feet high, rushing towards our vessel, causing it to roll so far that you feared she was going to go clean over; then back the other way tossing the boat violently from side to side. Then the great seas passed under the boat to dash themselves to pieces on the rocky shore, shooting up in a great white surging mass of foam about thirty feet high.

> Truly, "the heavens declare the glory of God and the earth showeth his handiwork. Day unto day uttereth speech and night unto night showeth knowledge. There is no speech or language where their voice is not heard." How can the infidel maintain there is no God when he sees such wondrous works?

Young Oswald mused in awe of the surrounding splendors.

This was no luxury liner they were traveling on, but a plain, working vessel, and as they were boarding in Vancouver, Oswald had looked over his motley shipmates with some trepidation. There were turbaned East Indians and pig-tailed Chinese, a wide variety of races and languages, many of them looking scruffy and unkempt. For Oswald, whose world up until now had been peopled almost exclusively with Anglo-Saxons, yes, these were decidedly different.

Now, to apply for foreign mission work was one thing, but to suddenly find oneself surrounded by foreigners — and what appeared to be a pretty distasteful lot at that — was not quite what Oswald was ready for. "Please bring me a white man for a cabin mate," he coolly directed the purser. The purser obliged — and a dead-drunk Swede staggered into Oswald's cabin, carrying a large whiskey bottle under his arm. Actually they all were thrown into close quarters, especially in the slovenly dining area where "two-bit" or twenty-five cent meals were slopped down on greasy, unwashed tables. The many passengers traveling steerage class were jammed together on the decks and passageways.

In Prince Rupert, just a few miles south of the Alaska border, Oswald was welcomed into the home of the Presbyterian minister, the Reverend C. Kidd. But the first morning, Mrs. Kidd discovered Oswald's bed had two lice probably picked up on the ship, and promptly banished him to the town bunkhouse where for a quarter he had a board to sleep on and was at least out of the weather.

Oswald enjoyed this frontier town, whose streets were laid out with planks nailed to the top of leveled-off tree stumps. The majority of houses, including the Presbyterian church and manse, were frame, with canvas or tent tops. With only a half-hour's notice, Oswald took the service that first Sunday morning for Reverend Kidd, and again the evening service.

Next morning Oswald set out with his little valise of Bibles going door to door among the tents and log cabins scattered haphazardly along the fringes of town. Sometimes he was welcomed by people who seemed eager to buy the Scriptures. But more often it was a rough answer, with a door or tent flap slammed in his face. In one cabin he encountered two big ruffians who gruffly cursed and scoffed: "Bibles can't do no one no good no how. They're just a _____ pack of lies and make a _____ of hypocrites."

Oswald spunkily retorted:

> Now look here, men. You may say what you like about the Bible; you may say it's a pack of lies. But that doesn't alter the fact that the Book tells me there's a God and I believe it. It also says that Christ died for all sinners, who, if they do not repent, must go to hell, but if they accept Christ they will certainly go to heaven. And I believe it. Besides, you're not going to come to any harm by having a copy of God's Word in your cabin.

He sold a Bible for a quarter. That afternoon the Chinese laundryman bought two New Testaments in his own language, as did a Japanese man.

Oswald hiked into the bush to visit the construction camps. When he walked into the bunkhouse at one camp, the men were playing cards. But Oswald simply walked up to the nearest table, plunked down his valise, opened it up to display his wares, and made his sales pitch. "Is there a man who would care to get a nice Bible from the Canadian Bible Society? Here they are, all fine Bibles, and you may all have a look at them." He went from table to table. "Sold only one fifteen-cent New Testament, but thank God for that," he recorded in the diary he had begun to keep.

One day Reverend Kidd offered Oswald his rowboat to visit two camps six miles up the coast, and Oswald set off in the morning, accompanied by a man he had met on the steamer with a fancy for the outing. Reverend Kidd tossed his gun in the boat as they were shoving off. "You just might get a shot at a duck."

Duck-hunting was so new to Oswald that he blew the head off the first duck. Another was only wounded and was flopping around in the boat. How to finish off this bird? Oswald brought the oar down with such a mighty thwack on the hapless creature that the oar went right through the bottom of the boat. The icy Pacific Ocean began gushing through the gaping hole. "Quick, put your fist in here!" Oswald ordered his friend, while Oswald frantically pulled the oars against the tide toward the beach which, thankfully, was only a quarter mile away. They were able to improvise a patch and get safely home.

Oswald thoroughly relished the rough-and-ready life, carrying his one blanket and little valise of Bibles as he tramped through the bush or hiked along the railway tracks or corduroy roads (logs laid sideways, close together). Alone among the tall timbers he could sing at the top of his voice and pray aloud for hours. He enjoyed sleeping in the bunkhouses with the men, and even though he knew little about getting people converted, he like preaching to the unsaved; and this was the condition of most of these men, whereas in churches he would have only the occasional unbeliever.

During these days, Oswald got in the habit of praying about everything, especially when in the darkness he lost the trail through the forest, and this was bear and grizzly country; or when he had to inch his way, also in the dark, on hands and knees across a narrow tree trunk bridging a treacherous mountain stream.

To reach the construction camps deeper in the interior, Oswald traveled by sternwheeler about 100 miles up the fast-flowing Skeena River close to the Alaska border. He preached in the dining halls at night and often during the day set out on poorly marked trails through the wild forest to little Indian villages.

Sometimes Oswald journeyed by tugboat or steamer to the

remote logging and fishing camps along the heavily forested coast, traveling often through dense fog and sleeping on the deck for several nights. He always enjoyed these voyages, especially when a big sea was running. He liked to stay on deck, as his diary indicates:

> with the rain teeming down, the wind lashing in as the little tug bravely climbed a steep wave, then bounded down head first, then up another. Sometimes the great waves broke over her decks as they flew high over the bow; often she rolled from one side to the other almost to the water's edge.

Oswald stepped ashore from one such journey in Port Essington and made his way to the large frame home of the Methodist missionary, arriving dripping wet on Reverend Freeman's doorstep. This became Oswald's home away from home, with Mrs. Freeman a "most quiet and yet cheerful woman," five delightful children, and Reverend Freeman with whom Oswald enjoyed many checker games. (Oswald had learned well from the men in the Embro station waiting room.)

Port Essington was an Indian community, and when Oswald preached at the Sunday services, it was his first experience of speaking with an interpreter. He felt he made a poor job of it, but soon mastered the simple trade language "Chinook" so he could move quite easily among the Indians during the next year when he scarcely saw a white man. *"Mika tikie macook Bible ookooksun?"* meaning "Do you want to buy a Bible today?" was his opening line. He soon discovered he would rather work among the Indians than the whites any day. "If they want a thing, they give what you ask without bargaining about the price." In village after Indian village, Oswald sold Bibles to almost every household.

In Port Simpson, a large Indian settlement close to the Alaskan border, Oswald served a short time as instructor in the Methodist Boys Home for Indian children. Among the other duties he had was working along with the boys hauling the dirty coal by hand-wagon from the dock.

As many as 700 Indians packed the hall where Oswald preached several times. The Indians were very faithful in attending church services; they were natural orators and good at leading a meeting, Oswald discovered. "And they are great singers; I love to hear them sing in their own tongue, especially 'The Hallelujah Chorus.' "

On December 25 as he sat among the boys and girls by the big Christmas tree while an Indian Santa Claus distributed presents all around, Oswald was missing his own family back home. "But this celebration is far more interesting and wonderful," he decided.

On New Year's Eve, 750 Indians gathered for a solemn midnight service presided over by the Anglican missionary, followed by a fireworks' celebration made even more spectacular when the store that had sold the fireworks suddenly burst into flames, showering the black sky with pinwheels and rockets. "In about one minute it was gone, but what a beautiful display!" the youthful Oswald enthused.

MY DEBT

Tell me, dear Lord, what Thou wouldst have me do,
How I can show my gratitude to Thee,
Repay the debt, the debt of love I owe,
For all that Thou didst bear and do for me.

Wouldst Thou that I to other lands shouldst go,
Bearing the tidings of Thy grace and love,
Thy glad Evangel, wouldst Thou have me tell,
Till by the cross my love to Thee I prove?

Cannot I suffer as Thou didst for me,
Take up my cross and bear it day by day;
Labour and toil until my work is done
That I my debt of love to Thee may pay?

Ah, yes, dear Lord, I can and gladly will
Lay down my life in sacrifice complete;
Yet all and more to Thee can ne'er repay
The debt I owe that I might be made meet.

OJS

FIVE
♦♦♦
AMONG THE INDIANS

Loneliness is the hardest thing a missionary has to contend with. . . . OJS

The following week Oswald, under the auspices of the Methodist Church, set off for the Indian reserve at Hartley Bay — a sixteen-hour boat journey down the coast. There he would teach school and take charge of the mission work. The Girls' School had added two quilts to his one thin blanket; he had twenty-four dollars' worth of groceries, a cookstove, an axe, hammer, nails, and fifteen jars of preserves, a gift from one of the Christian women in Port Simpson.

The little hamlet was beautifully situated on an island in one of the inlets, with mountains and virgin forest coming down to the ocean edge. The morning of his arrival, it appeared to be buried under snow.

A group of Indians waited silently on the wharf. Oswald presented his letters of introduction to the chief, then started up the path for the mission which consisted of a tidy log church and mission house which also served as a schoolroom. The snow was up to his hips, and it was hard slogging. Eagerly Oswald shoveled the snow away from the door of the mission house.

His new quarters held a bed with homemade mattress scarcely four feet long, four benches, a rough board sofa, table, chair and a row of shelves for dishes. Young Oswald's heart leaped for joy. This was even more than he had hoped for! He grabbed a shovel and in sheer exuberance cleared a broad path through the snow. Then he found a board to tack onto the foot of his bed to make it closer to six feet. He brought in his stove and heated up a tin of beans and hot tea.

That evening he called a meeting of the chief men of the tribe. As they filed in, Oswald, just turned nineteen, realized with a peculiar sensation that he was presiding over his first church meeting. However, the strange feeling soon left him as he spoke through an interpreter and helped them work out the details of responsibility for the church services and the school.

But Oswald was having difficulty keeping the fire going. The few sticks he'd gotten from the sawmill across the inlet were wet and refused to light. Then when Oswald ripped a plank off the old shed, the plank caught fire, but also filled the room with smoke. He could not get the place warm. He lay in bed that first night shivering from the bitter cold and desperately lonely. Every sound startled him. He lay awake listening, almost afraid to move. "Maybe I am a coward," he conceded.

But in the morning, the sky was an incredible blue and the snow hung heavy on the evergreens. The world was beautiful and it was Sunday. Oswald preached joyfully through an interpreter to a packed church, with Sunday school in the afternoon and a testimony meeting after the evening service.

Each day it gave him great joy to face the rows of happy young Indian faces in the schoolroom. They were always on time, and they were so very patient while their young teacher struggled with the language. He was a strange one, they must have thought, so scrawny with his white-blond shock of hair and bright blue eyes.

Some days Oswald would come in from outside work drenched to the skin, with feet so wet and cold that they were like lumps of ice. But before making the fire, he would find himself so overcome with joy that he would race around the room singing, "Glory to Jesus! Praise God from whom all blessings flow!" until he was out of breath.

Although Oswald had to gather and dry his own firewood, the Indians kept him supplied with venison and skins for mats. Wild ducks fed within a stone's throw of his cabin. He bought a twelve-foot dugout, although his previous canoeing experience on Toronto's Humber Bay was hardly adequate preparation for the strong crosscurrents and churning surf of these coastal islands. But by staying clear of the rough main channel, Oswald spent many pleasant afternoons and evenings on the water, particularly as spring began to come to the area and the ocean's surface often would be glassy smooth, mirroring the mountains rising up all around.

One such evening, he had the Chinese cook from the sawmill with him. (Oswald was tutoring him in English.) Suddenly Chung lost his balance and tumbled against Oswald, plunging that end of the boat under the cold waters of the bay. They were quite a distance from shore and Chung could not swim. Quickly, Oswald pushed the frightened Chinese to the other end of the boat which then righted itself and although two-thirds full of water, brought them safely to shore. (A dunking might not have done Oswald any harm because he had not had a regular bath all winter!)

One day Oswald discovered to his chagrin that he had not left his old bad temper back at the cross after his conversion, as he had hoped. It could still flare up swiftly and unexpectedly and did at the home of the sawmill owner who had invited him for a meal. He had hung his coat on a nail at the door, when a big Scotsman came in, grabbed Oswald's coat, and threw it onto the floor, hanging his own coat in its place. Oswald bristled, "How would you like me to do that to your coat?" "I dare you!" the Scotsman shot back. At that, Oswald's temper rose like wildfire, until he was so angry that he was shaking from head to toe with rage. Completely out of control, he dashed from the room and cried to God for forgiveness, and instantly the answer flashed *"You are forgiven."*

Peace was restored to the tempestuous young heart, but Oswald was unnerved. He had thought he had had the victory.

Another time an Indian baby died, and Oswald stood with the others on the shores of the Pacific, watching earth being thrown in on the little grave. Suddenly the young mother let out a dreadful shriek and began tearing out her hair in great handfuls until her whole head was a mass of blood. Oswald was appalled. The woman returned to the village, wailing loudly throughout the night.

Not long after this, a child of a Christian couple died, and Oswald took the little body in his arms and led the way through the forest along the trail to the burial ground, with the Indians following in single file. There in the rocky soil they dug another little grave and placed the tiny body in it. As the earth was thrown in, the mother stood by the graveside weeping. She was not wailing or tearing out her hair — just weeping silently. And when it was over, she returned to her little shack still weeping to herself. Oswald never forgot the contrast:

> What was the difference? Both mothers had lost a baby. Both mothers loved their babies as much as any mother. But the first was a heathen mother. She did not know Jesus Christ. "I'll never see my baby again," she wailed. But the other mother was a Christian. "He shall not return to me but I shall go to him." She knew that the great Shepherd of the sheep would take her little lamb in His arms and keep it until He could hand it back to her, and then she would have it for all eternity.

As the winter wore on, Oswald began wondering more and more what his future would be when he finished his term with the Bible Society. One night he was lying in his makeshift bed, not knowing what to do and thus praying very earnestly for light. Suddenly the answer came so plainly that it startled him. It was not a voice, but nonetheless, an unmistakable answer: *"Go to the Toronto Bible Training School."* Oswald was elated. Now his heart could be at rest for he knew what he would be doing in September.

With the coming of spring, the Indians left the village for their hunting grounds, the school was closed, and Oswald returned to his colportage work up and down the coast. But he recorded some useful observations about sending out missionaries:

> I went out green knowing little; I trust I learned something. I have come to the conclusion beyond a doubt that missionaries should be sent out two by two. I believe that I could have accomplished far more and I know life would not have been nearly as lonely had I had someone to share my life. Loneliness is the hardest thing a missionary has to contend with, and no missionary should be sent out to bear the terrible loneliness all alone.
>
> Oh, that God will give me someone filled with the love of Jesus to share the loneliness and solitude of far-away China!

THE CALL OF THE ORIENT

Send us the choice of your nation,
Give us your strongest, your best,
Men with a wide education,
The cream of your glorious West;
The cultured and trained of your college,
Athirst with an ardent desire
For the highest attainment of knowledge
That man has the power to acquire.

Send us your men with less learning
Tho' they have not a degree,
Men who for service are yearning,
And longing His kingdom to see;
For scholarly minds we are pleading,
Tho' few will respond to the Call;
But more of the others are heeding,
And the Spirit is working thro' all.

Send us above any other
The man who can love the opprest,
Our language so hard for another
Will hamper the strongest and best;
But language of love, tho' unspoken,
Will be understood by us all,
So, from hearts that are weary and broken,
For men who can love comes the Call.

OJS, 1913

Yet Oswald had never had as sweet a fellowship and precious communion with Christ as during those days when he shivered alone in his little cabin thousands of miles from home and loved ones.

SIX
♦♦♦
PRAIRIE PARSON

How it strengthens my faith to trust God for it all! OJS

"Go to Toronto Bible Training School" was the unmistakable instruction Oswald had received from God in the little cabin on the Indian Reserve at Hartley Bay in the spring of 1909. But in September of that same year, Oswald was enrolling instead as a freshman at the Manitoba College in Winnipeg. Within a week, he knew he had made a desperate mistake.

The change of direction had come about during the summer months of colportage work. After leaving the Indian Reserve, Oswald had worked for a few weeks along the northern coasts; then the Bible Society had sent him to Vancouver Island. Dashing to catch the ferry to Victoria at the south end of the Island, Oswald found himself by mistake on board a boat bound for Seattle, USA; nevertheless, he settled down to enjoy the extra ride and magnificent scenery, reaching his destination a day late.

Besides selling Bibles from door to door and joining with the Salvation Army as often as he could to preach on street corners during these weeks on the Island, Oswald, now almost twenty years old, was thrown into a new dependency on God for his basic daily needs:

> I have my room bill to pay, 25¢ a day; I've had only two cups of tea and a little toast today. But I have claimed God's promises; Philippians 4:19: "My God shall supply all your need"; and Psalm 37:25: "I have not seen the righteous forsaken nor their children begging bread." These two promises I hold up to God. He must feed me or I will be in debt, and that is impossible. His Word cannot fail.

The next day Oswald could record:

> Praise God! More Bibles arrived and I sold enough to pay off everything, and still have 30¢ over. God has not failed me. How it strengthens my faith to trust God for it all!

This seemed to be the pattern for the whole summer.

When Oswald entered a community, his strategy was to call on the Presbyterian and Methodist clergy first. This usually resulted in a lump sale of Bibles and Testaments, as well as an invitation to preach the Sunday services. Some of these ministers took a real interest in the devout young man, and Oswald shared with them his plans to prepare for the ministry.

"Manitoba College is just the place for you," a godly Presbyterian man advised. "They have a five-year Minister-Evangelist program and with the experience you've had this past year, you would be accepted without hesitation. And this would prepare you for ordination in the Presbyterian Church, whereas classes at the Bible Training School would not." This appealed to Oswald who previously had applied to Knox Presbyterian College, but had been turned down because he had no high school credits. "Perhaps the call from God was primarily to get me out of the bush and into a training program," Oswald rationalized.

To complicate his decision, he received a wire from the director of missions for the Methodist Church under whom he had served at Hartley Bay, offering him an apprentice-type pastorate at Greenwood, a community not too far from his parents' home in Mount Albert. "I don't know what I should do, Lord," the confused young Oswald prayed. "But if you provide me with the cost of the fare, I'll go out to the Presbyterian minister's place to get his advice." When the money appeared quite miraculously, he took it as the Lord's direct provision. After conversation and prayer, he confided to his diary:

> I have decided to go to Manitoba College, although it is the very last thing I want to do because it keeps me away from my loved ones for five long years.

And so Oswald enrolled at the college, with a full load of matriculation subjects including Greek, Latin, and French. "I study some five hours a day, often till after midnight, but I like it," the new scholar said with relish.

But just a week later the admissions committee decided they could not recognize his former work because it was not under the Presbyterian Church; he must either spend a year on the field or take the nine-year course.

Nine years! Sick with disappointment, he walked the streets of Winnipeg in a bitter agony of terrible darkness and confusion. What had gone wrong? How could he commit himself to this? For days he struggled, until God gave him peace that he should carry on; then he plunged into his studies, failing Greek but passing everything else. Most Sundays he was sent to preach and sometimes had to play the organ in neighboring churches. Often he struggled through prairie blizzards to arrive on time — his horse and buggy getting stuck in deep snowdrifts.

The highlight of his year was the visit of Jonathan Goforth, who had returned from China and was holding services on the Holy Spirit and prayer at the college. Oswald played the piano for two of the meetings. He also discovered the *Autobiography of Charles Finney:*

> This is the most helpful and inspiring book outside of the Bible. It has been wonderfully used of God to awaken me and has taught me to lay the very greatest stress upon prayer and the Holy Spirit to convert

> men. Oh, how feeble and weak I am of myself! I believe the greatest thing I need is the baptism of the Holy Spirit. If only I had that, I know God would use me.

Oswald began to devour the books, especially biographies, found in the college library. He noted:

> These accounts of the lives of good men give me the most inspiration and help, stirring me to fresh zeal along with self-sacrificing love.

He began to assemble his own collection of the works of John Wesley, Martin Luther, Gipsy Smith, Ira Sankey, C. H. Spurgeon, and David Brainerd.

He read constantly — in the wagon or on horseback — as he moved around the countryside from dawn until after dark, visiting parishioners in the two-church summer pastorate he had accepted just west of Winnipeg. The heat on the prairies was often oppressive, made worse by the onslaught of vast mosquito hordes and the bull flies that attacked the horses mercilessly. The homesteaders' houses he found poor indeed. Some were just dirt-floor one-room cabins shared with the animals and set so far back in the bush that the owners scarcely saw another soul. In other cabins, Oswald found open umbrellas being held up during bad rains. Still, he was welcomed to their lodgings and sometimes was offered only tea, bread, and butter, with a corner in the straw loft overhead. Oswald, who occasionally walked in his sleep, would tie a cord from his wrist to a log to keep him from toppling over the edge. Sometimes he brought children along with him to brighten his day.

His passion for evangelism was again flaming like a burning bush that would not be extinguished. He wrote:

> God has laid on me a burden for revival, and in order to accomplish this I must have His blessed Spirit. Oh, God, strip me of all that hinders the filling of Thy Holy Spirit.

For long hours young Oswald wrestled with God:

> I prayed till I was too weak and weary to do so any longer, then knelt at my bedside for support until I was nearly asleep. Then I lay down on the bed and prayed still, but weariness overtook me and I could only half-pray and half-sleep.
>
> God revealed plainly the one thing that has been cursing my life and which for weeks I have been unwilling to give up—the reading of the detective stories in the *Glasgow Weekly News*. I could not see how it was doing me any harm, but at last I solemnly promised God I would read no more. When the paper came, I found myself wishing I had not promised, but I threw it in the stove, and surrendered all to the will of God.
>
> Then with Bible open at Luke 11:13: "If any of you then being evil know how to give good gifts to your children, how much more shall your Heavenly Father give the Holy Spirit to those who ask Him?" I claimed His promise of the Holy Spirit for the purpose of winning souls for His glory. I claimed Him by faith; I believe He has filled me, although there were no manifestations such as Finney had. But the Word does not promise it. I believe He has filled me and that I will see manifestations in my words taking effect and souls being redeemed here.
>
> My life is changed since receiving the Holy Spirit—I cannot explain it but from that day I seem to have something extra, or rather, He has more of me. My mind has been at rest; a deep peace has stayed with me.

"We must start prayer meetings in both churches," a revival-bound Oswald announced.

"Utterly impossible!" retorted his skeptical parishioners.

"I see nothing impossible at all. God has changed worse hearts," Oswald very simply maintained.

The prayer meetings and Sunday schools were started, giving him two preaching services and two Sunday schools each Sunday, plus midweek prayer meetings. Oswald seemed to have a great deal of trouble traveling around his parish: twice his "gentle" horse bolted with the wagon; he was thrown from his horse, and was lost in the dark on the endless prairie more than once. Oswald felt God's protection especially close one day when he was out duck-hunting with a buddy from the college. An unseen youngster slithered through the grass ahead of him just as he fired his gun. Miraculously the bullet missed the child.

As the summer wore on, Oswald decided he could not return to the liberal college where his sensitive spirit had been deeply offended, particularly by the worldliness and scoffing ridicule of fellow theology students who jeeringly had nicknamed the sober Oswald J. Smith "Parson." Thus he set out a course of action:

> I have decided I will do what I planned to do last year — go to Toronto. There I will wait until God opens a door for me. If it is His will that I should stay in Toronto, I have plans for
>
> 1. Attending day classes at Toronto Bible Training School.
> 2. Getting a Sunday school of "Street Arabs," that is, poor boys and girls.
> 3. Getting some consecrated young men and women together and holding open air meetings as long as the weather permits. Doing mission work whenever possible.
>
> On the other hand, if He should open a door to evangelistic work, I am thinking of trying to get one of the ministers of a church in some town around to let me begin work in his church.

Accordingly, he preached his last sermon on October 2, riding twenty-nine miles that same day besides preaching and conducting Sunday school twice. The next morning he arose at 2:30 A.M. and drove twenty-five miles to a horse dealer, sold his horse and buggy, then walked over five miles to catch the train for Winnipeg. Coming in from the drought-stricken prairies, Oswald thoroughly enjoyed his first bath in four months. Then following a train ride to Fort William (now Thunder Bay), he boarded a steamer going down the lakes to Owen Sound and home.

But his train was late arriving in Toronto, and Oswald missed his connection to Mount Albert by a scant five minutes. This was Saturday night and a train would not be out until Monday. Oswald used the Sunday to look up his good friend Reverend Morrow, who invited him to tea and to speak at the afternoon Bible class. Finally Oswald arrived home.

SEVEN

♦♦♦

THE CALL OF THE ORIENT

"Not I, but Christ" is my motto!. . . OJS

Following a week at home, Oswald enrolled in day classes at the Toronto Bible Training School. In addition to academic work, he grabbed every opportunity for any extra instruction that might help fit him for the foreign field. He signed up for a first-aid-to-the-injured course; then with the Nursing-at-Home program he accompanied the clinic doctor into the homes of the poor, even assisting at the birth of several babies. Oswald was especially grateful for this experience because he wanted to be able to take care of his wife-to-be and do what he could for the people when he was "faraway in China."

A retired Christian dentist who was spending his life among the Jews of Toronto offered to teach dentistry to missionary students, and Oswald was first in line. As he drilled and pulled teeth, his heart went out to the delightful Jewish children: "Surely such beautiful young lives will not, cannot, be damned. God save them!"

From the first week of school, he was plunged into a busy schedule: speaking to women's and young people's groups, leading the Evangelistic Band he had formed, and preaching in the jails and missions and on street corners. Oswald taught a Bible class in the Central Prison at 9:00 A.M. each Sunday morning.

One of the greatest joys of these keen young men and women at the Bible school was to "gather round the piano and sing the dear old gospel hymns." Oswald simply could not understand Christian young people enjoying jazz and the popular music of the day: "It seems to me that spiritual people should be full of sacred music and should love to sing the praises of Jesus. Surely this is one expression of the spiritual life."

One of the most pleasing singers in the group was Jennie Tyrrell, three-and-a-half years older than Oswald and a graduate of the Training School. Jennie was a nurse in the Nursing-at-Home program, preparing for the foreign field, and as often as she could, joined in the activities of the Evangelistic Band. It was Jennie who sang, "Why Not Say Yes to the Saviour Tonight?" at Oswald's first evangelistic campaign shortly after he had turned twenty-one.

This campaign was something that had been on his heart since Winnipeg days, and he arranged it all himself, booking a church for the week, then paying to have 3,000 handbills printed. These he distributed with help from fifteen boys who had come to the Lord in one of his recent meetings. A few professed salvation, and Oswald carefully noted their names and addresses, adding them to his growing prayer list.

Oswald felt burdened to share the gospel with all he met—the barber, the people beside him on the street car, whomever. Occasionally these attempts at personal work did not come off too well. There was the time in the restaurant when he began witnessing to an argumentative trucker who had joined him at the table. Oswald's words riled the man to the point where he finally leaned across the table and yelled, "Shut up at once, or I'll soon shut your _____ mouth!" Oswald shut up and beat a hasty exit.

All the while, however, Oswald's preaching was improving. Apparently at first his preaching had been loud and boisterous, with a very rapid delivery. Now he had begun to be quiet and slow down, concentrating on expression:

> I don't know how in the world people used to sit and listen to me. To think I was a proud enough fool to believe that I could preach as well as some of the leading evangelists! God certainly has taken away that idea! I realize how full of mistakes my addresses have been, too much of self and the word 'I.' In every way I strive to better myself and make my preaching more agreeable to those who listen. I love to have people criticize me and point out my weak points. *"Not I, but Christ" is my motto-watchword!*

He studied the sermons of Charles Spurgeon and DeWitt Talmadge, and was also experiencing something totally new in his ministry:

> God is giving me sermons by His Holy Spirit. When least expected they flash before me; I grab my notebook and take down the headings as fast as I can, all within about three or four minutes. This morning as I was reading in John 3, within ten minutes I had the outline for three new addresses. Yesterday a sermon from John 1:46 was given to me: "Come and See." Praise God!

But I long for power in preaching — power to win somebody every time I preach the gospel and give an invitation, he prayed. And from then on, at almost every service some did come forward. He wrote in his diary:

> Oh, that my will will be so in harmony with Him, that my life will be so consecrated and surrendered to Him that the power of the Holy Spirit may so fill me that when I speak to a lost soul about Jesus, it may result in a definite acceptance of Christ as Personal Saviour, Lord and King!

During his summer vacation from the Bible college, Oswald became Canada's first Traveling Secretary for the Pocket Testament League. Going into factories, YMCAs, and churches, he urged young and old to join this worldwide organization of those who pledge to carry a Bible or New Testament wherever they go and to read at least one chapter a day. At the end of the first day he went back to his boarding house, a poor place with too many bedbugs for comfort, and wrote out a letter of failure and resignation. He just would never make a go of it. But then he remembered his first day with the Bible Society in Muskoka — he had felt the same way then; he had written a letter of failure at the end of that day too. But he had torn it up and persevered and God had blessed. "Please, God, I'll trust You again and You'll see me through. I'll stick at it even if I fail to make a cent all summer," he determined.

It was another good summer. One of the highlights for Oswald was the two-week conference at Woodstock College when the Presbyterian Church brought together fifteen missionaries from all parts of the world. Oswald was so moved that he gave two dollars for missions and then put a quarter on the collection plate as it passed when suddenly he realized he had nothing left. "Lord, I need a dime to get me through the day," he prayed. And in answer, when he returned to his room, his landlady was eager to purchase a twenty-five cent New Testament. "Over and above my need!" Oswald marveled.

That fall, Dr. John McNicholl, president of the Toronto Bible Training School, chose Oswald to take over the pastorate of the Congregational Church at Belwood, about fifty miles by train. He would leave on Saturday mornings and return Monday mornings. This work netted Oswald seven dollars a Sunday, with free meals for the weekend. Then in the summer, Oswald moved out to be a full-time pastor. To his delighted surprise, the people came regularly from long distances, and he always had a full house. Often he accompanied the doctor on his rounds and gained considerable instruction from him. Oswald discovered he had no heart for visiting parishioners: "This is the one work I do not like. To me it is lazy work to simply sit and talk to people. I wish for something more active." Soon he organized a union prayer meeting of the Protestant churches in town and a teacher-training class.

Oswald also arranged for thirty-five children from the Toronto slums to have a holiday on the farms of church members. His heart had been so broken when he had visited them in their poor homes during the school term: "If only I had a home in Toronto so I could bring in these children for a good meal every few days. I would gladly spend all my money in this way. I'd give anything to adopt some of them; I would love to have a dozen or more around my table," Oswald told his parishioners. Oswald loved children and they loved him.

As Oswald ministered in churches, missions, and jails, he was pondering the problem of how to reach the masses:

> Christ said, "Launch out into the deep; go into the highways and byways." But the modern churches are not doing this. We must discard our beautiful buildings, remove the pipe organ, and make the church a place where the common people will be at home.

Throughout these Bible school years, the bright spot in the life of this intense young man was his friendship with the sparkling, dark-eyed Jennie. They had quickly become a team in the Evangelistic Band, traveling to all the meetings together. Sometimes Oswald borrowed Uncle Tom's pony and buggy to clip-clop along the wooden blocks that paved Queen Street:

To Toronto Junction o'er the fields
We slowly drove along;
And tho' we knew not how to love,
Our hearts were filled with song.

The effervescence of first love awakened Oswald's creative talents, and he began to pen delightful little love poems to the girl he had asked to be his wife. "Dwell deep" was their motto, and from this Oswald penned the first verse and music of his first hymn "Deeper and Deeper," one that would stand among his greatest:

Into the heart of Jesus deeper and deeper I go,
Seeking to know the reason why He should love me so:
Why He should stoop to lift me up from the miry clay
Saving my soul, making me whole, though I had wandered away.

One day during his last term at the Bible training school, Oswald was in class trying to memorize his sermon for the next Sunday. He kept taking a peek at his notes, while at the same time listening intently to the lecture. But the professor heard his papers rustling, saw him glancing down from time to time, and finally exploded: "Smith, stop whatever you are doing and pay attention! And if you can't pay attention, you can leave the school!" he thundered.

Oswald gathered up his books and walked out of the class, out of the school, never to return, as far as he was concerned. But Jennie came by, and weeping, he poured out the whole story. Jennie pled with him to apologize and go back, to try to forget the humiliation and finish school. He took her advice. His apology was received politely, and he never studied sermon notes again in class!

At graduation, Oswald was given a "pass" in spelling. "They should have failed me," he admitted. Yet all his other marks were high, and Oswald was appointed valedictorian of his class.

Once more he had been turned down by the Presbyterian Mission Board for evangelistic work, and Knox College still would not accept him. But McCormack Theological Seminary, "Praying Hyde's" school in Chicago, recognized his credits. Thus in September 1912, Oswald, at the age of twenty-two, preached a farewell message in Dale Presbyterian Church with Reverend J.D. Morrow beaming his encouragement.

EIGHT
♦♦♦
DWELLING DEEP

O lonely soul, dwell deep,
God plans thy life, and He
Plans only what is best,
Dwell deep, He watches thee.

OJS

Soon after arriving in Chicago, Oswald stood in the crowd at Moody Bible Church for the ordination of "Borden of Yale," who was bound for missionary work in one of the loneliest parts of China. This unsettled Oswald: "How can I settle down to three years of quiet study? Oh, how I long to go to the foreign field!" Nevertheless he plunged in, all the while not being able to shut out the agony and hurts of the great city surging around him. He wrote about his impressions:

> *This last month I have felt the burden of a city;*
> *Its great sorrow has pressed in upon my soul;*
> *Its vice and sin have bowed me upon my knees in tears;*
> *I cried and cried to God to have mercy on the*
> *poor fallen girls, and the burden is crushing.*

Although he seemed most impressed with the plight of Chicago's lost young women, he believed firmly that winning souls should be a man-to-man and a woman-to-woman interchange. So he started with the men and boys, first taking charge of a boys' club in the downtown Bohemian Settlement House. He worked among nine- to fourteen-year-olds who were the "roughest and most destructive gang of street boys" Oswald had ever encountered. For several nights he simply stood still while they "broke furniture, fought and hollered to a fearful extent." The noise was continuous and "almost deafening." Finally Oswald got so discouraged he decided to give them up, figuring he had no gifts for boys' work. But when only six boys showed up instead of the usual gang, Oswald began to play games with them and "God began to tame them."

His next challenge was the men. Oswald rented a hall near the Loop in downtown Chicago, and once weekly at the noon hour the working men would crowd in—as many as 1,000. Often Paul Rader would preach. Oswald had been thrilled with Rader's preaching in the great Moody Church and the format was different from that of the big city churches he had known. Here were a wonderful orchestra, choir, and the exciting music which often featured Salvation Army band-style pieces in the thirty-minute prelude and bright new gospel songs, many of which had been written by Rader himself. Rader had been a prize fighter, and like Reverend Morrow was a man's man.

At the seminary, Oswald was attempting to keep a low profile, never even opening his mouth in the weekly prayer meeting until late November when Dr. McClure, the president, asked him to lead in prayer. McClure must have sensed something, and the next week invited the young Canadian to join them in their Thanksgiving dinner. This was the "most stylish meal" the barefoot boy had ever enjoyed, and that evening Oswald drew up his own Thanksgiving list: salvation came first, followed by victory over sin, the Bible, and prayer, peace, trust, and service. Next came his mother: "What I owe to her I will never know, but I believe it was on account of the pure, saintly life which she lived as a girl that I always had a tendency toward God." In eighth place was Jennie, the girl to whom he was engaged. Six weeks later, he discovered that he had been recommended to supply the pulpit of a large Presbyterian church in southwest Chicago.

It was a good thing he had come to the attention of the faculty when he did, because he was running out of funds rather drastically. He had started in September with eighty-seven dollars saved from his summer's work; the seminary had also given him a tuition grant of twenty-one dollars per quarter. He splurged twenty-seven dollars on a rebuilt type-writer, and before he knew it, was down to his last ninety-five cents with a debt of twenty dollars plus the cost of seven meals. His application for a job as a waiter was turned down. He cut his two meals a day to one — a five-cent cob of corn. He was most upset that he had not been able to keep up with his tithing. Feeling weak and drained, he pocketed his pride and wrote home for ten dollars to get him out to a friend's house over the holidays where some good home cooking would put him back on his feet.

There was no money for Christmas presents for anyone, even Jennie. Oswald was afraid she would not understand, and she did not. He had never told her how strapped he was financially nor why it was that he could not visit her as often as she would have liked. He had never shared with her, nor with anyone, the heaven-given vision that overshadowed every human passion.

The letters from Toronto became less frequent until finally one arrived: "Oswald, I'm afraid I don't love you anymore." Oswald was devastated. A flurry of frantic letters failed to resolve the misunderstanding. He could scarcely write his exams and get through the term. A poem written April 4, 1913, captured his pain as did another one written during this period:

HIS LOVE

Loved ones may go and all I prize most dear,
Life lose its charm and sorrow linger near;
Yet there is One whose love will still abide
Through cloud or sunshine, whatso'er betide.

Sorrow but drives me closer to His side,
His love remains, His heart is open wide;
Sadly I bow and tell Him all my grief,
For only He has power to give relief.

Dear God, the way is dark, I cannot see,
But still I feel that Thou art leading me;
'Mid deepest gloom as in the morning light,
Trusting in Thee I know 'twill all be right.

Thus, Lord, I turn my bleeding heart to Thee,
Asking that Thou wouldst shed Thy love on me;
Praying for grace to rise on angel wings
Far, far above the love of earthly things.

Chicago
April 4, 1913

WILT THOU BE NEAR?

Wilt Thou be near, O Lord, whate'er befall me,
Be near to guide, to keep me day by day?
O Saviour mine, no matter where I wander,
Wilt Thou be near lest I should lose my way?

Wilt Thou be near throughout my pilgrim journey,
Be near when all my heart is filled with fear?
And when I pray, O Saviour, wilt Thou hear me,
In all of life, wilt Thou, my Lord, be near?

Wilt Thou be near when I am crushed by sorrow,
When no one else can comfort and sustain?
When I am left bereft and broken-hearted,
Wilt Thou be near that I may not complain?

Wilt Thou be near when I am weak and feeble,
When all my dreams are buried in the past?
Be near, dear Lord, amid life's darkest shadows,
And in death's hour, oh, wilt Thou hold me fast?

OJS

Still in anguish, Oswald had to leave for Kentucky to preach to the mountaineers; yet to his great surprise, it became a summer of deep happiness and joy. God filled his life with a contentment and peace he had never known before. He suggested to Jennie that as a test of their love, they should not correspond for a year, and in a burst of superb optimism he wrote in affirmation:

The Saviour can solve every problem, the tangles of life can undo;
There is nothing too hard for Jesus, there is nothing that He cannot do.

The Saviour can lift every burden, the heavy as well as the light;
His strength is made perfect in weakness, in Him there is power and might.

The Saviour can bear ev'ry sorrow, in Him there is comfort and rest;
No matter how great the affliction, He only permits what is best.

The Saviour can satisfy fully the heart that the world cannot fill;
His presence will sanctify wholly the soul that is yielded and still.

He found himself rejoicing as he journeyed over the hills:

There is joy, joy, joy in serving Jesus, joy that throbs within my heart;
Ev'ry moment, ev'ry hour, as I draw upon His pow'r,
There is joy, joy, joy that never shall depart.

There is joy in serving Jesus, as I walk alone with God;
'Tis the joy of Christ, my Saviour, who the path of suff'ring trod.

There is joy in serving Jesus, joy amid the darkest night,
For I've learned the wondrous secret, and I'm walking in the light.
Yes, there's joy, joy, joy that never will depart!

But before the year of testing was up, Oswald received a registered letter. When he opened it, Jennie's engagement ring tumbled out into his hand. Oswald was stunned: *How can this be?* He cried as he walked blinded by pain along the darkened streets. Had not God given Jennie to him in answer to his prayer for a companion on the foreign field? Had he not passed many long nights dreaming of the day they would be together serving God in some darkened corner of the world? He had dreamed of having one love, only one love. Now was she to be torn from him?

Oswald was plunged into an agony of despair. Then up from sorrow's caldron came the fragrance of "Satisfied with Thee":

O Thou who art my Life and Stay, my one and only Friend,
I know Thy *love will never fail, Thy mercy never end.*

It matters not how dark the night, nor yet how drear the day,
Thy presence is my portion still, and Thou, Thyself, my Stay.

O blessed Lord, O Christ divine, how dear Thou art to me!
My soul is thrilled, my heart is filled,
I'm satisfied with Thee.

In "His Love Is All My Plea" Oswald reassured his heart:

His *love is mine forevermore, He makes the darkest hour seem light to me;*
He walks beside me night and day, the Love of Christ is all my plea.

From his heartache, both words and music poured out in

Alone with Thee when others have forsaken,
And naught is left save solitude to me,
My weary heart turns throbbing with emotion
To find itself at last alone with Thee.

Alone, dear Lord, ah, yes, alone with Thee!
My aching heart at rest, my spirit free;
My sorrow gone, my burdens all forgotten,
When far away I soar alone with Thee.

He finished off the five verses of "Deeper and Deeper," the hauntingly beautiful hymn he had begun two-and-a-half years earlier:

Into the will of Jesus deeper and deeper I go,
Praying for grace to follow, seeking His way to know;
Bowing in full surrender low at His blessed feet,
Bidding Him take, break me and make, till I am moulded and meet.

Into the cross of Jesus, deeper and deeper I go,
Following through the garden, facing the dreaded foe;
Drinking the cup of sorrow, sobbing with broken heart;
Oh, Saviour, help! dear Saviour, help! Grace for my weakness impart.

Into the joy of Jesus, deeper and deeper I go,
Rising with soul enraptured far from the world below;
Joy in the place of sorrow, peace in the midst of pain,
Jesus will give, Jesus will give, He will uphold and sustain.

Into the love of Jesus, deeper and deeper I go,
Praising the One who brought me out of my sin and woe,
And through eternal ages, gratefully I shall sing;
Oh, how He loved, oh, how He loved, Jesus my Lord and my King!

Once more he placed himself under the hand of God as expressed in "Full Surrender":

All I have I yield to Jesus, His forevermore I'll be;
To His will I now surrender, He is everything to me.
Full surrender; Oh, how easy, when I come, confessing all;
Casting every care on Jesus, Ever listening for His call. . .
Peace and rest in Him I'm finding, For his burden is so light;
He has broken every fetter, Made me victor in the fight.
Oh, the joy of full surrender; How it thrills me through and through;
Every talent for my Saviour, while I seek His will to do.

In his diary he recorded:

The way is dark, I cannot understand
But still I trust Thy love, O Saviour mine;
The fire is but to cleanse and purify,
So I submit to every trial of Thine.

And though my night of weeping tarry long,
Thy Word is sure, Thy promise cannot fail;
The morn will dawn and bring eternal joy,
Dear Lord, in Thine own time remove the veil.

. . . There is no love like His love to me. I am trusting Him for the one who is to share my life, if it be His will to grant me earth's greatest gift. I care not who she is, so long as she is His choice: my marriage must be made in heaven. I thank Thee for peace, peace, peace! But I long for the Spirit's fulness, the Spirit's power, so that nothing shall have the power to disappoint, or to rob me of His peace.

I want Thy plan, O God, for my life: May I be happy and contented whether in the homeland or on the foreign field; whether married or alone, in happiness or sorrow, health or sickness, prosperity or adversity — I want Thy plan, O, God, for my life. I want it; O, I want it!

Dear, precious Jesus, keep Thy child faithful to the end.
Take all there is of me!
Guard me from the evil one and
Fill me with Thy fullness!
Enable me to dwell in Thy presence,
To abide in Thy love.
I praise Thee for power over sin,
For opportunity of service.
I regret the failures,
the mistakes and the guilt of the past.
Oh, forgive it all.
Let me burn out for Thee!

ALONE WITH THEE

O. J. S. Oswald J. Smith

Deeper and deeper

NINE
♦♦♦
THE FIRST REVIVAL

God condescends to use me, unworthy and sinful though I am. OJS

Those few summer months in Kentucky were critical ones for the twenty-three-year-old seminary student. Somehow, despite the heartbreak of having lost Jennie, he finished the term at school. His last Sunday in Millard Church was a great one with ten of the leading young people making a commitment to Christ. Yet when he arrived in Cawood, Kentucky, a week later, he was "weak, ill, cast down, and full of grief" from having passed through the greatest sorrow of his life. Alone among the great hills, in the little Presbyterian manse, he buried his head in his arms on the kitchen table and cried out in an anguish of overpowering loneliness, "Lonely! lonely! lonely! Dear God in heaven, have mercy and send a friend to me soon."

Later in bed he cried out:

> I am tired, discouraged, despondent, sick. Is life worth living after all? What am I doing in this world? Almost nothing. My life seems useless, so worthless. Here I am half sick and of no earthly good. Why do I remain? Will I ever be of any use in the world? Oh, God, what a miserable failure I have been. I lay this torn, broken, defeated, selfish, conceited, ambitious, proud life at your feet. Dear Saviour, accept and fill it.

Then God met him, and the glory of His presence filled the little mountain cabin:

> Oh, the peace the Saviour gives, truly it "passeth all understanding." When I consider for but one brief moment the wondrous Life Beyond the Grave, and on its untold glories allow my thoughts to dwell, I wonder how earth's treasures 'ere had power to turn my thoughts from Him who gave so much. Then, as the rapture, the splendour of it all breaks in upon my soul, the greatest sacrifice, the hardest lot, or the very best that earth can boast — fame, wealth, power, home and all else that men count dear — seems to fade away in utter insignificance in the face of countless ages of unbroken peace, rest, union and contentment — the unutterable blessings of God's immeasurable eternity.

> My meat is to do the will of Him that sent
> me and to accomplish His work;
> And He that sent me is with me;
> He hath not left me alone!
>
> John 4:34, John 8:29, RV
> [Revised Version (American, 1901)]

As he journeyed through the hills, sometimes in the early morning sunrise, he would watch the sun climb from the mist-shrouded valley and touch the mountain peaks with gold. Sometimes he walked long miles beside the quiet rivers and rushing streams, beneath a canopy of chestnut, oak, and walnut trees with flowering berry bushes and rhododendrons adorning the hillside. Finally, bursting from his broken heart now touched by God's glory came the words:

> *I have walked alone with Jesus in a fellowship divine,*
> *Nevermore can earth allure me, I am His, and He is mine.*
> *In my failure, sin and sorrow, broken-hearted, crushed and torn,*
> *I have felt His presence near me, He has all my burdens borne.*
>
> *On the mountain I have seen Him, Christ my comforter and friend,*
> *And the glory of that vision will be with me till the end.*
> *In the darkness, in the valley, with my Saviour I have trod*
> *Sweet indeed have been the lessons that I've learned alone with God.*

I have seen Him! I have known Him! for He deigns to walk with me;
And the Glory of His Presence will be mine eternally.
Oh, the Glory of His Presence; oh, the beauty of His face!
— I am His, and His forever; He has won me by His grace.

Within weeks of his deep anguish, and tortures of failure and uselessness, Oswald found himself in the midst of his first revival. The Holy Spirit drew the men of this bootleg liquor area to cram the Turtle Creek schoolhouse night after night, crying to God at the altar for mercy. In two weeks of meetings, forty-one came forward to accept Christ.

It was hard going, visiting in the homes throughout the day, then preaching at night or whenever he had opportunity — sixty-four visits in a twenty-five day stretch. He was not sure he enjoyed some of the meals the hospitable mountain folk shared with him: plenty of squirrel and rabbit all fried in deep grease and washed down with sour milk. Often during the day he would walk four or five miles, then ride another six to ten on mule or horseback.

To his dismay, the boiling sun and intense heat of the afternoon frequently brought on "roaring headaches" so that he could do nothing but lie on his bed and cry to God for relief and strength for the evening service. *How will I ever stand the heat of the foreign field?* he wondered, recording in his diary:

> At last my head grew easier and I slowly walked the three miles and preached tho' still very weak. Praise God, three precious souls found Christ.

Often he felt ill and unable to go on, especially after he had had a bad toss from his mule, and injured his back, making him a cripple for a few days. But again he prayed, and God restored him.

The opposition to his work was quite intense in some areas, especially when he got too close to the very lucrative "moonshine stills" producing contraband whiskey in this Prohibition Era. One evening as people were leaving the service, shots suddenly rang out in the schoolhouse clearing, passing between the legs of one woman's mule and shattering the lantern in a man's hand. Another day, two of the new converts warned him of a plot to ambush him that night and "do him in" as he journeyed alone in the darkness through a rocky gorge. They urged him to stay home. But Oswald quickly concluded it was "his duty to keep his appointment to preach the gospel," and asked the Sunday school superintendent to accompany him on muleback. Later they were joined by a third supporter, and thus passed safely over the mountain.

At last Oswald came to the end of this "most profitable of all his summer ministries to date." Bidding good-bye to his little kitten and the tearful neighbor lady who had prepared most of his meals, Oswald placed his duffel bag containing his typewriter and few clothes over the mule's back, then set off in the rain for the "short ride" to the Harlan station just ten miles away.

He had again made many dear friends and hated to leave. "Gather them up like gems of the ocean, Value each token of friendship's devotion . . ." Oswald rhymed as he boarded the train for Chicago.

"God condescends to use me, unworthy and sinful though I am," Oswald marveled. "He chose me, not I Him. I am determined that He shall have all there is of me."

Smith at age fourteen with his brothers and sisters. Hazel, who later died, wears the dark dress.

Top: Smith at age eighteen in Stanley Park, Vancouver, 1908.

Bottom: Wash day for Smith in Vancouver, 1908.

Top: A lumber camp in British Columbia.

Bottom: Smith (center) with coworkers in ministry to the lumberjacks.

Top: Smith and a Kentucky mountain girl eating watermelon, 1913.

Bottom: Smith with his mother, Maud Laidley Smith.

Left: The Reverend J. D. Morrow of Dale Presbyterian Church, Toronto.
Right: Smith at Dale Presbyterian Church.

Left: Daisy the Deaconess at Dale Presbyterian Church.

Right: Smith and Daisy on their honeymoon.

TEN

♦♦♦

"JESUS ONLY"

Let us cast ease aside; let us go out and win men and women for Jesus Christ! OJS

Toward the middle of October in his second year at the seminary, Oswald was appointed pastor of South Chicago's First Presbyterian Church with the princely salary of sixty dollars per month. It took almost an hour each way on the streetcar, but Oswald happily used the time for reading: Dante's *Inferno,* Victor Hugo's *Les Miserables,* and Milton's *Paradise Lost.* He read from the great poets for at least thirty minutes daily.

Besides having a full load of studies at the seminary, Oswald spoke four times each Sunday and at midweek prayer meeting. "But it is not nearly enough," he wrote. "I wish there were more Sundays in the year that I might preach all the sermons and messages God gives me." His greatest rejoicing was in seeing transformed lives. By the next spring, he had a core group of twenty keen young people, most of whom he had led to the Lord and had trained over the winter in personal evangelism. Now they stood on the street corners as fishers of men. The young pastor challenged his congregation:

> If you do not win a soul for Christ this summer, you have missed one of the greatest opportunities of your life. The warrior said, "England

> expects every man to do his duty!" But listen, this summer Jesus Christ expects every Christian to do his duty! Let us cast ease aside; let us go out and win men and women for Jesus Christ!

In addition to street corner meetings and services seating 250 on a vacant lot "under the blue canopy of heaven," Oswald organized a neighborhood campaign. A 500-seat tent could not hold the crowds that came to hear the local Baptist and Congregational ministers who shared in the preaching with Oswald.

After that summer, twenty-five new converts were received into the membership. Before Oswald was finished, the church that had been a mission church for thirty years became self-supporting. (Oswald helped meet the budget by taking a 25 percent cut in his own salary.)

But Oswald was bone weary: "I have been tired, so tired in the work of Christ, but not of it. I go to bed tired, get up tired. I am tired and weary all day. Last night I could scarcely crawl up the stairs to bed." Actually, Oswald had been weak and sickly all summer. He had plunged too quickly into the work following the collapse from total exhaustion and the strain of the broken engagement at the end of the school year. A kindly parishioner now took him into her home for two weeks while a doctor came twice daily to treat his throbbing headache and profound weakness.

As could be expected in a parish setting, Oswald had times of deep discouragement when he had to deal with problems among the membership, most of whom were older than he. They did not take kindly to his reading from the pulpit the names of elders not attending prayer meetings, and told him so in no uncertain terms. Such times brought the young pastor to his knees in humility and failure. Feeling utterly broken and wretched, he wept and prayed until God lifted him up. "When I remembered that my Lord was misunderstood so often, then I, the servant, must expect to be misunderstood and blamed, even when I have done my best."

There were other humbling times such as the northside women's meeting when Oswald sang his solo three or four notes too high, and some of the ladies laughed and laughed. "God knows how I got through all four verses. I don't." Worst of all, a few students were there, and Oswald was mortified to face their ridicule at the seminary.

He often smarted at the memory of the day back in Galt, Ontario, when he had had the opportunity to address 300 clergymen. For some reason he had become frightfully nervous and could not remember a thing he had planned to say. What came out was mixed up and made little sense. If only he had had enough sense to have a few catchwords with him! He often felt he had spoken badly, totally missing the mark: "Why, God? Is this the way you choose to conquer my pride?"

Many heartbroken, soul-searching poems were born in such an hour, and Oswald shared some of these poems and melodies with his music teacher, Dr. W. B. Towner, director of music for Moody Church. (Oswald first studied voice, then arranging, pulling off the highest marks in the seminary.) Towner encouraged Oswald, helping him polish his work, then collaborating to have some joint efforts published. Frequently Towner would give Oswald a melody and subject such as "Christ is coming back again," and request he write the words. Sometimes these lyrics would flash into Oswald's mind during lectures or just before he preached and occasionally while he read his favorite biographies of famous Christians. During his second year, he was reading Count Zinzendorf's ringing statement "I have one passion — it is Jesus, Jesus only" when in a flash the hymn "Jesus Only" was born. Towner supplied the melody. With some hymns like "Deeper and Deeper," Oswald had to struggle long months to get precisely what he wanted.

JESUS ONLY

For salvation full and free,
Purchased once on Calvary,
Christ alone shall be my plea—
Jesus! Jesus only!

He's my Guide from day to day,
As I journey on life's way;
Close beside Him let me stay—
Jesus! Jesus only!

May my model ever be
Christ the Lord, and none save He,
That the world may see in me
Jesus! Jesus only!

He shall reign from shore to shore;
His the glory evermore;
Heaven and earth shall bow before
Jesus! Jesus only!

CHORUS
Jesus only, let me see,
Jesus only, none save He;
Thou my song shall ever be
Jesus! Jesus only.

In addition to hymns, Oswald began to publish simple gospel messages. Unable to find a tract that he felt would catch the reader's attention and also clearly explain the way of salvation, he drafted one himself and sent it to Moody Bible Institute. Oswald put up the first ten dollars to purchase 2,000 copies and Moody carried the balance of forty dollars for 10,000 pamphlets entitled "The Question of Questions."

His fellow students sometimes teased "Ozzie," as they called him, for being too serious and "mystic-minded." Nevertheless he joined in their fun, going on hikes and picnics to the beach or boating across the lake and having a cook-out on the shore. Although warmly affectionate and demonstrative with those he knew well, Oswald was painfully shy in a group of strangers, and would sometimes hide away at a party so he would not have to mingle. He was keenly aware that his shortcoming often left him feeling out in the cold. "But I've been alone so much in the past that it's hard; by God's grace I am going to overcome this and be as sociable as others," he pledged at a skating party as he forced himself to join the group around the bonfire.

Still he spent many long hours alone — developing photographs in the darkroom he rigged up in his closet or perusing the art gallery or studying Van Dyke's *How to Judge a Picture* and the *History of Painting.* His great love of poetry led to his teaching a Saturday night class on the poems of his favorite poet, Alfred Lord Tennyson.

As often as they could, several of the seminary students would slip over to the great Moody Church where the dynamic Paul Rader packed in the crowds night after night. Rader preached with the flair of a showman, striding back and forth across the platform. He dramatized the Bible stories with great vividness, and was often backed up with sound effects from the musicians.

Then Billy Sunday came to Chicago. With a rapid-fire delivery, he would preach easily for an hour and a half, running up and down the platform, never still for a moment. Sometimes he would take a great leap right up on top of the pulpit. His emphasis, his appeal was to men, and far more men than women came forward when Billy Sunday gave the invitation. Oswald Smith was greatly impressed.

Yet throughout all his activities and studies, the passionate call to a lost world burned in Oswald's heart like an ember smoldering, waiting only for a fresh breath to blow it into bright flame. His shelf of missionary biographies was growing longer each year. Of all the lives he had studied, none touched his heart like Judson of Burma and David Brainerd, the missionary to the North American Indians. Oswald's missionary vision had shifted from China to Africa during his Toronto Bible Training School days when he had been asked to lead the weekly African mission study group. The cry of that great "dark continent" had gripped his heart, so much so that during his first year at McCormack, he had written a novelette set in Africa. In it, he is imprisoned for the gospel's sake and Jennie dies tragically in his arms. He never published this piece.

Later at McCormack, a stereopticon slide presentation of India's downtrodden women made the strongest appeal:

> India, poor weeping India! My purpose to give my life to the non-Christian world is stronger than ever before. I give myself, body, soul and intellect and all I have for any part of the field in which He wants me to labour. I can't give money for I have not got it, but I can give myself.

Yet all the while, a struggle was going on. "Have you not given me special talents to be an evangelist? Surely I am not to bury these in the foreign field?" Oswald asked God. But then a missionary challenged him: "Oswald, if your desire to be an evangelist is only to speak to large crowds, then it does not amount to much." Finally, Oswald faced up to the truth. He did have a selfish motive:

> My longing to be a great evangelist is surely my besetting sin, the "vainglory of life" of 1 John 2:16, the ambition for fame, popularity, power, greatness. How I have cried to God to give me victory over this. Oh, how vile I am in myself, how selfish is my heart.
>
> "I am crucified with Christ" — I wonder if I can say that. Yet, is it possible to be conscious of certain talents and gifts which one possesses, with the one great yearning to use every single one for God, and at the same time to be humble and wait His time to use them? I do not know, I do not know.
>
> *O to be humble, to seek only His will;*
> *To be willing to be hid and unknown;*
> *To remain in the background*
> *To await His time*
> *to get rid of all desire for fame here*
> *and to get the heart set with intense longing*
> *on the foreign field and His glory.*
>
> Oh, God, take away this devilish worldly ambition; take away this vision of my preaching in Massey Hall and to other great throngs, and send me far away where the people are yearning, pleading for the help I can give. Here, nearly all have heard the gospel at least once. Oh, to give opportunity of salvation to those who have never heard!
>
> *The passions of my soul have all*
> *been kindled into a flame:*
> *I would bleed;*
> *I would sacrifice*
> *I would burn out for Christ!*

Oh, may the compassion of Christ fill my soul! I would spend day after day tramping the streets of the great city, visiting the poorest of the poor, the sick, the oppressed, the weary, worn and tired; bringing cheer and comfort, leaving blessings behind, pointing the sin-sick to my loving Saviour who alone is able to heal the broken heart, bind up the wounds, and make men happy. Service! Service! Service! That is the great keyword. It must be the dominant note of my life.

Lord, come and take:
give me Christ instead of self,
trust instead of worry,
humility instead of pride and vanity,
purity instead of impurity,
patience instead of impatience.
Let me have no will, no ambition of my own.
I have placed my life, my steps in His hands.
I care not where He leads me for I have come to the place
where I am perfectly willing to go to any part of the foreign
field or to stay at home:
to take up evangelistic work, teaching, or pastoral, in city, town or country.
My blessed Saviour is molding this ambitious, stubborn life
to glorify Him. May He burn me out.

ELEVEN
♦♦♦
CHOICES

God make me a conquering man, and enable me to conquer myself. OJS

During his last term at McCormack, Oswald attended a missionary meeting where a map of the world filled the front wall. From it he caught a fresh glimpse of world need; it was not just a choice among China, Africa, or India. Slowly the light broke and Oswald saw that *his work was to be world work:*

> I must be a missionary to the whole world. My own dear country calls me — would that I might set it on fire for God. But *the world is my parish.* Even if I live in one place, *I must reach beyond my local parish to the world.*
>
> Can I be deluded? Surely not. *I feel Him pushing me on.* I count myself God's world-man to go anywhere. It is mine to obey orders; His to give them. If only I can reach lives for Christ! If only I can touch young hearts for service!
>
> *O God, help me to step carefully,*
> *to decide slowly,*
> *to listen to the Spirit's voice,*
> *and to go with certainty.*
> *Let me not make a mistake.*
> *And above all,*
> *make me a "Man of God."*
> *No matter where I go*
> *may I ever*
> *keep the world vision in mind.*
> *Amen.*

As graduation approached, Oswald found he had three choices for future service. One, he could remain at South Chicago, where the work was progressing so well that the elders and congregation felt he should continue. Two, he had been offered a church in Juneau, Alaska. Oswald had applied to the northern mission fields when the Presbyterian Church had turned him down yet another time for overseas/foreign service. Third, he could go to Toronto to assist Reverend Morrow who had just finished the basement auditorium in the new Dale Presbyterian Church. The salary in Chicago would be $1,500; in Juneau $1,200; and in Toronto $600.

Oswald had written a little stanza for himself:

The world is wide in time and tide
And God is Guide: then do not hurry;
That man is blest who does his best
And leaves the rest: then do not worry!

Still, he was in agony, for he could not decide among the three. Then while reading his *Daily Light,* a verse leaped off the page: "And thine ears shall hear a word behind thee, saying, This is the way, walk ye in it . . ." (Isa. 30:21, *KJV*). I will instruct thee and teach thee in the way which thou shalt go! I will guide thee with mine eye" (Psa. 32:8, *KJV*).

"How wonderful!" Oswald responded. *"This is the way* — He promises to show me where He wants me." Two days later, the Scripture was presented during a lecture: "When they desired him to tarry a longer time with them, he consented not" (Acts 18:20, *KJV*). "Praise God!" Oswald exclaimed. "That takes care of South Chicago. Now, is it Juneau or Toronto?"

Oswald had a confidant in Dr. Henry Hepburn, pastor of the church Oswald had joined when he first arrived in Chicago. Hepburn had become a valued friend and counselor, and so Oswald turned to this man of God for help in making the decision. After prayer, they agreed that

Toronto was the choice, with Juneau set aside "for now." That night Oswald wrote in his diary:

> However, I do not look upon Dale [Toronto] as permanent. I shall do my level best while there, but I see it as a door to the greater field that God has for me. Somehow the regular pastorate does not seem to be my life work. *I must be travelling and enthusing others.*

Oswald's ordination on April 30, 1915, the day following graduation, held much meaning for him:

> I spent the whole day in prayer and fasting that I might be ready for the night, reading Psalms 90 and 91, John 13 to 17, and the pastoral epistles, 1st and 2nd Timothy and Titus. *God make me a conquering man, and enable me to conquer myself.*

Two of his poems grew out of this period:

I MUST BE TRUE AND FAITHFUL

I must be true and faithful,
My Master calls me on;
He bids me go where darkness reigns
To tell to souls in error's chains
Of what He did on Calv'ry's tree,
And how He sets poor sinners free.

Oh, here am I, Lord Jesus.
What wouldst Thou have me do?
It is Thy will that I should go,
Or wouldst Thou have me here below
Remain at home to give and pray
That others may Thy call obey?

I hear the voice of Jesus:
"Go ye to all the world,
And tell the News on ev'ry side
Of how I suffered, bled and died,
To make provision full and free
That men might live eternally."

I saw them in their darkness
By Satan's pow'r oppress'd;
In heathen lands, both far and near,
Without one ray of light to cheer,
And, lo, a voice within me cried,
"Go, tell them of the Christ who died."

I dare not tarry longer,
The day will soon be gone,
And darkness fall on land and sea,
The darkness of Eternity,
When harvest time will be no more,
And all my work on earth be o'er.

WE WOULD PRAISE THEE

Blessed Saviour, we would praise Thee
For the wonders of Thy grace;
All along our pilgrim journey,
Thou hast been our Hiding Place.
Often have we been forsaken,
Made to drink the cup anew;
But Thy love has failed us never,
Thou, O Christ, art always true,

Thou hast mingled joy with sorrow
While the years have passed away;
Often has the path been thorny,
Fierce and long the bitter fray.
But the glory of Thy presence
Has been with us day by day;
We have found Thy grace sufficient,
Thou, O Christ, hast been our Stay.

When the love of others failed us
And our hearts were filled with grief,
In Thy fellowship, Lord Jesus,
We have always found relief:
And today our hearts are singing
Of Thy goodness thro' the years,
We would praise Thee, blessed Saviour:
Thou, O Christ, hast dried our tears.

Thou hast weaned us from earth's pleasures
By Thy pow'r and grace divine;
Thou hast filled us with Thy fulness
And our hearts are wholly Thine.
Oh, how precious is Thy presence!
More than all the world beside;
Oh, how great Thy tender mercy
As we in Thy love abide!

And then Oswald Smith set off for Toronto, not just his home, but now his stepping-stone to the world.

TWELVE
♦♦♦
THE PREACHER AND THE DEACONESS

Souls come first, but the next great craving of my heart is. . .for a helpmeet. OJS

Oswald Smith preached his first sermon at Dale Presbyterian Church on June 6, 1915. He marveled that while only twenty-five years old, he had been chosen to be an associate paster in Canada's second largest Presbyterian church, with 800 to 1,000 people packing the basement auditorium for the Sunday evening service. But working with J.D. Morrow involved some activities not usually associated with the ministry. Right away Oswald was pressed into service taking his turn with the "Pay As You Enter" box which Morrow had gotten from the streetcar company and used for collecting money to finish his church. He would stand at the corner of Yonge and Shuter Streets in the heart of downtown Toronto singing and playing a little hand organ from early afternoon until long after the theaters closed. Morrow also discovered a superb spot from which to catch people as they left the Woodbine Race Track, feeling flush with their winnings. He took in a great deal of money this way. Oswald loved Morrow and wanted to do everything he could to help.

Morrow was a splendid evangelistic preacher, who held his audience captive as did Paul Rader at Moody Church. Sometimes he interrupted himself to sing a song he had written;

then with the audience reduced to tears, he would pick up his message and go on with it. But Morrow did not know music, and so Oswald wrote it down for him and arranged publication, together with some of his own compositions. Very quickly 2,500 copies of "Dale Hymns" were off the press.

Oswald also had three of his own poems of comfort printed up in a little four-page pamphlet for pastoral work. "Very, very neat" was his pleased comment. And he was delighted with the new *Alexander's Hymns* which contained two of Oswald's selections, the first to be included in a hymnal.

Morrow shared the pulpit equally with this eager young man who still had so many sermons flashing into his head that he did not know when he would ever get to preach them all. Oswald's one passion was for souls, and only a few were being saved. (There was one service at the reformatory where forty accepted Christ in response to Smith's preaching.) "But God never intended a minister to preach without results: souls must be awakened. Sinners must tremble. Lost ones must be saved and Christians consecrated and led to dedicate themselves for service. I cannot be satisfied with less. Oh, God! Send a revival to Dale!" was his desperate prayer from the first week.

His heart was still seized with a missionary passion. "It doesn't seem fair," he wrote in his diary that first summer:

> *Every man should have a chance to be saved.* Here in the homeland, most have had that chance. But out there — Oh, God, take me if thou wilt and let me go. What a joy it would be to tell the story to those who have never heard. There is no honor to equal it here! Four times I have applied and have been rejected. Perhaps next time it will be different.

Yet on the whole Oswald was delighted with his lot: "I feel as if I have left the rolling billows of the ocean and arrived in a safe harbour where the waters are tranquil and calm." He was enjoying being with his family again. They had moved to Toronto's east end and Oswald had fixed up a cozy study in the attic. That Christmas all nine children and their parents were together. Oswald carved the turkey and played the piano for the younger children to sing; then after supper he read the first and last chapters of Dicken's *A Christmas Carol* to the family. It was a happy day, even if Oswald had to interrupt it for a funeral and a sick call.

Early in the new year, Morrow went to Florida for a vacation, leaving Oswald in charge. The next day, a young couple came to the vestry requesting marriage, and Oswald was delighted to perform his first wedding. Somehow this came to the attention of a fellow minister who called Oswald, advising him that the marriage was not legal because Oswald had not yet been received into the Toronto Presbytery and that Oswald should urge the couple to "re-marry." Oswald quickly searched them out at their Toronto address, only to find they had left. The next morning Oswald set off for Hamilton to find the husband who was in the army barracks there. Somehow he could not trace him. Then he went to the girl's home in Grimsby; the bride had not told her parents she was married and so was greatly perturbed when Oswald showed up on the doorstep. The girl confessed all, then with Oswald went to Hamilton to find the young man and a minister who was properly authorized to perform a marriage. Oswald did not get home until midnight.

Oswald's chagrin at the event was lessened considerably by the company he'd had along with him for the day — Daisy Billings, Dale's prim and petite deaconess, just four months younger than Oswald. He had met her soon after his arriving back in Toronto, and had not been much impressed with the severe, drab blue uniform she wore. (Morrow, too, thought it "looked best hanging on the wall!") Still, she was most efficient in her duties, and was greatly loved by the people. Before Oswald's coming, Daisy had preached once a month, and was called a "crackerjack."

Like Oswald, Daisy Billings was a serious-minded Christian. Over the months they were often thrown together on church business. He found her company most agreeable and enjoyed her family, who were pillars in the Christian and Missionary Alliance Church. Daisy had studied at their Nyack training school, then had spent a few months preaching to the coal miners of West Virginia before coming to Toronto to train as a Presbyterian deaconess. She had been on the staff of Dale just a year before Oswald arrived. All in all, they were having some pleasant times together, especially when she left the uniform at home and looked little more than a girl of twenty-two.

But once again, Oswald was letting himself get run down. With Morrow away for all of February, Oswald had full responsibility for not only the church, but also the building program which was nearing completion; then the details of the opening ceremonies had to be worked out. By the middle of March, Oswald was facing total exhaustion again, and the terrible, debilitating headaches and mental depression returned, along with the deep fatigue.

The doctor kept him in bed so that he missed hearing Daisy preach the last sermon in the basement of the church. "Her praises were sung to the skies; she must have preached a great sermon. I wanted so much to hear her!" Oswald wrote regretfully.

Then the doctor sent him down to a noted health clinic in Clifton Springs, New York, for a month's treatment in the mineral baths. But the "rest cure" Oswald himself devised during the last week seemed to work the miracle, and he decided to stick with it for the rest of his life — a two-hour rest each afternoon. He noted in his diary:

> But oh, how I hate this lazy life! I never knew before just how much I really loved work. I used to feel condemned if I took an hour or two off through the day; it was go, go, go from early morning till late night. And this has gone on for seven years, constant, steady. No wonder I have not known what it was to feel well for the space of a week! Now my prayer must be "Lord, what must I leave undone today?"
>
> I understand my system now and realize just how it must be cared for: I will cut out all pastoral calls except sick calls; for all else the people must come to me. My teeth and tonsils must be attended to,

> and I am on a strict diet for the rest of my life. And so with exercise, rest, and diet, I expect to avoid future breakdowns and do my work without interruption. I must put the brakes on, slow up, if I am to stand the test of time and hold out.
>
> *But oh, how my heart burns for the foreign field. Would that I had the strength to go! Oh, may He fill me and make me a missionary here.*

Now, for some time Oswald had been looking for living quarters closer to the church and a little quieter than home with eight boisterous brothers and sisters. Shortly after returning from Clifton Springs, he found just the perfect house. The next day he walked Miss Billings over to see it.

It's very nice, she thought. *It will do just fine for that Chicago girl who came up to see him in the winter.* She was baffled when one week later a bouquet of flowers, along with the request for a date with the associate pastor, was delivered to her house. What Daisy did not know was that during Oswald's long stay at Clifton Springs he had decided that if she would have him, he would marry her.

From the day Oswald had first trusted Christ, he had prayed two prayers: first, that God would guide him to his life's work; second, that God would give him a wife to share that life. "No good thing will He withhold from those who fear Him," God had promised. Further, the Scripture stated, "Whosoever findeth a wife, findeth a good thing." Oswald coveted finding this "good thing":

> I would value more, and rather have a woman's love than all the fame that the whole world could heap upon me. *Souls come first,* but the next great craving of my heart is the yearning for a helpmeet. God grant that she may rise to my largeness of vision, with an understanding of the great ambition of my heart.

Then Oswald had gone through the agony of becoming willing to go through life alone if that was the way he could do God's work best.

Finally, at Clifton Springs God had revealed to him that the one for whom he had prayed these long years, the one whose love would truly satisfy for all time — this perfect "helpmeet," — was right under his nose, and had been for almost a year.

And so one evening in late May, Oswald took Daisy to a fallen log along the shores of Lake Ontario and there asked her to share his life. The answer? Yes! Daisy had loved this gangling new preacher from the start, in spite of her resentment at him coming. She had assumed that Morrow needed no other help than what she could give. But she was impressed with Oswald's luminous, piercing eyes and his confident bearing. When he preached, there was a fire that sent shivers up her back.

One week later on June 1, 1916, they rented a canoe and paddled up the Humber River to a high hill overlooking the Old Mill. There Oswald placed a ring on her finger. He wrote:

> Precious girl! She is more to me than she will ever know. I never, never knew another like her. She is far, far sweeter than I ever dreamed.

Once more the poems flew from Oswald's pen — no longer sad, but lyrical rhapsodies of new love. Daisy responded enthusiastically: "To think that soon we need never part again. I would like to see not another human being for at least a year after we are married. Oh, Oswald, I'll go with you anywhere in the Lord's work no matter what suffering it costs. But I can never let you go alone!"

The two twenty-six-year-olds spent many happy hours together fixing up the house on Garden Avenue. Oswald painted the outside and planted a little vegetable garden; Daisy chose paint and wallpaper, and a cousin came to help with the work.

Then, a month before the wedding, Morrow called Oswald into his office. "You know I am chaplain of the 'Sportsman's Battalion.'"

"Yes."

"You know that I have been promising the boys I would

join them overseas just as soon as I had this church building completed.'' Oswald knew. ''Well, I'm leaving at the end of September. When you get back from your honeymoon, you'll be the acting minister of Dale for all the time I'm gone.''

At this time Morrow was fed up with the constant opposition from some members of the session who accused the energetic, enterprising minister of going ahead on his own in matters where his church officials should have been consulted. They were particularly upset when this happened in financial areas.

It fell to Oswald to chair the stormy meeting requesting a leave of absence for Morrow and setting the salary of the interim pastor at $1,500 annually. Still he was penniless as the wedding approached, and had to borrow $100 from a former teacher at the Bible college, who happened to be independently wealthy and who had become a close friend over the years.

On the wedding day, September 16, more than two-thousand friends jammed Dale Church to witness the 8:00 P.M. ceremony. They waited and waited while Daisy paced the floor at home wondering what had happened to the limousine they had hired to take her to the church. It had gone to the wrong address, but at 8:25 finally arrived at her door.

The young couple had announced a honeymoon trip to Quebec City (Oswald's father had arranged a free railway pass). After the ceremony, while Morrow and Daisy's father searched the sleeping cars at Union Station, trying to find the newlyweds, Oswald whisked his bride away to their own little home because ''no girl should have to spend her wedding night in a train berth.''

Saved!
Oswald J. Smith
Roger M. Hickman
1. Saved! saved! saved! My sins are all for - giv'n;
2. Saved! saved! saved! By grace and grace a - lone;
3. Saved! saved! saved! Oh, joy be - yond com - pare!
Christ is mine! I'm on my way to heav'n;
Oh, what won - drous love to me was shown,
Christ my life, and I His con - stant care;
Once a guilt - y sin - ner, lost, un - done,
In my stead Christ Je - sus bled and died,
Yield - ing all and trust - ing Him a - lone,
Now a child of God, saved through His Son.
Bore my sins, for me was cru - ci - fied.
Liv - ing now each mo - ment as His own.
Refrain
Saved! I'm saved through Christ, my all in
through Christ, my
all; Saved! I'm saved, what -
all in all;
ev - er may be - fall; He died up - on the
cross for me, He bore the aw - ful pen - al - ty; And
now I'm saved e - ter - nal - ly, I'm saved! saved! saved!

THIRTEEN
♦♦♦
REVIVE THY WORK, O LORD!

Prayer will do the work. The battle is not ours but God's. OJS

Oswald was inducted as acting pastor on October 16, 1916, but less than two months later, resigned. He could not control the board meetings which had been out of hand even before Morrow had left. Moreover, this sternly erect young preacher with piercing blue eyes and shock of blond hair strode the platform preaching repentance and revival — he was a little more than some of the staid congregation had bargained for. Certainly he was attracting crowds, more than Morrow ever did, with over two hundred on Sunday mornings and closer to twelve hundred in the evenings. Oswald would preach at night, and for the morning service would bring in some of the finest men of the day including Jonathan Goforth, Roland Bingham, and John McNicholl.

But many of the members did not like the big banner he had hung right across the front of the sanctuary, with bold red letters: GET RIGHT WITH GOD. Sunday nights he abandoned the hymnbooks in favor of song sheets with the bright new gospel songs such as "O That Will Be Glory" and his own new revival hymn "Saved!"

The choir began objecting strenuously to the new gospel songs and to the singers Oswald brought in for special music.

One night the choir outright refused to go on, and he felt he had no choice but to resign. "I never will have a choir if I can help it," he vowed. Three weeks later, the session ruled that the choir must submit to the minister and Oswald was reinstated. But "we had no Christmas this year," he starkly recorded.

Then just as all seemed to be quieted down, one Sunday morning Oswald forgot to introduce the soloist, and the whole choir was up in arms again. The choir director resigned, and the senior elder resigned from the choir and all his offices. Oswald was also having difficulty getting the man of his choice appointed Sunday school superintendent.

Oswald felt there was a warring faction composed of those to whom the church was little more than a social club, and these were mostly lodge brothers. He often felt that lodge loyalty determined many appointments and decisions rather than a seeking after godly leadership and spirituality. There were some groups that he felt actually hated each other.

Oswald reasoned:

> I can do one of three things. I can bow down to the worldly element and be ruled by it; or I can overthrow it and insist on spirituality; or I can leave the church.
>
> I'm not in Dale to fight until I have to; but by God's grace and help, I'll take the second course and overthrow the worldly faction.
>
> I take my stand today for
> 1. A spirit-filled eldership
> 2. A Christian managing board
> 3. A saved choir with consecrated leader
> 4. A redeemed membership
>
> DALE WILL YET BE A MONUMENT TO PRAYER.

There was a group standing in prayer with Oswald — those whose lives had been touched and transformed under his ministry during the past two years.

But these first four months at the helm had indeed been stormy ones, and again the battle took its toll: Oswald could not sleep, and his head throbbed and ached all night. Utterly exhausted and unable to carry on with the work, he took a month's leave of absence, going to Daisy's family in Peterborough where he chopped ice or played with the children and pulled Daisy on the sleigh through the snow. There he met George Stenton, whose deep Christian fellowship he enjoyed. Stenton had written some hymns which Oswald was happy to correct and send away to his own music publisher, and Oswald wrote some music himself.

Back at the church, he plunged in with renewed vigor. Night after night, "Oswald Smith's Soul-saving Gang" gathered in the "upper room" to pray. On holidays they fasted and prayed all day and evening. He wrote:

> Prayer will do the work. The battle is not ours but God's. Let us stand still and see the salvation of Jehovah. Jehovah will fight for us (2 Chron. 20:15; Exod. 14:13, 14).
>
> *Revive Thy work, O Lord! And manifest Thy pow'r;*
> *O come upon Thy church, and give a penitential show'r!*
>
> *Revive Thy work, O Lord! And every soul inspire;*
> *O kindle in each heart, we pray, The pentecostal fire!*
>
> *Revive Thy work, O Lord! And give abounding joy;*
> *O fill our hearts with perfect love, And burn out all alloy!*
>
> *Revive Thy work, O Lord! And make Thy servants bold;*
> *Convict of sin and work once more As in the days of old.*
>
> *Revive Thy work, O Lord! Fulfill Thy promise true;*
> *Let Jesus Christ be glorified, And great things for us do!*

Joining in prayer with Oswald and the people at the church were several older men whom Oswald had come to know and love as he met with them each Friday afternoon in the west end YMCA, for one-and-a-half hours of prayer, crying to God for revival first in Toronto and then across the nation. "Oh, God, make me your instrument," Oswald pleaded, and these men supported him in his desire. They shared with Oswald books on revival, and the writings of the Puritans began to revolutionize his life. He discovered John Fletcher, vicar of Madeley, Switzerland:

> Aside from David Brainerd, none has so stirred me to prayer and holiness of heart as has the seraphic Fletcher. He is truly one of the most remarkable characters in all history. His spirituality and whole-hearted devotion to God, in the estimation of many have been unsurpassed.

In agonies of soul-searching, he fell on his face before God and cried:

Have I grieved Thy Holy Spirit?
Have I quenched His pow'r within?
If I have, O Lord, forgive me,
Cleanse my heart from ev'ry sin.

O my Saviour, come I pray Thee,
As I at Thine Altar bow;
Hear, O hear my heart's confession,
Pardon, cleanse, and fill me now.

Do I lack the grace He giveth?
Have I pow'r to win the lost?
Is my message unavailing?
Fill me, Lord, at any cost!

Do I yield to sin's allurement,
Havings lost the pow'r to win,
Since I grieved Thy Holy Spirit
When I let the tempter in?

Lord, I come in deep contrition,
Yielding all I have to Thee
Making now a full surrender —
Thine forever would I be.

Finney became his constant textbook — Finney who put off his wedding to preach, who often prayed the night through with his faithful prayer partners.

This touched off such a seeking after God that Oswald was sometimes up and out of the house before breakfast; often these men from the YMCA met at 5:00 in the afternoon and prayed until midnight and even until 1:00, 2:00, and 3:00 in the morning, agonizing with their faces on the floor before God — meals forgotten. Oswald asked George Stenton to come and be his prayer warrior, even as Finney had his Father Nash to back him in prayer.

And the power of God began to be mightily in evidence, with much sobbing and brokenness as seekers lined the altar. Twelve came for salvation the first night that Oswald announced an after meeting. Night after night people cried out for God, not wanting to go home. Some fell on their faces before the altar; others fell back, smitten by the Spirit. They were coming without an invitation. Sins were confessed and old wrongs, righted. None of the leading elders attended prayer meetings, but they objected to what they heard had gone on: "We're Presbyterian and do not believe in conversion." Even so the meetings continued, and Oswald crystallized the mood of the people in his hymn "With Thy Spirit Fill Me":

Lord, possess me now, I pray,
Make me wholly Thine today;
Gladly do I own Thy sway,
With Thy Spirit fill me.

Lord, I yield myself to Thee,
All I am or hope to be
Now and through eternity,
With Thy Spirit fill me.

Lord, commission me, I pray!
Souls are dying every day;
Help me lead them in Thy way,
With Thy Spirit fill me.

With Thy Spirit fill me,
With Thy Spirit fill me;
Make me wholly Thine, I pray,
With Thy Spirit fill me.

A broken Oswald asked:

> But do my nearest and dearest believe in my religion? Do I get irritated still? Lord, undertake for me. Make me a sweeter, more tender

> and loving husband, a more Christlike man in my home, an example of godliness and true spirituality. Oh, how far short I fall! May I not be a stumbling block to my wife but rather, make me a pattern of holiness and love. Grant us a happier and more perfect union. Oh, that my heart might be filled with perfect love, for where love is perfect there can be no malice or temper, jealousy or pride. Oh, how I yearn for more love. How my heart hungers for righteousness. How I long for more of God!

One day, Daisy discovered a little love poem on the kitchen table:

> *How glad I am tonight, O dearest one,*
> *That I can call you "wife," my own true wife;*
> *Mine only, all, and held by bands of love*
> *That naught can e'er unloose in death or life.*
>
> *What nearer, sweeter union could there be?*
> *Wife, husband, home, and love the best of all,*
> *All knit in one, a bond with none more dear,*
> *By God ordained long years before the Fall.*
> *— O darling mine, 'tis sweet to call you "wife."*

Nonetheless, Daisy was smarting, in spite of her adoration for her new husband. Not only had Oswald never asked her to preach, keeping the pulpit for himself, but also what had happened to those dreams she and Oswald had shared of lovely evenings together in their own little parlor? "I don't want to see anyone else for a whole year," she had written to him on the eve of their wedding. But now she was left alone while others had moved in to share his life, to be the soul-mate she had hoped to be, and she felt trapped at home with their child. Daisy had found herself pregnant almost immediately after their honeymoon, and had been sick for most of the nine months. She had been able to do some deaconess work, but now even this had been taken from her. It was a far cry from the days when the gay, personable Morrow had driven his devoted little deaconess about town on the back of his motorcycle.

Besides, she was not at all sure she agreed with the course Oswald was on. Holiness teaching was not new to Daisy; she had grown up with it. She had personally experienced the blessing of the Holy Spirit in a wonderful way when just in her late teens. She knew what it was to sit at the dinner table surrounded by family, but to be so caught up in the things of God that she scarcely knew what was going on around her. Her father too had been wonderfully anointed. And at Nyack there had been a good deal of emphasis on seeking the infilling of the Holy Spirit.

But the very practical Daisy had put all that aside when she had come to the Presbyterian Church. Moreover, she felt that the day-to-day work of Dale was suffering with Morrow overseas and with Oswald giving himself almost totally to seeking revival within his own soul and the church.

And then there was this matter of his missionary vision: even before marriage they had been talking of going to Alaska. But that was before Morrow announced he had enlisted and would be requesting a leave of absence and thus needed Oswald to "hold the fort in his absence."

"Daisy, if I can't go, I must be a missionary here," Oswald had insisted. "Dale is not a missionary church, because Mr. Morrow somehow never caught the vision. God help me make Dale a missionary church!"

"The supreme task of the church is the evangelization of the world" — Oswald had been trumpeting this since his first summer at Dale. But then he had added: *"Missions is not to be confined to an organization within the church. It is the chief work of the whole church."* This view created a problem with the Women's Missionary Society.

Then when he took up his first missionary offering from the general congregation, amounting to $600, the die was cast. "If we look after foreign work, God will look after the home work," Oswald firmly believed. This attitude created a lot of opposition, however, and some who previously had stood with him now turned against him: "Fancy sending $600 out of the church when we need it so badly right here!" It was true that Dale Church was in financial need. Morrow had left the church in fairly severe debt, and Oswald had wondered how it could survive.

Morrow returned from overseas in the spring of 1918, too ill to resume preaching duties. He hardly knew how to react to what was going on in his church. There were many who had felt, and publicly stated, that only Morrow could fill Dale Church, yet Oswald had kept it filled while he was away. Financially it had not gone under, although it was not out of debt either.

Eventually these two good friends had a serious misunderstanding. There were even public accusations in which Oswald was charged with having plunged the church deeper into debt. It was a bitter, bitter blow to Oswald but he would not fight Morrow, saying, "He was a great man, and I loved him." And so only three years after he had come Oswald resigned. At twenty-eight, he was crushed and heartbroken.

FOURTEEN
♦♦♦
THE DOOR CLOSES

O God, has my ministry come to an end? Are you putting me on the shelf? OJS

The weeks leading up to his leaving Dale Presbyterian Church were extremely difficult ones for Oswald. In his diary he had recorded:

> We get no light, no gift of faith, no opening of heaven, no spiritual outbursts anymore. We are still up against a wall where we have been for weeks now. The conflict is hard. All, all is dark.
>
> I have been giving nearly all my time to prayer, mostly alone. How unworthy I feel, how far away from God. I wonder that He should ever choose so useless and weak a vessel. Yet in spite of growing darkness I feel a calm confidence in God.

Then in the midst of the turmoil, one Sunday night Oswald's preaching was interrupted by a young woman crying out to God for salvation. An awe seemed to sweep through the audience as men and women began weeping and sobbing aloud. "How wonderful that God should give this taste of revival when all is so dark!" Oswald marveled. He wrote that

> the battle is not yours, but God's! 2 Chron. 20:15. "Stand still and see the salvation of the Lord. . . . The Lord shall fight for you" Exod. 14:13, 14 — these verses tell me to leave things in God's hands and take no action myself. He will deal with "the Egyptians" who oppose me.

Thus when he went before the session of Knox Presbyterian, who had been contributing to his support and had the oversight of Dale Church, Oswald refused to discuss his differences with Morrow; even so, the session unanimously recommended that Dale not accept Oswald's resignation. Nevertheless, to Oswald's stunned sorrow, his resignation was accepted by the board. "None of my friends were at the meeting," he recorded that night.

He preached his last sermon at Dale Church on October 27, 1918. "You Need Jesus" from John 7:37 was his parting shot, to conclude a stormy, yet wonderfully blessed three-and-a-half years. "And the best part of Dale was that it was there that I found my dear wife," Oswald could say.

Earlier in September, Oswald had known that his resignation was in the offing. While desperately hoping that God would intervene and turn things around (because "if *God* had opened the door of Dale, then no *man* can shut it," he kept reassuring himself from Revelation three), Oswald had begun looking for something to do, just in case that door should be closed. He was asked to go to France to take charge of a "hut" behind the lines for the Soldiers' Christian Association. He shared the fact that he was considering this with a close friend. Imagine his chagrin when he decided to accept the post, only to learn that his confidant had already quickly applied and had been accepted, thus snaffling the job from right under Oswald's nose.

Oswald was left with nothing, and winter was coming on. To ease the financial load, he moved his family from the Garden Avenue honeymoon nest into a snug apartment. The house had proved hard to heat, and had needed many repairs. The $1,500 from Dale was not enough to go round especially when Oswald was helping his parents buy a house. Sometimes when short of coal, they had to let the furnace go out while Oswald, Daisy, and baby Glen huddled through the night around the little stove in the kitchen. Daisy and Glen had both been very ill.

Through all this, Dr. Ralph Hooper had stood by as a close

friend. Hooper was the family doctor, but more — he was one of the prayer warriors who had met with Oswald at the YMCA or in his study at the church or at home whenever Hooper could steal away from his practice. He was also a first-class preacher, and put this above his medicine. Oswald's friends from Toronto Bible Training School days also became more precious than ever. (Oswald happily had been appointed president of the Alumni Association.)

One day several Christian businessmen approached Oswald, requesting that he serve as pastor for their group which had broken from the Plymouth Brethren. They were meeting independently in Beulah Tabernacle, a beautiful little building on Charles Street, half a block east of Yonge in downtown Toronto. There was a strong missionary emphasis among these dedicated men of God. Oswald felt the call was of the Lord.

During the days at Beulah Tabernacle, Oswald attended a "Victorious Life Conference" and the ministry of George Trumbull, editor of the *Sunday School Times,* blessed him abundantly. There Oswald discovered that his trust must be "moment by moment" and that his faith must be exercised constantly, for "the just shall live by faith."

In addition to Trumbull's teaching, Oswald had come to know William Newell since Oswald had helped to raise $1,100 for publishing Newell's great work on Romans. As Oswald now considered the teachings of that book, he gradually realized that all his pleading and entreating, his groaning and weeping while he tarried at the altar, trying to persuade God to pour out His Spirit, was almost like the prophets of Baal who had cut themselves and cried aloud to no avail:

> What a false impression of our Father God to think of Him as unwilling to bestow His gifts, when He is far more willing to give than we are to receive. "How much more will your Father give the Holy Spirit to them that ask Him!" God loves to give; it delights His Father heart.
>
> I need no longer "tarry," waiting for the Holy Spirit to come. *He is here.* The question is one of real surrender, of confessing and

> renouncing every sin and clearing my life of any obstacle so that the river of the blessed Holy Spirit can flow through my life. He longs, He yearns to enter and fill each room in my heart just as soon as I open it to Him. Praise God, I need not struggle, plead and wait. I need only take! *As I yield fully to God, He will fill me.* Whether I feel different matters not: I will reckon that God has accepted my surrender and has filled me, according to His promise.

One night after Trumbull's meeting, Oswald decided to put this to the test:

> I stood on Romans 6:11 and Galatians 2:20, dead to sin and alive to God by faith. It was a real and glorious experience. I rejoiced with great joy and much liberty. Again and again I sang of His love; I prayed and sang and wept, for the presence of Christ was very real. He seemed to fill all the room where I was and to be with me each moment as I walked the streets.
>
> But yet, this teaching stops short of the "Anointing," or the "Enduement of Power from on High," which Wesley, Finney and others had, and which made them the mighty men of God that they were. And *I want this Power without which there can be no revival, no deep conviction of sin.*

These were humbling days for the man who had pastored a large aggressive church and now found himself once more working with smaller groups, speaking to mothers' meetings and at the jail and missions. Worse still, when in January 1919, the idolized Paul Rader came to town for a campaign at Massey Hall, Oswald was pushed aside while some of his former colleagues graced the platform. He was not even permitted to usher or to do personal work in the inquiry rooms. "Oh God, have you no more use for me? Has my ministry come to an end? Are you putting me on the shelf?" Oswald cried despairingly.

Then he decided to sell hymnbooks in the aisles. One evening when the song leader, Arthur McKee, asked the audience to sing a new song, "Saved!" he announced, "Do you see the author's name at the top, *Oswald J. Smith?* Well, there he is, the man in that aisle selling hymnbooks." To

Oswald's mortification every head turned around. But he was immensely gratified to hear his favorite testimony hymn sung for the first time, with 3,400 voices fairly lifting the roof. He wrote in his diary:

> How wonderful to think of those days when I was sixteen and used to try to compose hymns as I went back and forth to school. Now after thirteen years I have the exceeding great joy of hearing one of them sung in the great Massey Hall where I was saved. Oh, how passing strange!

That night God spoke to Oswald, reassuring him that, indeed, he was not going to be put on the shelf.

But what was he to do? Oswald had now turned twenty-nine. Winter was passing into spring, and with it came the growing certainty that Beulah Tabernacle was not God's place for him after all. He did not sense there the burning passion for souls that he craved. Barton Street Baptist in Hamilton asked him to consider a call, but Oswald "felt led to decline." William Newell suggested that Oswald travel with him as an evangelist. Then the next day, St. Clarens Church of Christ offered Oswald a pastorate at $1,600 per year, but he refused that also.

"Oswald, you really must do something — anything!" an exasperated Daisy finally protested. After all, times were hard. They had not even the thirty-five dollars to pay the apartment rent, and so had had to put their furniture into storage and move in with Daisy's parents who had settled in Toronto's west end. The bills were piling up from the printers — Oswald was always printing tracts or booklets of some sort. There was a lawyer's letter demanding payment for car repairs. Daisy was so upset that she packed some bags and took Glen to stay with relatives in Peterborough.

And then along came a letter of "fearful accusation" from the pastor who had taken over his pulpit in Chicago. Oswald wept and sorrowed deeply at this "last great blow since leaving Dale." He recorded that

> the battle is hard. Crushed again and again by Satan. A real contest. Day by day he has thrown something unexpected at me. I have been brought very low indeed.

Daisy was right — they had to do something. Although Oswald was quite ill with a cold, they packed up their few belongings and caught a train the next day for British Columbia.

Enroute, Oswald had a few things to straighten out in Chicago, and so headed directly for the home of his former chief elder. He also met with other elders and Sunday school superintendent to clear up the false charges. Still, he was not permitted to preach in his old church. "But I believe the day will come when God will lift His hand and let me do so," he affirmed. "How I would love to proclaim the message once again from that pulpit!"

FIFTEEN

♦♦♦

WITH THE LOGGERS

If they do not come, we have no choice but to go to them. OJS

Oswald's mission in British Columbia was with the Shantymen's Christian Association. Back in January, during the Paul Rader meetings, he had met the SCA superintendent William Henderson. On learning of Oswald's earlier experience in British Columbia, Henderson had shared that the Shantymen were looking for someone to go into the coastal logging camps under their auspices.

At first Oswald had put it out of his mind; the idea was certainly not very appealing when both he and Daisy were hoping for another large city pastorate. But every so often the thought would pop to the surface. Oswald had even gone out on a $215 limb to print 35,000 tracts with six of his messages he thought would be ideal for the lumberjacks — just in case. Miraculously the $215 with train fare came in to pay that bill, and they arrived in Vancouver on April 1, 1919.

It turned out to be a miserable spring and summer for Daisy. Moving five times in the first three months — from damp basements and single rooms before finally settling into a fairly comfortable furnished home at Kitsalano Beach — did not help her. Oswald was away most of the time for periods of three to fours day or a week. There was even one sixteen-day stretch that seemed an eternity. When he was home, he was busy correcting the proofs for a poetry manuscript he was having printed; he was also hurrying a second book to the publisher.

In his absence, Daisy did some speaking, and often visited with two Presbyterian deaconess friends she had come to know during her training in Toronto. But most of the time she felt wretched: she was pregnant again and Glen had been seriously ill, but most of the misery was in her own soul.

For weeks Daisy found herself unable to read her Bible or pray. She felt deserted, left behind, trapped between the baby's fevers and too little money while her racehorse husband surged ahead in great leaps and strides, his eye on the goal, with blinders to all distractions. She lamented in a letter to Oswald:

> To think that once I knew how to lay hold of God for answers to prayer better than you! But somehow my heart seems numbed, my spirit cast down, my grip on God gone. Somehow I cannot attain to the life of prayer and faith I once had. I have tried many times to get it back.
>
> Now my life seems so useless, so void, so blameable. My darling, I know I have grieved and disappointed you, not because I wanted to, but because I seem bound by a power that has tried to keep you back.
>
> But this separation is teaching me a lesson. Ever since we have been married, I have leaned upon you and not upon my Lord. I have put you in place of the Lord Jesus, and no wonder I have failed — failed as a Christian, failed as a wife, as a mother, as a helper to you in the Lord's work.
>
> But today I have prayed for you and your work as I have not done for a long time. I long to know the Lord as I used to know Him.

At the end of June, having settled Daisy into the Kitsalano house, Oswald that same evening set out on his "sixth missionary journey." This time he was accompanied by his dear friend and co-worker Dr. Ralph Hooper, who had sold his car and left his medical practice and family to rough it in the bush with Oswald.

And rough it they did, often hiking ten and twelve miles

through rugged forest and along railway ties, skinning over the slippery log booms (they got a dunking more than once!), and riding the logging trains through the silent forest and narrow canyons, standing on a little six-by-ten-foot platform and holding on for dear life as they whizzed at dizzying speeds over spindly trestles and around hairpin turns with the sheer rock dropping away hundreds of feet to the rushing river below. At night they slept on the beach or in floating bunkhouses, sometimes shivering on the floor under a mattress for a little warmth or squashed into a single cot. At times they preached on empty stomaches, but more often they feasted on the bounty of the logging camps. Oswald often reported feeling desperately ill, but they had to press on. For as he wrote,

> God's word to us for the unsaved is "Go out! Go out!" Our duty is not done when we minister only to those who come into our churches. If they do not come, we have no choice but to go to them. Our Lord "went out" and so must we. And oh the job that fills our hearts as we follow in the footsteps of our Master, going from camp to camp even as He went from village to village. "Stay here, Lord," they said to Him. But He replied, "Let us go into the next towns, that I may preach there also" (Mark 1:37, 38).

They never took a collection at their meetings and gave away many gospel portions, especially in Japanese and Chinese, and felt more welcomed among these people.

On the whole, their reception was anything but warm. Rarely did the men give them a decent hearing; sometimes they would just stay away or crank up the gramophone or drown out the preachers with the power saws and engines. Oswald found this the hardest field he had ever tackled:

> We talk and preach and pray, and give away tracts and gospels, and yet we find no conviction, no penitence, no breaking down, no seeking for God, no visible outcome. How we realize our own helplessness and failure. *We must have the Enduement of Power from on High.* Nothing less will be equal to the task.

One morning when Oswald was "fasting and praying out in the woods, seeking the Power," a vivid impression "with much joy and exaltation of the spirit" came to him that he was to return to Toronto. In a vision he saw the poor district surrounding his old Toronto parish: ". . . and my heart went out to minister to them. I must return to Toronto to start a work. Perhaps it is Dale."

"Let's go right now," Daisy insisted when Oswald shared the vision. But Oswald felt he had a commitment to finish out his term. Oswald's sister came out to stay with Daisy, and two other friends from Toronto visited; even so, as the summer went on, Daisy, feeling more uncomfortable with each passing day and wanting to get settled before the new baby, pled with her husband: "I cannot think the Lord intends these separations. It is agony until I see you again. I don't care what you do in Toronto, so long as I have you with me. Please make this your last trip and don't leave me anymore."

Thus on September 1, upon completion of their "tenth missionary journey" which included another ten-mile hike along the railway ties, with neither lunch nor supper, Oswald left Vancouver for Toronto. He was accompanied by Daisy and Glen.

Oswald reviled himself: "I'm such a failure as a missionary. I'm too cowardly even to give out tracts on the train. After the hundreds of thousands of tracts I've had printed! The Lord have mercy on me!" He made up for it the next day by doggedly going through the cars and giving two tracts to every passenger. On the whole, he felt the summer experience had been good:

> It's taught me many things I needed to know, most of all, how to visit, the great value of it, and how to make my visits count for God. How to preach in the open air, unafraid. How to be tender and more loving, and lead my people as a true and faithful shepherd. How to live the life of faith and look to God for daily guidance, trust Him for all and see His hand in everything. I will love my home as never before; let a man suffer hardship as we have this summer and he will not be in a hurry to leave his comfortable home again. And I will

appreciate Daisy as never before. How much more I love her! How much nearer we have been drawn together! I feel sure that God will make our united lives happier than ever before.

What the future holds I do not know. To my prayer "Lord, what will you have me to do?" the only answer I have yet received is "Arise and go into the city and it shall be told thee what thou must do" Acts 9:6. So we are going to Toronto and leaving everything in His hands.

SIXTEEN
◆◆◆
WAITING ON JESUS

It is not so much where *I am to labour; surely, if God has anointed me for service, He can use me anywhere.* OJS

Once more Daisy's parents made room for the little family, and Oswald began looking for something to do. Dale Presbyterian still had not called a pastor, and the congregational meeting was scheduled for September 24; Oswald was among those being considered. The previous week had been an anxious one; Oswald had slept little, "thinking till his mind was almost vacant." At the voting, he did not even come close. "The Lord knows best," wrote Oswald and closed that book. Reluctantly.

The next day he was in Roland Bingham's office, accepting a fifteen-dollar-a-week job as editor on a half-time basis of the monthly magazine *The Evangelical Christian.* Bingham was the founder of the Evangelical Publishers, the Sudan Interior Mission, and the world-famous Keswick Bible Conference in Muskoka, Ontario. Later that same day Oswald was appointed secretary of the Shantymen's Christian Association at a salary of twenty dollars a week. Thirty-five dollars total! "The Lord is good. More than I deserve or am worth!" Oswald exulted.

Three days later, he headed into Northern Ontario on

behalf of the Shantymen. After sitting up all night on the train, he checked into a hotel first thing in the morning to get a little sleep. But the bedbugs cut it short, and he set out to walk fourteen miles into a logging camp. "Bully for you!" the men cheered when the gaunt young preacher staggered exhausted into the clearing. Most of them attended the meeting, with perfect attention. All that week he slogged many miles — mostly on foot — through the mud of the forests, going from camp to camp and getting soaked to the skin. Arriving home early Sunday morning, Oswald had a pleasant day with his family. After church that evening Daisy dumbfounded him by announcing that in his absence she had bought a house just two blocks from her mother's. Where she had gotten the down payment, Oswald did not know.

Throughout the fall Oswald worked on the magazine, asked for a cut in salary, and later refused his pay from the Shantymen's because he did not feel he was doing enough. There was a restlessness, with rumors that Knox was going to buy Dale and put Oswald in charge. The Presbyterian Church asked him to become superintendent of their Jewish Mission, but Oswald again was "not so led." On an occasional Sunday he was asked to preach, but more often he sat in the audience.

Night after night he paced the floor: "Where is this work you showed me in the vision and called me so clearly for? How long, Lord, how long?" Often he walked the streets of the area he had seen in his vision, crying out to God. Once he went into the neighborhood YMCA and checked out the large 750-seat auditorium, but the rent was a prohibitive twenty-five dollars a night.

On his thirtieth birthday, Oswald papered the kitchen in their new home, then sat down and wrote:

Waiting on Jesus when I am weak
Claiming his promise to those who seek;
Waiting on Jesus when I am strong,
Trusting Him only all the day long.

Waiting on Jesus when I'm opprest,
Finding in Him sweet comfort and rest;
Trusting Him fully, whate'er befall,
Jesus my Saviour, Jesus my all.

Waiting on Jesus lest I despair,
Knowing he ever heareth my prayer;
How can I doubt Him when He is near?
No one so loving, no one so dear.

Waiting on Jesus, rapture divine!
Wonder of wonders, Jesus is mine;
Trusting and praying, whate'er betide,
Walking each moment close by His side.

In mid-December, Oswald was elated to see the copies of his first book, *Voices of Hope,* a collection of poems handsomely bound in deep-red leather. But within the week he had a thunderous phone call from Roland Bingham, who managed a large Christian bookshop connected with the magazine, and who had also arranged to market Oswald's book in other stores. Bingham had just perused his copy, and was furious. "These frothy love poems, these sappy mewlings of a moonstruck teenager have no place among the works of Oswald J. Smith!" he stormed. True enough, some of them were admittedly intimate, especially those penned during his days with Jennie, but Oswald had blithely tucked these among his deep searchings after God.

"You must get these books out of my store. I refuse to sell them. Take them out of every store and destroy them!" Bingham thundered.

Oswald was appalled. Not just his honor was at stake; he had borrowed several hundred dollars to have these books printed on the speculation that they would turn a profit during Christmas sales. He wrote that

> these poems represented hours and days of work over a period of many years, reflecting the deepest experiences of my heart. I can't tell you how precious they were to me. This book was the dream of my life. To give it up would be like tearing out my very heart itself.

And not only would there be the loss of revenue — how was he to pay back the borrowed money?

How he wrestled:

> Yet if there is any question about them, if they would in any way hurt my ministry or spoil my Christian influence, then I will not let them go out. With great fear and trembling, by His grace, I place it all on the altar.

Oswald went to all the bookstores where *Voices of Hope* had been placed, gathered up all the books, and lit a big bonfire in his backyard where he watched his dream literally turn to ashes before his eyes. He kept only three copies.

One he sent to his trusted counselor and former pastor in Chicago; one other, to his favorite English professor at McCormack Seminary, asking their opinion. He was cheered by their response:

> Too much of the sentimental, they say? Too immature? Critics said the same of Tennyson and Longfellow. Maturity will come, and some day you will bring together a stronger group of writings than these. Probably you have been wise to withdraw them, but do not fret. *OJ, you have done well.* So forget the voices of criticism; there are those who love you and are proud of your success.

But he was still in debt. His good friend Dr. Hooper slipped him fifty-dollars to help him over Christmas.

And then, the day after Christmas, the *Toronto Globe and Mail* carried an article by Oswald, describing the dangerous work of the lumberjack as he takes the tops off the tall firs in British Columbia's forest. So vivid was the account of this "high rigger" that the editor asked Oswald for more copy, at ten dollars a story. But Oswald's wrestlings over his book had led to an even deeper commitment:

> I must be God's only. God has shown me that I must be utterly abandoned to Him, entirely at His disposal, God's man through and through. I must write nothing, publish nothing, read nothing that is not spiritual and does not glorify Him. *All* for Jesus, *all* my words

and thoughts and doing, *all* my days and *all* my hours. Take myself and I will be ever, *only, all* for Thee. My poems must be renounced, the treasures of my life. The dreams I have had of writing for big papers and magazines must be surrendered. The intellectual pleasures I derived from Dickens and the great classic authors must go. Others might indulge in these things, but I dare not. God has called me. My interests can no longer be divided. I must be His absolutely and without reserve. Having placed my life on the altar, I dare not take it back. It is devoted entirely to God.

IN CHRIST

In Christ I live, to Him I give
Myself and all my treasures;
He died for me on Calvary,
And weaned me from earth's pleasures.
My soul is filled, my heart is thrilled,
I'm His, and His forever,
And all I own to Him alone
I yield and naught can sever.

In Christ I dwell, and all is well,
He gives me joy for sorrow;
I fear no ill, for He is still
The same today, tomorrow,
And so my song the whole day long
Shall be a song of gladness;
In deepest grief I find relief,
He gives me balm for sadness.

In Christ I rest, my soul is blest,
Nor can I doubt His leading;
Tho' fears assail, He will not fail
While I His voice am heeding.
And when at last, earth's trials past,
I go with joy to meet Him,
Oh, happy day! life's bitter fray
Forgotten as I greet Him.

No more of James Fenimore Cooper's *The Last of the Mohicans;* no more *Adventures of Sherlock Holmes* or *The Count of Monte Cristo;* no more Longfellow and Tennyson — these books that had been his constant companions to be enjoyed as he jogged along on horseback over the prairies and mountains or by lamplight in a lonely cabin or to escape from the heavy pressures at the end of a long day. He wrote:

> But God has made me willing to make the sacrifice and given real joy in surrender. He is weaning me from the world and causing me to be wholly devoted, utterly abandoned to Him.

But then the editor of the *Globe and Mail* called again: "We want to launch an appeal for aid to starving Armenia. Would you write the lead articles?" *Surely this is different,* the writer in Oswald decided. And feeding the hungry would bring glory to God. Hardly knowing where Armenia was, Oswald grabbed an atlas and the dispatches off the wire service. For two weeks his compelling stories splashed across two columns of the *Globe and Mail's* front page. Readers responded by sending in an unheard of $250,000 for relief.

Oswald's check for fifty dollars for the series came just in time. Mother Billings and the nurse moved in to assist with the delivery of their second child, Hope Evangeline. It was a cruelly long, hard delivery, and Oswald was not able to be with Daisy as he had been to help with the birth of Glen. Instead, Oswald and Glen were lying in the next bedroom, both desperately ill with the dreaded influenza that was sweeping the country in 1920. Oswald got up too soon and suffered a severe relapse. He was aware of the doctor and nurse working over him hour after hour, while he himself was praying for healing, believing that God still had a work for him to do.

During his recuperation, Oswald became more deeply convinced than ever that God indeed had a special work for him. He resigned from the magazine, determined to give himself only to the ministry:

> When God has called a man to the sacred office of the Ministry, then nothing else can take its place. I am thinking now of an intensive work, a spiritual work where souls would be saved, sent out as mis-

sionaries, and the people trained to give largely to missions. A work that is carried on along scriptural lines entirely.

Before, I have always craved a spectacular service in a large public way. The pulpit work alone I have seen as valuable, despising the pastoral ministry. Now I see its importance, and long to be a real pastor, a true shepherd. That now seems to me to be the most important work in the whole world.

With his friend Hooper, he gave himself increasingly to prayer and study of the Word, reading and studying an entire epistle each morning:

The Bible is becoming the Book of books to me; the message that I have to proclaim is clearer, more definite and more glorious than ever before, but I am fully conscious that unless I have the Unction, the Enduement of Power, my message will be unavailing and profitless. With it, souls will be convicted and saved, the believers led into the fulness also. But I must first experience it myself.

It is not so much *where* I am to labour; surely, if God has anointed me for service, He can use me anywhere.

Oh, for the Spirit's mighty pow'r,
The Unction from above!
Oh, for the gracious heav'nly show'r,
The fulness of God's love.
This only, this our one great need!

SEVENTEEN

♦♦♦

LAUNCH OUT INTO THE DEEP

Lord, I have nothing, only thee. . . . OJS

"There is simply no way I can let you go off with Dr. Hooper again," Daisy had said. Yet at the end of May, she was at the station, waving him a kiss as the two men set off for Kentucky on behalf of the Shantymen's Christian Association.

And once again Daisy was in torment, hating the separation. Now she began to think that Oswald no longer loved her and just wanted to get away from her, or that maybe God was punishing her for not being a good enough wife to this great man of God whose spirituality she felt was dwarfing her. But then, perhaps she had only herself to blame, because she had been the one who had challenged Oswald that he must have been mistaken about his vision out in the British Columbia forest, this vision that God wanted him in Toronto to start a work with the common people. Almost a whole year had passed and nothing had happened to confirm the vision.

"I can't argue with that," Oswald had agreed. "Certainly no pastorate is available. The only open door is with the Shantymen, so unless something else turns up, that's what it will be." Thus Oswald and Hooper had set off for twelve weeks back in the Kentucky hills, which Oswald had come to love during his seminary days seven years earlier.

"I'll try to be brave," Daisy had promised. "Our lives seem so short. How long will it be before we are settled together somewhere? I hope we'll never have to part again. I'll do the best I can for the children, and you enjoy your work. Little Glen says, 'I have no Daddy to love me,' but we will sacrifice your companionship if that is His will for us."

Both Oswald's and Daisy's families rallied round the young mother with her new baby, and Daisy's younger brother Don often stayed overnight. Daisy took in boarders to help augment the small allowance from the mission. (Sometimes this came late and she had to borrow from her mother.) The love letters flew back and forth almost daily. After mailing one particularly sad, despondent letter, Daisy felt so remorseful that she rushed off a telegram reassuring Oswald that his little family was managing. "Surely some blessing will come out of all this trying time," Daisy wrote. "I trust that heaven is rejoicing over repenting souls; may the Lord give you an abundant harvest."

And down in Kentucky, those prayers were being answered "exceeding abundantly." Oswald had found it unusually hard to say good-bye to Daisy and the children, especially knowing how upset Daisy was at his going. He, too, hated the separations, and was always intensely lonely for his loved ones. But he rejoiced in the work of giving out tracts and preaching in the open air and in the homes and little churches. Once again the going was rough and involved hiking many miles and riding muleback over the mountains. At one point Oswald became violently ill and Dr. Hooper had to treat him for food poisoning. He was soon back on his feet, but then Hooper succumbed and did not respond to treatment in the hospital, so Oswald brought him back to Toronto. Thus the projected stay of twelve weeks was cut to twenty-five days; however in those twenty-five days the two men visited over 500 homes and held sixty-four services with 3,250 mountain folk attending; thirty-three professed conversion and nine were restored to the Lord. "Whether it was Satan driving us from the field or God's permission, I don't know. I only know we were compelled to leave by the doctor's sickness. God always seems to bring me back to Toronto," Oswald mused.

However, apart from his beloved wife and children, there did not seem much to come back for. Thus Oswald spent the summer traveling about the vacation resorts, holding services on the hotel lawns and verandas, or paddling a canoe around the lakes and giving out tracts to the cottagers. But he was praising God that it seemed fairly certain he would be given a Baptist pastorate in the fall; then in early September he discovered that it had been given to another. It came as a bitter blow, and was very hard on Daisy especially. With so little money coming in, they were often short on food and sometimes missed meals altogether. With two children, it was a desperate time. "I feel so unworthy and useless. Lord, I have nothing, only Thee."

The reading from the *Daily Light* was particularly precious to them that dark September 4:

> Said I not unto thee that, if thou wouldest believe, thou shouldest see the glory of God?; Rest in the Lord, and wait patiently for him; He shall not be afraid of evil tidings; his heart is established. John 11:40; Psa. 37:7; Psa. 112:7. Praise be His name, we will trust, and wait, and see the miracle!

Now, Oswald was reluctant to share with anyone what was really going on in his heart — that God had met him once again in a very special way during the last week of the summer, assuring him that the time had come to launch out into the deep and let down the nets. The starting date had been set for the first Sunday in October; the name was to be the "Gospel Auditorium."

Earlier Oswald had not been able to understand this word from the Lord in view of the pastorate he had agreed to accept; thus when he found that it had been given to another he took this as a seal from God and secretly rejoiced. Like Nehemiah, he told no man what was in his heart as he began to make inquiries about the hall he had chosen in the Queen-

Dovercourt area not far from Dale Church. It was to this area and the desperate need of the working people that his heart had continued to be drawn. He drew up a constitution:

> ORIGIN:
> Born of God on the 1st Sunday of October, 1920, after almost fifteen months of continuous waiting upon Him in definite believing prayer, in response to an unmistakable Call.
>
> PURPOSE:
> First — A testimony to the faithfulness of God and the reliability of His promises, that He may be glorified.
> Second — The salvation of souls, the edification of believers, and world-wide evangelism.
>
> METHODS:
> First — A work of faith, wholly dependent upon God. Its needs are brought to Him in prayer, and to Him alone.
> Second — No collections are taken up and no solicitations for funds authorized.
> Third — No debts are incurred, the work being enlarged only as the Lord indicates His will by sending in the means.
> Fourth — One-tenth of the total income is set aside for Missions.

He began to pray in the money for rent and publicity, determined that never again would he go in debt. He had been saturating himself in the life of George Mueller and reveled as his own prayers for daily needs began to be answered in a previously unknown way — ten dollars handed to him by a woman on the street, fifteen dollars arriving in the mail from an unknown person and so on. The money trickled in, and when he had sixty dollars, he booked the Royal Templar Hall and ordered handbills printed. Then he told Daisy and his good friend Dr. Hooper, with whom he had been praying daily. Hooper was staggered by Oswald's audacity. "Where are you ever going to get twenty-five dollars for rent each week?" he demanded. "If you had something coming in regularly, it would still be a lot of money. But you have nothing." Nevertheless, Hooper helped him go door to door giving out the announcements.

On that momentous October 3, 1920, a fearful Oswald viewed the 750 empty seats still totally empty twenty minutes before service time. He was alone: Hooper was preaching elsewhere, Daisy was home with sick children, and none of his old friends had joined him. Peering through the crack of the door he was kneeling behind in desperate prayer, he saw a couple come in, then others, until sixty-five took their seats. Oswald led the singing, played the piano, and preached. The offering in the box at the door totaled $5.73, hardly enough for the $25 rent.

But Oswald was heartened, and announced they would push on with the 7:00 weekly services. He managed to enlist a fine pianist and a woman Bible teacher; his old Sunday school superintendent from Dale began an 11:00 A.M. Children's Service. A Wednesday night cottage prayer meeting, a Tuesday night tract band, and a Sunday afternoon women's Bible class were added. He brought in the best gospel music talent in the city, and the crowd began to build. And Daisy caught the vision.

EIGHTEEN
◆◆◆
THE VISION FULFILLED

Lord, I'll trust you. OJS

Oswald's faith was often tested to the limit:

> No money in hand for church notices in the papers so omitted rather than go into debt. Last day of month; no money. Must close with a deficit. Some doubt and uneasiness. God help me!

Quite miraculously, the rent money always came in, and 10 percent went faithfully to mission work. But the offerings marked "personal" in the little box at the door were sparse, and unless the money was marked that way, he refused to take a cent. Many days there was simply no money. Then a ten-dollar gift would arrive, or a couple would come in off the street to be married and that would be five dollars from heaven. But the total income for the Smith family for October was still only $31.25; for November it was a little better with $68.33. In early December, a fifty-dollar gift and a barrel of Northern Spy apples caused Oswald to rejoice: "God has not forgotten!"

But when Daisy told him that she was pregnant once more and Hope was not yet a year old, it was a somber Oswald who went before the Lord and laid it all out. "Is it worthwhile? Is there another way?" Oswald cried to God. Shortly after this, he discovered a copy of *The Alliance Weekly* among his mail on the dining room table. The cover carried a photo of the founder, A. B. Simpson. Oswald had never seen the magazine before and wondered who had sent it. But as he held the magazine in his hand, he had a distinct impression, a distinct word from God: *"This is to be your work."*

It was such a new thought that again he kept it to himself for a few days, praying about it almost constantly. Dr. Simpson was known to Oswald, who remembered well the day Simpson had spoken at the Toronto Bible College. And then Daisy had attended the Christian and Missionary Alliance training school at Nyack, New York, and had shared with Oswald a good deal about the movement. Undoubtedly, it was solidly evangelistic, and its ministers stood four-square on the fundamental faith, with no "higher criticism" or modernism.

Oswald could easily identify with Simpson, a former Canadian Presbyterian minister and graduate of Toronto's Knox College. Simpson's passion for the "lost in heathen darkness" had driven him to resign from a large, fashionable, but visionless, New York church and to launch the worldwide fellowship which now had 500 missionaries. As he looked into it, Oswald was impressed with the economics: only 6 percent of the funds were kept at home. "I think the Alliance could suit you very nicely," Daisy agreed after they had prayed together. "They see that their ministers are taken care of financially, too."

So Oswald contacted the Canadian office and found that just a few blocks down the street from his rented hall, one of the Alliance churches—Parkdale Tabernacle—was struggling to stay alive, with only twenty-four members attending. With minimal negotiation, the two groups were merged, and Oswald, now thirty-two years old, took over as pastor the first Sunday in 1921.

Almost immediately Oswald was plunged into a totally new experience with the church's annual missionary convention. While he sat on the platform and watched, the ushers went up and down the aisles handing out pledge envelopes. When

Oswald was handed one, he turned it over and read: "In dependance upon God, I will endeavour to give to the missionary work of the church $_____ during the coming year."

That leaves me out, Oswald figured. After all, the Lord knew that the weekly twenty-five dollars the church was paying him, although a vast improvement over their finances for the past two-and-a-half years, would barely cover expenses — and there soon would be a new baby to provide for. But just as Oswald was scrunching up the envelope, the Lord spoke to him, *I'm not asking you to give out of what you have. Will you trust me to put extra money into your hands so that you may give it to foreign missions?*

Oswald's heart beat faster: *All right, Lord, I'll trust you. How much should it be? "Fifty dollars"* came the immediate response. That was more than half a month's salary! *I must have heard you wrong....* But, no, fifty dollars was the strong impression. The voice of the Lord whispered, "This is the way. Walk in it."

Oswald felt clammy all over. His hand shook as he straightened out the crumpled envelope, reached for his pen, and wrote in the amount. That began a new experience in faith as each month he had to pray in an extra four dollars, and each month God sent the money in some miraculous way.

The missionary convention was soon followed by another new experience for Oswald with the advent of the Bosworth Brothers Evangelistic and Healing Campaign which had been arranged by the Canadian office of the Christian and Missionary Alliance. The services were to be nightly except Saturday, with prayer meetings every morning.

So great were the crowds each night that after the first week they had to move into the 3,400-seat Massey Hall, and sometimes even then people were turned away. After some meetings, almost half the audience was at the front, either crying to God for the infilling or baptism of the Holy Spirit; others had come for salvation, but the biggest crowds were for healing.

Oswald had never been exposed to this, and felt very confused by it all. He definitely wanted God's best — all that the Holy Spirit had to give him. "The lame are walking, the deaf are hearing, the cancers are gone — these things no one can deny," he reported. Oswald tossed away his own eyeglasses when his normal vision was restored. But he still had questions, particularly when he took some members of the team with him on his sick calls, and they refused to pray for those in the hospital; they would not even deal with souls about salvation.

Nevertheless he rejoiced in the great blessing that the meetings had brought to the congregation: "May God make the Alliance Tabernacle a centre of blessing for the whole city!" At the conclusion of the campaign sixty-one converts were baptized by immersion; the last to be immersed was the new pastor Oswald J. Smith, the Presbyterian who had never before seen the need for a believer's baptism. From then on, Oswald no longer baptized babies, but would dedicate them to the Lord. They would be baptized years later upon their personal confession of faith in the Lord Jesus Christ as Savior and Lord.

With interest so keen, Oswald decided to continue evangelistic campaigns again with meetings every night. He brought in outstanding speakers from all over the continent, augmenting them with the delightful music ministry of groups like the Cleveland Colored Quintette, whose rhythmic gospel songs were an immediate hit with Toronto audiences. To accommodate the growing crowds, they decided to erect a ninety-foot square tent on a vacant lot one block west of Spadina on College Street closer to downtown and right on the streetcar line. "Please bring a chair," Oswald requested. On opening night, July 3, 1921, people struggled off the streetcars, carrying more than the 1,500 chairs that the tent could comfortably hold.

Oswald had extra cause for rejoicing: Daisy had just delivered another son, Paul Brainerd. Hooper had not been available for the birth, and a woman doctor had been sent in his place. This time Oswald was able to be present. This delivery was easier for Daisy because the doctor had given Oswald a wad of cotton batting soaked in chloroform to hold at Daisy's nose in order to put her under.

Oswald suddenly felt guilty, remembering the rush they had been in at Glen's delivery. Dr. Hooper had had a meeting to preach at, while Oswald had been anxious to hear R.A. Torrey speak in Niagara Falls. Daisy had had a nurse with her, but still, Oswald felt he should not have left her so soon after Glen's birth.

"How could we have been such infernal religious fanatics?" a smitten Oswald confessed to Daisy. "Can you ever forgive me?"

NINETEEN

"EVERYTHING FOR JESUS AND JESUS EVERYTHING"

The Lord did not tell us to build beautiful churches but to evangelize the world. OJS

The meetings in the tent continued every night until it became obvious that the Parkdale Church had become outgrown permanently. A new building was required — "a great spiritual centre where starving thousands will find bread enough and to spare" — as Oswald described this answer to his prayer of a lifetime. He had been greatly impressed in Chicago with Rader's Gospel Tabernacle, a great barn of a place which sat 5,000 and was packed out every night. The building Oswald envisioned would be erected in Toronto's central west end, and would be plain and inexpensive, "because the Lord did not tell us to build beautiful churches but to evangelize the world." The 80-by-130-foot cement block structure would seat 1,500, with no pillars or posts, Unlike Rader's building that had cinder floors and was heated by large stoves set about the walls, the Alliance Tabernacle would have a heating system and cement floors.

At one point, when funds ran out Oswald halted construction, refusing to saddle his people with a mortgage. But a half day of prayer wrought the necessary miracle, and the building was opened on time by Paul Rader, who was becoming one of the most powerful influences in Oswald's life. "God puts something into a dollar that is given from the heart that makes it explode in the souls of others," Rader enjoined as he preached from Romans 12:1 with a powerful plea for utter and complete sanctification to the will of God. "The most acceptable thing anyone can do is simply to give himself" he said. "Only thus can he be pleasing to God; only in this way find the highest satisfaction and good in life, which come from a mind and heart at one with the Almighty."

Within six months, an elevation was constructed to give an additional 500 seats. Although a Sunday school was held Sunday afternoons, there were no special facilities because Oswald's vision was to "fish for men, not minnows." The only space taken from the main auditorium was for a small pastor's office, a bookstore, and choir loft.

The last $3,745 indebtedness was wiped out when Oswald suggested that everyone contribute one week's salary; thus within eighteen months of opening, the Tabernacle was debt free. "And we must stay debt free so we can channel all our funds into getting out the gospel," Oswald insisted. The $5,658 for missions in 1922 was doubled to over $10,000 in 1923.

"Everything for Jesus and Jesus Everything" from A.B. Simpson was the motto for this great new soul-saving center at 85 Christie Street. Truly they were reaching the unchurched, the working folk who did not feel comfortable in a richer congregation. Night after night, the auditorium was packed, with people standing around the walls and looking in the windows. During a series of meetings conducted by the Welsh revivalists Fred Clarke and George Bell, 1,000 followers paraded from the Tabernacle down the main streets, carrying large placards which read JESUS IS COMING—ARE YOU READY? and YE MUST BE BORN AGAIN. Seventy cars draped in banners followed. "Trim your lamps and be ready for the midnight cry," they sang. This was all good copy for the newspapers, and Oswald Smith was fast earning the reputation as one of Toronto's most colorful and successful ministers.

Oswald began developing several outreach programs from the Tabernacle. The Wayside Mission sent men to the sparsely settled districts of Northern Ontario to preach the gospel. A converted rabbi was engaged to lead the Seekers After Truth Mission among the Jews of Toronto. The Young People's Evangelistic Band held open-air services and gave out over 100,000 tracts the first year. A monthly magazine *The Prophet* was begun. The Tabernacle Publishers began to print Smith's tracts and pamphlets. These were sold in the bookstore along with a good selection of books for both the "saved" and "unsaved" and the new sacred Victrola records featuring such artists as the Colored Male Quintet, and Fred Syme whose rich baritone voice led the Tabernacle congregation in the lively singing of the many new gospel songs which had been introduced in the States and in Canada. In January 1925, an annex to the building was opened with additional seating to bring the capacity to 2,500; it also included facilities for the new Canadian Bible Institute to train young people for service at home or on the foreign field.

Two branch churches were started. Oswald said, "With our own work free of debt, it is natural that the mother should bear children." Thus a church in Toronto's east end was opened, and another in the new Forest Hill area north of the city where there was no religious service of any kind.

With all this activity, people took it for granted that Oswald J. Smith personally was thriving financially. But the truth was that he renounced his salary during the building campaign, once again taking only those gifts that had been earmarked for his personal use and placed in the offering box at the back of the auditorium. When the Board of Managers found that these were averaging only eight dollars a week, they insisted he take a regular twenty-five dollars each week. This began to be augmented by love offerings from other congregations as word of the success of the Toronto church spread through the Alliance and Smith was invited to hold evangelistic campaigns in churches all across Canada and the States.

In October 1923 he received a unanimous call to the prestigious mother-church in New York City, with an annual salary of $2,080. For a moment Oswald was tempted because surely this would increase his sphere of influence. But again God spoke to him: "Seekest thou great things for thyself? Seek them not; I, the Lord will exalt thee in due time." The answer must be no, Oswald quickly decided. For certain, God had called him to minister in the city of Toronto, to build this center for evangelism and base for worldwide missions. In Toronto he would stay.

One key to the growth of the work was Oswald's training of personal workers to deal effectively with the multitudes of seekers who came forward almost nightly. He gave special instructions.

"First, you take your place beside them at the altar, and then make your way with them into the inquiry room. There you *kneel* with them." (Oswald never forgot how he wanted to get down on his knees when as a sixteen-year-old he went forward for salvation in Massey Hall.) "Then deal with them individually from the Bible, taking them through the main Scriptures that show first that all have sinned; then that all our sins have been laid on Christ."

His favorite verses, from Isaiah 53:5, 6, were followed up with John 1:12 and John 3:16 (*KJV*):

> But he was wounded for our transgressions, he was bruised for our iniquities: the chastisement of our peace was upon him; and with his stripes we are healed. All we like sheep have gone astray; we have turned every one to his own way; and the Lord hath laid on him the iniquity of us all.
>
> But as many as received him, to them gave he power to become the sons of God . . . .
>
> For God so loved the world, that he gave his only begotton Son, that whosoever believeth in him should not perish, but have everlasting life.

"That's about all they can master at first hearing," Oswald advised. But he made sure that new converts went away armed with first-class booklets to study at home and reassure their souls of salvation, usually some of Oswald's own condensed sermons: "Only One Way" or "What Does It Mean to Believe?"

"Make sure they have a Bible," he finally enjoined; the church had New Testaments to give out if needed. "And be sure you record their name and address; then visit them in their home before next Sunday, and offer to sit with them in the service." In this way Oswald developed a strong core of confident personal workers, always ready to stream forward with Bible under arm as soon as the first seeker stepped into the aisle.

Another secret was the group of godly elders who rallied around, kneeling for prayer in the pastor's office before each service. What a blessed change from the lodge brothers who never attended prayer meetings in his former charges!

Paul Rader was a frequent visitor at the Tabernacle, and like the other visiting evangelists, received a flat fifty dollars for the week. (Occasionally some turned up demanding more, but Oswald simply canceled the meetings and sent them packing.) Oswald in turn was often called on to fill the pulpit in Chicago for Rader's increasing absences after he became president of the Christian and Missionary Alliance worldwide.

Oswald could always leave his church with confidence, knowing that he had strong men in charge and that the visiting musicians and preachers would keep the crowds coming. One of the most colorful guests was Madam Maria Karinskaya, a Russian opera singer who had found the Lord and now wished to sing only for Him. Aboard ship bound for America, she had been "discovered" by Jonathan and Rosalind Goforth, who were returning from China to visit their home church, Knox Presbyterian, in Toronto. Oswald had kept in touch with the Goforths over the years and they sent the prima donna over to him.

She had a magnificent contralto voice whose power and range held her audiences spellbound, and her costumes were striking. Then one dramatic evening, in response to a stirring appeal by Oswald, Madam Karinskaya removed the jeweled headdress that had been a gift from the Czar, and kneeling, presented it to Oswald. "Now I can go into the service of the true King," she said. Then she sang a lament for her beloved country — "Russia, Dark Russia."

And once again Oswald's heart was broken. He felt he must minister to those in darkness. How could he sit in the midst of this bounty and blessing when there were so many who had never heard? Yes, he was sending more and more money. Still his prayer was "Dear God, *let me go!* 'With a hundred thousand souls a day passing into Christ-less guilt and gloom, without one ray of hope or light, with future dark as endless night' — [A.B. Simpson] *Oh, God, let me go!*" But where would this prayer take him?

TWENTY

♦♦♦

RUSSIA, DARK RUSSIA

Russia, dark Russia,
Land of sorrow, sin and night;
No Christ, no Saviour
And no Gospel Light.
I have seen the vision
And for self I cannot live;
Life is less than worthless
Till my all I give.

Hark! they are calling —
I can hear them night and day,
Moaning and dying —
Let me haste away.
Weary, tired and hopeless
Groping still in darkest night;
To my sad, lost Russia
I must take the Light.

Millions are dying —
I can hear their bitter wail;
How dare I face them
If to help I fail?
Can I let them perish,
Souls for whom the Saviour died,
Live in ease and comfort
While they are denied?

No one to tell them
Of a dying Saviour's love;
No one to point them
To a life above.
Then farewell, dear homeland,
I must break each tender tie,
And to Russia hasten,
There to live or die.

OJS (1924)

Oswald had been learning more about the needs of Russia through William Fetler, founder of the Russian Missionary Society, which was taking the gospel to the Russian people not only within the Soviet Union, but also in the Eastern Europe border states/countries. The work had had its beginning among the 2.5 million Russian prisoners-of-war held by Germany during World War I.

So vivid was Fetler's portrayal of the need that Oswald was stirred to the core. "Come to Latvia and work with me," Fetler begged.

"No, my work is here at the Tabernacle. But I want to see the field," Oswald countered. Thus, in June 1924 Daisy drove him to the station where he caught the train for Quebec City, thence to board the *Empress of Scotland* bound for London, England.

Oswald was blessed, like Dwight L. Moody, to have three godly women who felt called of the Lord to pave the way for him with their prayers: his wife, Daisy, his deaconess-secretary Miss Alice Porter, and Chrissie French, a new convert from the Tabernacle, who felt led to give herself to the Smith household to stand with Daisy and the children since Oswald was being called away so often to preach. Thus as Oswald journeyed into the strongholds of darkness, these three joined together to surround him with prayer, to hold up the shield of faith against the fiery darts of the enemy, pulling down the forces of evil so that souls could be saved.

But what a tug it was for Oswald and Daisy to part again. "Why, oh, why is God taking you away from me when you are more to me than words can ever express?" a tortured Daisy had pled. "I only wish I were worthy of you and filled in your life the way I ought to. I fall so short of my own ideal for myself as wife and mother, and often wish, really and truly, that I were taken away so that before you are old you might have a more ideal woman."

Why indeed did these separations have to be? Oswald knew why. In his diary he recorded that

> there is something within me calling, ever calling; I am restless, like a hunter's dog on the leash, straining to get away. It is that irresistible "must go." *The divine fire burns within my heart.* I rise from my desk and rapidly pace the floor, praying, crying to God as I see the distant fields. I feel that come what may, I have no choice but to go.

As the train clattered along, Oswald took pen and notebook and dashed off another love poem:

Did you break your heart today
Ere you tore yourself away
When you knew I could not stay?

I am brokenhearted too,
For I long so much for you,
And I know not what to do.

When I saw the teardrops start,
I would clasp you to my heart,
Never from you would I part.

How my heart goes out to you
For I know you suffer too,
And your love is strong and true.

Walking along the deck of the ship, Oswald realized it was good that he had gotten away because he was more tired than he had imagined following the three hard years of building up the Tabernacle. For the most part on board ship he kept to himself, reading or writing poems and book chapters. Sunday he was asked to take the service in the lounge.

Before traveling on to Riga, Latvia, where his missionary journey was scheduled to begin, Oswald treated himself to two weeks in Switzerland and France. There he feasted on the staggering beauty of the Alps, hiking up the mountainside to gather wildflowers and scampering over the glaciers. The picturesque little villages enchanted him, and he took pictures of every new wonder. In Paris he drank up the magnificence and exquisite art of the Louvre and the Palace of Versailles.

Much refreshed, Oswald arrived in Riga on the shores of the Baltic at midnight, and was overwhelmed by hundreds of Christians who stood on the platform, singing hymns of welcome. He and Fetler then boarded another train to travel through the night. Arriving at daybreak in the city of Libau, Fetler immediately hired a 1,000-seat hall for a meeting that night. He quickly had handbills printed, and then he and Oswald went along the streets giving them out.

Oswald could not believe that anyone would turn out on such short notice, but long before the announced time, the few available chairs were taken. Most of the chairs had been removed so that even more men and women could jam into the building, filling every inch of space. For over three hours they stood, eager for the Word of God. There were no hymnbooks, so Fetler read out two lines at a time and the crowd poured out their hearts in heavenly praise. "Surely the Russians are the finest singers on earth, after the Welsh!" Oswald enthused.

Oswald preached with an interpreter. At the invitation, scores pushed their way to the front to kneel, confessing their sins and yielding their lives to Jesus Christ.

This was just the beginning. Day after day, night after night, in as many as four services and taking up ten hours of the day, they preached to great crowds that packed out each building, standing in the aisles, jamming the galleries, peering in the windows, with services lasting three to six hours. And still the people cried for more. Each day Oswald and Fetler rose at 7:00 A.M. for two hours of prayer. They traveled into Poland, lurching through the night, curled up on the hard wooden bunks of a third-class train, then sat jolting for hours in a horse-drawn haywagon along corduroy roads through the dark, bandit-infested forest. They journeyed into areas that were under martial law. Where one group of believers had gathered, there the police stood too, with loaded rifles and fixed bayonets, listening carefully to every word Oswald preached as it was translated first into Russian and then into German.

For one five-day conference, 1,000 German Christians had gathered, some from 200 miles away. Whole pigs were roasted and the tables were spread with an immense feast. Then Oswald preached for over an hour on the Holy Spirit. He later recorded in his diary:

> As I spoke, my own heart warmed and I felt the fire of God burning in my soul. As I prayed at the close, it seemed as though a great tidal wave of blessing broke upon the audience: first a single sob, then another and yet another, until at last individual expressions were lost in the moaning and weeping all over the congregation. When I opened my eyes, I saw tears flowing down their cheeks, as they were broken and mellowed by the Spirit of God. They needed no urging then, no coaxing. I only had to give the word of invitation and they responded by the scores. There was no room at the altar; it was impossible for them to move in the dense crowd. But they lifted their hands and gave every evidence of whole-hearted response. How many opened their hearts I cannot say, but I do know that God worked in a mighty way.
>
> They pled with us to stay. Never have I felt such a tug at my heart to remain anywhere. But other fields were calling, other audiences waiting to hear the message. And with our souls afire with the spirit of revival we climbed on the wagons, the rain pouring down heavily.

One night while traveling on the train to Warsaw, Oswald awakened with violent pain; probably the foreign food had upset him. His colleagues moved him into a compartment, but so excruciating was the pain that Oswald fainted dead away. For hours he stayed that way, floating briefly to the surface, then fainting again, until in his agony Oswald "cried mightily to God." Suddenly the torture ended, and in great weakness Oswald rested until morning and all the next day. After that, praise God, he was preaching again.

Often during these days Oswald felt a special touch from

the Lord; great joy so filled him that at times he could scarcely continue his private prayer. Then he would be interrupted: "It is time to preach." Thus he would go from the glorious Presence to the waiting hearts, and God poured out a revival blessing.

One Sunday night when Pastor Fetler was preaching, Oswald noted: "a mighty wave of revival swept the audience so that hundreds fell on their faces and wept before the Lord. Strong men sobbed aloud and with agonized faces pled with God to forgive and receive them." Then Fetler called on him to speak, and he "exhorted them to a new consecration to the task of proclaiming the glad tidings." Amid much weeping they repeated the words with Oswald:

Lord, I give myself to Thee
Friends and time and earthly store;
Soul and body Thine to be
Wholly Thine forevermore.

The meeting lasted six hours, and 400 responded to the invitation. The next day a procession of hundreds made their way to the river where once again Oswald preached and Fetler baptized the converts.

All in all, this major missionary journey was one of the happiest experiences of Oswald's life. He would never forget the hundreds of believers singing hymns on the platform and waving handkerchiefs as the train pulled away from the station in late August. This trip was to change his life. He had tasted real Holy Ghost revival. He had seen village after village without one gospel witness. If the missionary fire had burned within him before, now it was kindled into a great zealous blaze. He came home charged with a flaming passion that no amount of adversity could dampen or snuff out:

> How I thank God for the privilege of proclaiming the unsearchable riches of Christ to these famished people! What a joy it was to preach the gospel to such eager listeners! I hear their pleading invitations to return and tell them more. How ripe is the harvest! But where, oh, where are the reapers?

Have you heard the Master's Call?
Will you go forsaking all?
Millions still in sin and shame
Ne'er have heard the Saviour's name.

Some may give and some may pray,
But for you He calls today —
Will you answer: "Here am I,"
Or must Jesus pass you by?

Have you heard the bitter cry?
Can you bear to see them die,
Thousands who in darkest night
Never yet have seen the light?

Soon 'twill be too late to go
And your love for Jesus show;
Oh, then, quickly haste away —
Tarry not another day.

OJS

TWENTY-ONE

♦♦♦

"THEY HAVE TAKEN AWAY MY CHILD"

"The night is dark and I am far from home". . . but God knows it all. . . . OJS

Though Oswald returned home, his traveling days continued. He toured North America showing his "lantern slides" and sharing his great burden for those lost and dying who never once had heard the simple message of God's salvation through the death and resurrection of His Son, Jesus Christ.

Everywhere he went now, young people were challenged to give their lives for the ministry of evangelism. With eyes blazing he would pace the platform, vividly recounting the exploits of the great pioneer missionaries such as Judson and Brainerd, and the great hunger he had seen in Europe. "If you cannot go, you must send a substitute; you must pray and give," Oswald demanded. And at each service they streamed to the altars to dedicate their lives.

At the Tabernacle, the missionary fires were kindled even brighter, with annual offerings skyrocketing from $16,756 in 1924 to $34,000 by 1926, with an additional $4,000 to build a church for evangelical Christians in Riga. (On a swing through the western United States and California with Fetler, Oswald raised another $50,000 for the Russian fields.)

And once more, it was all this money going out of the church that began to get Oswald in trouble again. Some of the

Alliance people were unhappy that money was going to missions not sponsored by the Christian and Missionary Alliance — and this was against Alliance policy. A few of the more staid Methodist members of the board were getting tired of the continuous campaigns, the many altar calls, and prayer meetings. "We'd like just straight church services, with more Bible teaching," they demanded.

Oswald countered:

> But we have Bible study every Wednesday and Friday night. Within the church there must be a balance between Evangelism, Bible Teaching, and Missions. *But the great emphasis must always be on Evangelism, because the church that does not evangelize will fossilize!*

For several months there existed among the Board of Managers an unrest of which the congregation was unaware. Oswald was beside himself; the disagreements, misunderstandings, and accusations hung on him like a lodestone. The unrest was particularly bad when he returned from an out-of-town campaign.

Moreover, he simply could not understand the dissension: Had he not built the congregation from 25 to a regular 2,000 with often hundreds more outside unable to get in the doors? This was probably the largest church in all Canada. Was not the church debt free with thousands to spare for missions? Were not souls being saved almost every night? What more could a board ask of a minister?

During this time, little Paul became desperately ill; in fact most people had given up on him. Oswald took his turn sitting by Paul's bed hour after hour, lying down for snatches of sleep but getting up whenever Paul cried out and comforting him until he went off again. Paul recovered, and one evening when he was only five, walked down the aisle after his father had preached to take his place at the altar with the others seeking salvation.

Along with Dr. Hooper who now served as associate pastor, Oswald had W. C. Willis, the church treasurer, who was his stay in difficult times. Each morning on his way to work, Willis would stop by the church office for prayer with him. Often Oswald would take the streetcar to the west end of the line and then walk the two miles across the fields to the Willis home for a day or two of rest and quiet.

Yet Oswald was at his wit's end to know how to deal with the problems among his Board of Managers:

> Foolishly I had taken onto the board men who were not Alliance background but had come from the big denominations, and did not have the vision for missionary work that the Alliance people had.

Now they were insisting that the Tabernacle concentrate more on local work. They began to attack Oswald's public ministry, his private life, and the lives of those who stood firmly with him. He always had hated fighting and could not stand not to have peace. In fact, he could not function in the midst of turmoil.

A year before, the Alliance had asked him to take over the job as superintendent for Central and Eastern Canada. "There'll be more scope for your evangelistic talents," head office had urged. At that time, Oswald had refused. Now he saw it as an escape from a burden which he felt he could not sustain much longer.

But he was torn:

> Surely my board won't let me leave. They asked me not to take the church in New York; they won't let me take this job either. But if they want me to stay, they will have to force the resignation of these few troublemakers.
>
> Yet, is it God's will for me to leave? I want only God's best for the Tabernacle. God forbid that anything, anyone should interfere with the progress of the work.

Seeing no other way to deal with the problem and being open to God's leading, Oswald handed in a letter of resignation, stating that he was accepting the job as superintendent, but looked forward to a continued happy relationship. Secretly and desperately, he was depending on the faithful supporters on his board to reject any idea of his leaving. Certainly the congregation would not want him to go.

But what Oswald did not know was that the policy of the Christian and Missionary Alliance was never to reject a resignation. "If God is leading a man out, so be it; we will not interfere," they figured. And this was the position his board had to assume.

Oswald was stricken dumbfounded and unbelieving. In a gesture of appeasement he had signed away the work born out of the travail of his heart, the child of his prayers and tears.

Heartsick and numb, he walked the streets in a daze. At midnight he came to the church and stood outside with tears streaming down his face. His heart was being ripped apart: "Dear God, what have I done? What have I done? How could I have signed all this away?"

Oswald was in anguish. "They have taken away my child," he wrote in a dark lament. Somehow there had to be a way to get it back. And he had tried very hard, but there seemed to be no way. The door was tightly closed:

> "The night is dark and I am far from home" — even so has it been these past months. Sad, sad experiences. Oh, what a fight, what a terrible battle! But God knows it all, blessed be His name.
>
> With all my heart I turn this day to the Lord Jesus Christ; my body, soul and spirit I present to God as a living sacrifice. For my many, many sins and failures I plead nothing but the blood. With a contrite, broken heart I come and He forgives. Humbly I bow to His chastisement.
>
> I believe that God this day lifts me out of a horrible pit and takes me from the miry clay, and that I am now, by His grace alone, placed on the rock Christ Jesus, never again to be moved. Hallelujah!
>
> From this day I walk with God.
> To be like Jesus,
> to enter into a prayer ministry the like of which
> I have never known,
> to become the father of numerous spiritual children,
> to live in the centre of God's will,
> to preach Jesus to the perishing multitudes,
> to have but one passion,
> to live a quiet, victorious life —
> This now is my ambition. God grant it. Amen.

Top: Tent service on College Street in Toronto, summer of 1921.

Bottom: Construction of the Christie Street Alliance Tabernacle.

Top: R. A. Torrey, whose life and testimony so deeply affected Smith.

Middle: William Fetler, founder of the Russian Missionary Society.

Bottom: Paul Rader, Smith's close friend, during his early ministry.

Smith (center), the beloved Dr. Hooper (right), and the song leader of Rader's Tabernacle, Chicago.

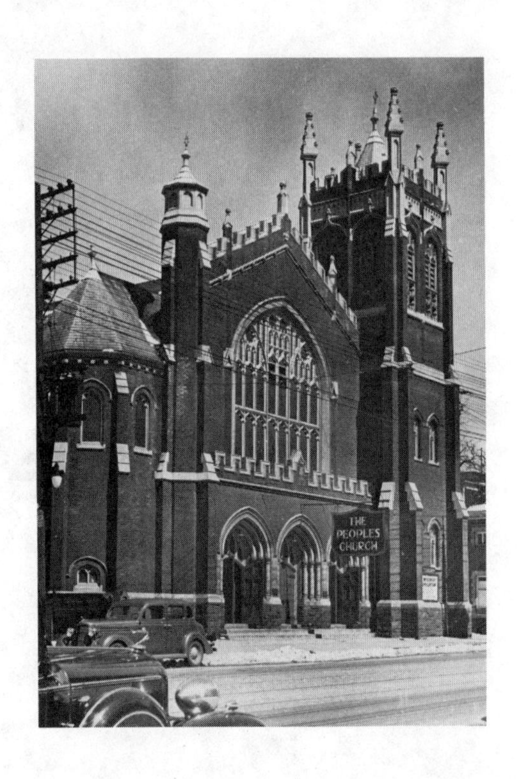

Peoples Church rents the 1,500-seat auditorium of the Central Methodist Church, 100 Bloor Street East.

A crowded missionary convention at the Bloor Street auditorium.

Smith and his three children.

TWENTY-TWO

♦♦♦

THE GLORY OF HIS PRESENCE

Surely You have not given me the vision to let it perish! OJS

Oswald threw himself into the superintending work, touring the churches and counseling with the ministers, but he found that rather than doing more evangelism, he had given up his preaching to do management. He felt he was "just no good at bossing his fellow-ministers."

Finally he resigned from the superintendent's job:

> I am not called to this: I am a pastor and evangelist; somewhere I must have a headquarters, a church to serve as a centre from which I can go out and hold evangelistic campaigns; with someone to hold the ropes at home while I am making visits to the foreign field.

At the end of November he accepted a pastorate with a congregation he had come to know and enjoy while on tour — the Christian and Missionary Alliance Gospel Tabernacle at Eighteenth and Georgia Streets, Los Angeles. He commenced April 1, 1927, after completing a tour of the Southern states. Oswald and Daisy rented out their house, packed up their belongings, and with the children and Chrissie boarded a train for the coast.

But as soon as Oswald entered the church, with devastating

clarity he immediately knew: *This is not for me. I'm in the wrong place!* He ran to the phone and called the movers in Toronto. "Don't ship our furniture. We're coming home!"

To his dismay the answer came back: "You're too late; your goods left yesterday."

"What will we do?" a stricken Daisy asked.

"We'll stay a year and make it a good one; I can do no less when these kind folks have brought us all this way." However, he did not yet tell his new board about this unexpected turn of events.

Oswald plunged into his new field with a fresh vigor because again God had met him in a special way just a few weeks earlier in March. He had been preaching in Tampa, Florida, when suddenly the Holy Spirit had come upon him:

> My heart was filled with an unutterable love; it seemed as though my whole body was bathed in the Holy Ghost. Somehow I finished my preaching and called for a season of prayer at the altar. I was melted, broken, awed, and as my soul rose to meet Him, the tears began to come. I could do nothing but weep and praise my precious, precious Lord. The world and all its troubles faded from my sight. My trials appeared oh, so insignificant as God, God Himself filled my whole vision. Oh, it was glorious. I began to pray, but only exclamations of praise and adoration poured from my lips. I saw no one save Jesus only.
>
> I slipped home to the pastor's house where I was staying, and there I continued to walk back and forth, my face uplifted, my heart thrilled, praising and blessing God.
>
> I must get away by myself, I thought, so I left the house and wandered I know not where. It seemed as though I wanted to love everybody. Every now and again as I walked along the street praising God, the tears would start to my eyes; and time after time I was choked with unutterable outbursts of worship and love that seemed almost to overwhelm me. I sang deep in my own soul my own chorus:
>
> *"Alone, dear Lord, ah, yes, alone with Thee!*
> *My aching heart at rest, my spirit free;*
> *My sorrow gone, my burdens all forgotten*
> *When far away I soar alone with Thee."*

> Finally I came back to my room and quieted down somewhat. I did not speak in tongues, but there was a sweet, settled peace in my heart and a light that never shone on land or sea in my soul. The glow passed, but the fragrance remained.

There seemed indeed to be an anointing on his ministry after that, and the altar would fill whenever he gave the invitation. Without coaxing, souls came seeking the Savior.

And this was evident in the new pastorate as the work grew speedily. Less than six weeks after his installation, a partition in the church had to be moved to accommodate the increasing crowds.

Oswald immediately organized three crucial groups: the Personal Workers whom he trained himself; the Prayer Warriors to be available for prayer at all times, particularly before each service; and the King's Messengers to distribute tracts throughout the city.

At the end of May, scarcely two months after his arrival, Oswald booked the largest hall in town, 2,000-seat Trinity Auditorium for Sunday afternoon services, at $125 weekly. He reserved it for four months, going right through the summer. The meetings were preceded by a thirty-minute organ recital, and featured the bright gospel music of a large orchestra and chorus choir, together with such artists as the Ramseyers with "the throbbing appeal of cornet and trombone, the rich thrumming of the harp and lilting piano duets often played in march or waltz time to the delight of the audience." The Russian prima donna, Madam Maria Karinskaya, thrilled these West Coast audiences with her magnificent voice, especially when she sang Oswald's "Russia, Dark Russia" to the tune of "Juanita." One of the most popular musicians was the "golden-voiced boy soloist," little Paul Brainerd Smith, who stood on a chair behind the podium and sang with a voice clear and true, filling the auditorium.

Los Angeles had never seen anything like it. Reporting on these unique services, one newspaper described Oswald as

> not only a brilliant speaker but a successful author and profound student of Biblical prophecy. He is an accomplished author, editor and hymnwriter. More than 100,000 of his ten book titles have been sold including *The Man God Uses, The Revival We Need, The Spirit-filled Life,* and *Hymns with a Message.*

His report on revival in Russian lands illustrated by seventy-five stereopticon slides was sure to draw a crowd, as was any one of his powerful sermons on prophecy. "Is the Anti-Christ at Hand?" was a favorite topic in the series.

By the second Sunday afternoon, the 2,000 seats were filled and 300 were turned away. The next Sunday, they decided to move the Tabernacle's evening service into Trinity Auditorium, so great was the interest. Only two-and-a-half months after Oswald's arrival in town, the Tabernacle Board of Managers decided to sell the present church property which was proving inadequate and to secure a downtown site for a "Metropolitan Tabernacle" to seat 2,000 people.

Along with building up attendance, Oswald challenged his congregation to unprecedented missionary giving: "I never mentioned tithing — just the need of the work and our obligation to get out the gospel around the world." And their pledge went from $5,500 to $17,500 that first year.

Oswald and Daisy thoroughly enjoyed California. "Los Angeles is an ideal summer resort," they wrote. Their home was situated on a quiet street, with fig and walnut trees in the large back garden. The generosity of their people quite overwhelmed the Smiths as they were showered first with a new Nash car, then a spacious, beautifully furnished home. They were making many new friends, including the R.G. Le Tourneaus who sang in the choir, and Charles and "Honey" Fuller of the "Old-Fashioned Revival Hour." The day drew near when Oswald felt he must tell the board of his decision to return to Toronto. "Are you sure this is the right thing, Oswald? Look at the blessing God is heaping on us, and the people are so happy. We've never had a more loving fellowship," Daisy pointed out.

"Daisy, I was out of God's will to come here," he

explained. "In spite of that, we have made the time count, or rather, *He* has made it count for Him. But I must return to Toronto. The call of God is on my heart and will not be silenced. Toronto is my city."

Besides, loyal supporters from Christie Street had kept writing to him, imploring him to return, saying that although he had been replaced, the crowds were not holding up and somehow there would be a way to reinstate him.

Thus, in late October he tendered his resignation to be effective April 1928. Following some special services along the coast, the Smith family left for Toronto, driving their new Nash car. But unfortunately the mechanic had decided to overhaul it just before leaving and had failed to replace all the pieces correctly. The engine continued to heat up so that they had to stop at every creek to fill the radiator. Then Hope came down with the mumps. Through the burning desert heat and traveling over hundreds of miles on unpaved roads, it was a thoroughly wretched trip.

With hope building that he would be asked to pastor the Christie Street church — "his child that was ailing" — Oswald returned to Toronto and preached the first Sunday in June in his old pulpit. But he would not be allowed back in. Finally, after two years, that was made irrevocably clear to Oswald. The work was lost to him forever.

Oswald was faced with the fact that at almost thirty-nine years of age, he had resigned from three large, thriving pastorates. For what? A vision that seemed more elusive that ever? *How can Daisy still believe in me, trust me to care for her and the children when I keep botching it up like this?* he wondered. *How hard it must be for her.*

He could continue as field evangelist for the Missionary Alliance, but he had no wish to be one of the more than 1,000 "strolling evangelists" of the day. He wrote:

> I carry the burden of the "Missionary-Evangelist." I must have headquarters. I want to travel to the foreign fields to get the vision firsthand and then return to broadcast the need and stir hearts all

> over the country on behalf of missionary projects. Only this will bring into use every talent and gift that God has given me.

But the heavens seemed closed to his pleadings for direction. It was a desperate, dark hour for Oswald, one of the darkest of his entire life. In a poignant poem he pleaded with God:

> *TARRY, DEAR LORD*
>
> *Tarry, dear Lord, oh, linger by my side,*
> *Turn not away but still with me abide;*
> *Dark grows the night; the light I cannot see,*
> *Stay then, O Lord, and tarry Thou with me.*
>
> *Though friends forsake and I am left alone,*
> *No one who cares and naught to call my own,*
> *Yet, Thou, dear Lord, has promised to abide,*
> *Come then, oh, come, and tarry by my side.*
>
> *Be Thou my Help when other helpers fail,*
> *Guide Thou my steps for I am weak and frail;*
> *Mid calm or storm, in comfort or in pain,*
> *Grant me, O Lord, Thy presence to sustain.*

Then the opportunity for meetings opened up to him in Truro, Nova Scotia. He went with a heavy heart:

> The battle had been unusually severe, the assaults of the enemy terrible. I could not drive him away. My heart was lonely. I was fearfully homesick and longed to get back with my family.
>
> I was alone in my room reading a Sunday school paper about the fullness of the Spirit, and this stirred me tremendously. And then He revealed Himself. I felt the Spirit flood over me. At once my heart was filled to overflowing. I walked the floor praising the Lord in the fullness of joy of the Holy Ghost. Peace like a river flowed over my soul.
>
> Regarding the future, my heart was at rest. All murmuring and complaining ceased. Oh, what a Comforter He is! It was a real anointing of the Holy Spirit.

And it came, all unsought at Oswald's hour of deepest despair and need.

Almost immediately he had a call from his dear friend Paul

Rader asking, "Can you preach for me in Chicago?" Preaching there always had been a great joy for Oswald, and he was cheered once more to be a part of this great thriving work. The musical artistry thrilled him with such professionals as Homer Rodeheaver, Merril Dunlop, Lance Latham, and Clarence and Howard Jones, all staff musicians. The large choir and the orchestra were dazzling as always. "Oh, God, make it real for me. Surely You haven't given me the vision to let it perish!" Oswald cried.

He decided to offer his services to Rader, who had pulled out of the Christian and Missionary Alliance when he felt he had been poorly used, and had started his own missionary organization, "The Worldwide Christian Couriers." "Wonderful!" Rader responded to Oswald's offer. "We'll set you up in Canada as the director of operations there. We'll rent Massey Hall to be the base for evangelism and worldwide missions that you have envisioned."

It was agreed. Oswald resigned altogether from the Alliance "after eight happy years," reminding them that what they had on Christie Street was because of his call to establish a work for God in the city of Toronto. But that work was not yet finished; thus he had no alternative but to pursue it with a new effort.

The reply from the head office of the Alliance was most cordial: they had been pleased with the spirit of Oswald's letter and wished God's blessing upon him, with much fruit in his new field of service.

I'LL FOLLOW THEE

I'll follow Thee, dear Lord,
For Thou didst die for me,
It matters not how hard
Or rough the way may be.
In sorrow or in joy,
In darkness or in light
I'll follow, follow on
Tho' day be turned to night.

I'll follow Thee, dear Lord.
When life is bright and fair,
For Thou didst follow me
When no one seemed to care.
I'll bear the heavy cross
Nor seek to lay it down,
Tho' others turn aside
And miss the victor's crown.

I'll follow Thee, dear Lord,
Across the desert drear,
In lands beyond the sea
Where e'er Thy voice I hear;
My heart shall gladly say,
"Dear Lord, I'll follow Thee,"
And then at last above
Thy blessed face I'll see.

OJS

TWENTY-THREE
♦♦♦
THE PEOPLES CHURCH IS BORN

We stand for
the Salvation of souls,
the Edification of believers
Worldwide Evangelism
and the Second Coming of Christ. OJS

On September 9, 1928, Oswald J. Smith stepped onto the platform of Massey Hall, and the Peoples Church was born. At that time it was actually called the "Cosmopolitan Tabernacle." The 2,000 who came to hear him preach that first night came back for more, often almost filling the hall. Again Oswald spoke with great clarity and force, spicing his sermons with tales of adventures in the northwoods and the Russian mission fields. Since his anointing with the Holy Spirit in Truro, each time Oswald preached his heart was flooded anew with the overwhelming love of God. The resulting power was evident as souls responded readily.

Oswald also brought in top-name speakers such as Paul Rader from Chicago and Clinton H. Churchill, the popular pastor from Buffalo, New York. Again the exciting new gospel music was featured, with the Ramseyers coming up from California to thrill Toronto audiences with their singing and playing. Billy Sunday's favorite hymn, "Brighten the Corner

Where You Are," was always a hit, along with "Since Jesus Came into My Heart."

Oswald had learned from experience that launching a work in a small building would take years to get it on the map; "but start in a large, well-known auditorium and you don't have to advertise because it's already known. It takes only a short time to get the whole city interested in what you're doing." And very soon the whole city of Toronto knew about Oswald J. Smith's new Cosmopolitan Tabernacle with the newspapers covering every activity of this "permanent evangelistic centre," reporting sermons in detail and crowds of 3,000 to 4,000.

Oswald set out their position very simply:

> We stand for the Salvation of souls,
> the Edification of believers
> and Worldwide Evangelism;
> and we emphasize especially the four great essentials, viz.,
> -Salvation
> -The Deeper Life
> -Foreign Missions, and
> -Our Lord's Return.
> There will be no church membership. We are separate from all churches and denominations, reaching out for the thousands of people who never enter a church door.

For both Oswald and Daisy, it was truly a time of coming home at last. Oswald looked back over their twelve years together and captured it in poetry:

> *Twelve years of furnace heat;*
> *Reverses came, we suffered pain and loss;*
> *Men turned against us, friends forsook our cause,*
> *Misunderstandings, disappointments sore,*
> *Defeats and broken vows, distresses, tears,*
> *Heartaches and burdens, trials and testings fierce,*
> *This was our lot, until our hearts cried out*
> *In dark despair.*
> *Yet through it all God knit us heart to heart*
> *And taught us how to love as ne'er before.*

Twelve years of trial — and yet of joys entwined,
Not all despair, nay much of heaven's best,
Dark days and bright, affliction, joy and health,
Yet in it all, through good or ill, His grace.

Thank God for these twelve years of furnace heat,
For love we now as lovers ne'er have loved
Except their love be tempered as was ours.

Then let us live as God would have us live,
O dearest, mine; and think not of the past
With all its failures and its blighted hopes,
nor dread the future.
For we are still but youthful, and the joys
Of perfect, changeless love may yet be ours!

Yet how soon were Daisy and Oswald to part again — this time for five months. Toward Christmas, Rader decided that Oswald should make a tour of the Russian and Spanish mission fields on behalf of the Worldwide Christian Couriers. Thus, after four months of packing out Massey Hall each Sunday night, the meetings were suspended, and Massey Hall was rebooked for the great missionary convention when Oswald would return in June 1929.

In mid-January Daisy journeyed with Oswald to Chicago for a last week together before his long trip. During this farewell week, Oswald preached at the Gospel Tabernacle every night, and the altars were full. Then they boarded the train for New York; in Cleveland, Daisy left the train to travel home to Toronto and spend five months alone with the children.

Again it was a cruel parting. "I don't want to stand in your way if the Lord is calling you out. But I need you, and the children need you. Love for a man is a thing apart; 'tis a woman's whole existence," Daisy wryly observed as again she was stung by his excitement, even eagerness, to leave her for the anticipated missionary journey. Try as she would, it was hard for Daisy to understand the inner fires that were driving this man she loved more than life itself.

"Certainly I'd rather stay in Toronto with you and the children," Oswald tried to explain. "But it isn't just Rader sending me: God is calling me and I must obey."

There's an urge upon my spirit that compels my feet to go;
And to Europe's teeming millions I must God's salvation show.
As He called the great apostle, so He chooses men today;
I am one whom He has chosen and I dare not disobey!

OJS

TWENTY-FOUR

♦♦♦

SEND ME OUT

I hide my face in humility and cry: "Who is sufficient for these things?" OJS

Wearing a fur-lined topcoat given to him by a Christian brother and carrying several hundred dollars for aid to the almost million Russian refugees crowding into France, Oswald sailed from New York to London, sharing the cramped tourist quarters with three strangers. "Funds must be saved for the Russian mission fields," Oswald stated simply. About such frugality there was never a question, and Oswald found himself critical of mission personnel who indulged in the luxury of better accommodation and meals and expensive cables home:

> God keep me absolutely clear of fault-finding and unwarranted criticism of mission societies and leaders. Criticism is a sure road to a dried-up, frozen-over, ebbtide spiritual experience. There may be some with whom we cannot conscientiously work, but we at least leave them alone. God has not appointed us their judge. God help us to keep our hands off, to practice what we preach, so that we really labour together in the unity of the Spirit, for only thus can the world be evangelized.

He was impressed to encounter on ship a group of young Mormons who were headed for Germany to do missionary work; they had had only ten days training and were paying all their own expenses. He learned that on an average, the Mormons sent out seventy-five missionaries every three weeks. Oswald wrote home:

> What an example to the Church of Jesus Christ! Would to God we could send out our seventy every three weeks. How quickly the field would be covered! Let us be stirred to action, even if it be by the Mormons.

In London, the February cold crept into Oswald's bones — with no heat in buses or trains and little central heating in the cheap hotels. Oswald thankfully slept in his fur-lined coat.

He met with the editors of several Christian publications: *The Christian Herald,* the largest religious publication in the world at the time with a circulation of 250,000 copies weekly; *The Life of Faith,* and *The Christian.* These were magazines that already had published several of his articles and had arranged to carry reports of his extensive mission tour.

Oswald also made arrangements with Marshall, Morgan, and Scott to have some of his books published in England. The usual royalty payment would be waived to keep prices at a rockbottom twenty-five or fifty cents for wide distribution in developing countries; the money also would pay for distribution of the Scriptures in these needy areas. Oswald was delighted when a Christian brother slipped him a tiny, finely bound collection of Wordsworth's poems, a lifelong treasure to be drawn from his pocket and enjoyed on weary journeys. He had regained the liberty to revel once more in the classics, which he found to be the very lifeblood of his creative soul.

Then it was on to Paris, and an eighty-cent-a-night hotel where he checked in with his one change of clothes. (Actually, all he ever owned was: a Sunday suit and shoes, an everyday suit and shoes, plus a couple of shirts and ties. On shorter trips he carried only his briefcase with toiletry articles, one shirt, and a change of underwear tucked in with a couple of books to read, writing materials, and his *King James* Bible.) Down the block he found a cheap Russian restaurant: "The prices are one third that of any other, so I simply will have to get used to the food."

In Paris, and throughout France and Switzerland, he ministered to both the nobility of Russia and the common people, all of whom had fled from Russia following the takeover by the Bolsheviks in November 1917. Sometimes he teamed up with Pastor Fetler, but more often he was on his own. He spoke in mission halls, theaters, factory dining halls, private homes — wherever the missionaries managed to open a door. The schedule was a rigorous one. Sometimes he had to rise at 4:00 A.M. to catch a train, jolting along in third- or fourth-class seats through the day and night, preaching long hours, often with only one meal a day.

In one city the meeting lasted until midnight when the missionary called a halt to get Oswald a cup of steaming coffee with some ham and french bread, for he had eaten nothing since noon. Then the group of new converts plied him with questions until 2:30 A.M.; they followed the conversation with prayer until 3:00 A.M. The fire had gone out and Oswald was shivering from head to toe. Fortunately there was a small fire in the old-fashioned boxstove in the place where Oswald was to spend the remainder of the night. By pacing back and forth, he gradually got warm enough to drop into a fitful sleep.

He traveled all the next day to Lyon where again the service went until midnight, but Oswald had to leave to catch a 1:30 A.M. train to Paris where he arrived in the morning feeling very weary, with a severe sore throat. But there was little time to rest before he was scheduled to preach again. So it went. Yet in spite of Oswald's headaches, sore throats, extreme chilling, hunger, and lack of sleep, God blessed mightily and scores responded to the messages.

Oswald was deeply pained by the desperate need of the missionaries he encountered. One pair was trying to exist on eight cents' worth of food a day; another couple with a new baby had virtually nothing. He was glad he had funds along so that he could distribute some as he saw need. And he determined in his heart that when he got home, he would do something to increase their support.

Before going on to Germany and Latvia, Oswald decided to treat himself at his own expense — not with mission money — to a quick Cook's Tour to Italy. There he climbed to the brim of Mount Vesuvius, taking photographs while the cinders were blowing onto him and belches of flame were erupting up through the dense smoke clouds. "What huge fires must ever rage in the bowels of this volcano! Who feeds them? How are they kept blazing? As I stood on that horrible furnace, it was not difficult to imagine the reality of hell," he wrote. Next he shot three rolls of film in resurrected Pompeii, the ancient [600 B.C.] city which had been buried 2,000 years earlier during a startingly sudden eruption from Mt. Vesuvius.

That afternoon, a mysterious fear began to steal over Oswald, an awareness of terrible personal danger lurking nearby. He paced the floor, with the deepening conviction that he must leave Italy and proceed at once to his destination in Berlin. "After an hour-and-a-half of prayer, I decided I must forego Rome for this trip. Went to bed in agony," his diary tersely records.

But in Rome there were still two wonderful hours between trains, and Oswald hired a cab to catch a glimpse of the city's magnificence, with its lovely fountains and statuary and old narrow streets giving way to broad modern boulevards. Reluctantly he boarded the midnight train to Venice where he had two precious hours to snatch a trip on the canals before going on to Berlin. And for once, he treated himself to a sleeper.

This brief visit to Italy also had included some very enlightening conversations with English-speaking Italians about the great improvements the new dictator had introduced. These talks provided rich material for later discussion of the new leader's place in prophecy. Could Mussolini be the Anti-Christ?

In Berlin, Oswald found letters from home waiting for him.

Eagerly he tore open Daisy's letters, then turned to the children's scrawled notes signed with dozens of "hugs and kisses": "We'll be able to beat you in checkers when you get home. . . . We're having a lovely time with Chrissie. . . . We wish you were here to read us the funnies/comics. . . . We are all well and hope you are well and have enough money. . . . We are not forgetting to pray for Daddy." And from Hope a postscript: "If you get to Russia, I would like you to bring me a new dress." Oswald picked up Daisy's letters and poured through the lonely pages once more:

> I love you tonight with a much greater intensity than ever and long for you with an unutterable longing, for I have found a love in you that I would not exchange for any other. You stand on a pinnacle alone as far as I am concerned. You have been so good to me in every way — it is wonderful to love and be loved. But I shudder to think of the awful distance that separates us. Perhaps God is punishing me for not being the wife I should have been to you. I sometimes get thinking of heaven where you will be so far above me that I will never see you, and it depresses me so.
>
> I try to be brave, but I feel so defeated by it all. I know we are not here just to live selfish lives in ease and luxury while others are suffering without God and without hope. For this reason I am glad you are away doing all you can to tell others, and we are all praying that you may be used in the salvation of hundreds of precious souls. I want you to have God's best for your life no matter what the cost or sacrifice. I believe the time is fast approaching when we shall have no more time to work. But I miss you every minute. Please try to rest your brain and don't take any campaigns that will tire you. Eat well and go to bed early. Make the most of this trip, for I'm afraid I won't let you go anymore without me!

With tears coursing down his face, Oswald tucked the letter into his case. Dear, dear Daisy, would God never let her understand? How the loneliness pressed in! Once more he fell on his face before God: "Are these separations really necessary? Have you really chosen me and sent me to these people or am I here out of my own eagerness?" Graciously God met him and healed the breaking heart: *"Yes, my child, I have called you to take my message. And I am going to bless your ministry in a way you have never dreamed."*

A few days later while still in Berlin, Oswald was overcome with a heavy chest cold, so that he lay awake all one night "fighting the hardest battle of his life," struggling to breathe, afraid that he might have contracted the flu that was sweeping Europe and killing many. As he tossed from side to side in agony, he could only cry, "Oh, God, please put it on the heart of someone back home to pray for me."

The next day, although weak, he was well enough to travel from mid-morning until midnight and was able to confer with the president of the evangelical movement in Russia, Reverend J.H. Proknanoff. And when he awoke from a sound sleep the following morning, he was almost totally cured. In his regular report home to Rader, he praised God for this wonderful recovery. After his conference with Proknanoff Oswald deemed it wise not to enter Russia at this time even though he had hoped to persuade the Soviet government to allow the printing of Bibles. They would have to work out another way.

Enroute to Latvia, he pondered the situation:

> Never in my life have I felt so small, so utterly helpless. What can I do? How can one frail man get the Gospel to so many millions? Will Europe ever be evangelized? Oh, to do something! To be used of God! I seem like a pebble on the beach. Like a grain of sand in the desert. Like a drop of water in the ocean. Like a worm before a mountain. I hide my face in humility and cry: "Who is sufficient for these things?" God! I am nothing. "He is able."
>
> *SEND ME OUT*
>
> *Lord, send me out with heart aflame*
> *To win them to Thy fold;*
> *Of Jesus and His wondrous love*
> *The Story must be told.*
>
> *Lord, send me out, I care not where,*
> *With pow'r to win the lost;*
> *To tell them of redemption free*
> *Procured at awful cost.*
>
> *Lord, send me out, it matters not*
> *How hard the task may be;*
> *The Gospel of Thy grace, I know*
> *Can set poor sinners free.*

SEND ME OUT

Lord, send me out, oh, let me go,
I dare not still delay;
The day of grace will soon be o'er
Then let me speed away.

OJS

TWENTY-FIVE

♦♦♦

REVIVAL FIRES IN RIGA

Oh, these teeming multitudes — how they have won me! OJS

Finally, Oswald was once again in his beloved Riga, the Baltic seaport of the former Russian Empire. (Prior to the armistice of World War I, Latvia had been Russian territory, with its life and people Russian.) During that first week of April it was bitterly cold with the sea frozen over and ships caught in ice sixteen-feet thick.

At the train station to greet Oswald was Pastor Fetler accompanied by fifty students singing a hymn of welcome. With great joy, Oswald walked through the new Salvation Temple with its 1,500 seats, besides the 200 in the choir loft. This was the meeting place that he had raised so much money to help build for Russian evangelical Christians after his last trip.

From the first night Oswald preached to great crowds both in Riga and in the other cities they traveled to, holding four services most days. After catching a train one midnight, he and Fetler traveled for ten hours, stretching out briefly on the hard boards which passed for sleepers. Arriving stiff and sore, they rushed straight to the 10:00 A.M. service at which Oswald preached. In the afternoon he preached again. When they reached the great hall that night, they found it packed from end to end with some two thousand people standing. Since there was no heat in the building, Oswald preached in his fur-lined coat.

So great was the response that they decided to dismiss the service and hold an after-meeting for the seekers. Only a few people left the auditorium. In the little area they managed to clear at the front, men and women knelt to freely give themselves to Christ. It was a glorious never-to-be-forgotten experience for Oswald. The service ended at 11:15 P.M. Then they proceeded to a dinner prepared by the Latvian sisters and got to sleep just before 2:00 A.M. They were up at 5:00. Catching a *droshky* (a four-wheeled Russian horse-drawn carriage), they drove over a rough road to the station and thus on to the next meetings.

Oswald was thrilled that several of his books had been printed in the Russian and Latvian languages, including *The Revival We Need,* and *When He is Come,* as well as several gospel tracts. Now was the time, the missionaries decided, for his book of gospel messages, *From Death to Life,* to be translated and placed in every Russian home: "These people are educated and can all read; this is a golden opportunity." Thus when Oswald and Fetler set off for meetings in the province of Latgalia on the Russian border, they took with them a translating team. On the train and during droshky rides, work progressed. In the hotel typewriters were set up to speed the translation.

Latgalia turned out to be the spiritually darkest area Oswald had ever visited — given over to both witchcraft and an almost pagan Catholicism. With less than a dozen paid workers and only 450 believers, most in the population of 550,000 had had no contact with the simple gospel. The crowds were wild and noisy; the men kept their hats on, and the girls took turns standing up, laughing, and mocking during the entire service. Sometimes the interpreter could scarcely be heard above the disturbance. For nine days Oswald preached to this rowdy group, remembering his days of being heckled back in the British Columbia bush. His sermons had to be very simple since most did not know even the children's Bible stories, and hence there was no foundation upon which to build. In most places many responded to the invitation, although some laughed in his face.

Sleeping accommodations in the villages varied considerably. "No one needs to be lonely at night; there is plenty of company," Oswald reported. He spoke not only of the crowded quarters, but also of the vermin that swarmed everywhere. Still he wrote:

> But oh, these teeming multitudes — how they have won me! My heart has been stirred, my soul burdened by this virgin mission field that I have now seen with my own eyes. How great is the harvest! How few the labourers! Would to God I could spend months touring from place to place throughout Latgalia, telling the story to the tens of thousands who have never heard of God's salvation!

But Oswald realized that he would have to "do what John Wesley had done: organize the work." Thus on the spot he organized the Russian Border Mission and appointed the pastor of the largest Baptist church in Latvia to be superintendent, promising him funds to open a Bible school to train preachers—thirty initially—for all over Latgalia. Oswald promised to send books, tracts, Bibles, and bicycles for the evangelists.

And then in Riga the revival began. The first morning the hall was almost full as evangelists, Sunday school workers, and Christians from all parts of the country gathered for a special Worldwide Christian Couriers Conference on "Soulwinning and Deepening the Spiritual Life." The second day there were more. By the fourth morning there was no room—the choir seats were filled, and even with extra chairs set out, people were standing in the aisles. Oswald recorded:

> And then the power of God fell on the audience. Men and women knelt everywhere, and oh, such prayers! Such tears! Such testimonies! How they sang! Again and again choruses of gladness, victory, and triumph were joyfully sung. "Hallelujah," they cried aloud. "Glory be to God!" It was heaven on earth. Mighty rivers of bless-

> ing. The Holy Spirit Himself came and made His abode with them, praise be to God.
>
> At the four o'clock service they were back, and once more the power of God was present. Tears flowed freely. Joy unspeakable and full of glory was depicted on many a countenance.
>
> At 6:30 I preached again, and at eight, four times in one day. Soon after I returned to my room there was a knock at my door. One of the students entered and told me how God had spoken to him. He described his great hunger of heart — "I have determined to pray all night for I will not cease until I know the power of the Holy Ghost in my life." As we prayed together, he sobbed aloud.
>
> Then came another knock on the door — would I meet with some in an adjoining room? There I found the office staff on their faces; to them also God had spoken. Again, there was agonizing prayer; sin was dealt with and put away, and a full surrender made, for again the Holy Spirit had His way. Presently in trooped all the students in a body, and kneeling down, in Russian, German, Latvian and English they poured out their hearts to God. Oh, what a melting time! How they wept before the Lord! What joy it was to be in such an atmosphere of revival and to see the Holy Spirit Himself at work!
>
> Finally they left, to continue in prayer in their own rooms; how late I do not know. At twelve o'clock I returned to my room and with joy and gratitude in my soul, went to bed. What a blessed day it had been.

The next morning again the altar was packed. With hands uplifted, they sang "Blessed Be the Name," At four o'clock Oswald preached again, with many standing. Once more the altar was lined with seeking souls. At seven o'clock, the power of the Spirit was very real, and a holy hush fell over the audience. An after-meeting was announced for the lower hall, and the upstairs auditorium filled up again, and once more that night Oswald was compelled to preach. Again scores knelt at the altar and with contrition and joy accepted Christ. When Oswald returned to his room at the mission house, he found a group of Russians on their faces before God, praying quietly and earnestly. Oswald joined them until midnight, then slipped away to bed.

Day after day they sang Oswald's hymn "Saved!" which had been translated into Russian and Latvian. Sometimes they sang it twice through at a time.

Easter Sunday was a particularly memorable day. It began with a 6:00 A.M. service, which seemed especially early for Oswald because he had attended the colorful Greek Orthodox midnight service the evening before, enjoying to the full the glorious singing of the choir, the pageantry of the priests in their gorgeous robes, and the lighting of the candles. It was 2:00 A.M. when he finally got to bed. But there were over 1,200 in the early morning service and many responded to the invitation.

At 10:00 A.M. the congregation had swelled to 1,600; Oswald baptized twenty-one and served communion. That service lasted four full hours so that Oswald had only time to eat a little and throw himself on the bed for a quick nap before the 4:00 P.M. service. At the fourth service, lasting from 7:00 until after 10:00, they prayed for the sick. He recorded:

> But, oh, what boundless joy as so many came to the Saviour! Henceforth I am determined to be a man of one message: the gospel. Other things, though important, must be laid aside, and the glorious gospel of the grace of God proclaimed in the power of the Holy Ghost. That is my supreme task. For many years I have read books by leading religious writers of a more or less heavy character; but lately I have turned to the simple but forceful and soul-stirring sermons of D.L. Moody. I have discovered that most religious books are very difficult to translate into a foreign language, but the works of Moody and Spurgeon are easy and far more effective. They preached the gospel with no side issues. God keep me simple in my preaching!

Pastor Fetler also reported on the blessings of that Easter Day:

> When Mr. Smith gave his Resurrection message, he did not manifest any signs of weariness or abating strength. God was in the message, and a number of souls gave themselves to Christ.

At the end of the meeting, Fetler suggested to the people that they bring a written testimony together with a thanksgiving offering to the afternoon and evening services. But,

Oswald turned these gifts back into the work. The testimonies, though, he kept and treasured. One wrote:

> I thank God for the many, many blessings which I have received from your preaching. When you have preached it was in my soul so that I must pray, pray, pray without to break up. It is in my heart something like flame-fire and I want everybody tell from our Dear Saviour's great love.

From another:

> How many blessings Latvia is received from you, how many people have you brought to God, and how many, many have you given back the health through your prayings! We can't thank you for all this but the great God will pay you. Little time ago I didn't believe God, but since the time I heard the story of your life, I am broken.

And another:

> We are thankful to our Heavenly Father for leading you to come to Riga. Your visit was a wonderful blessing to us. God has spoken to our hearts through your preaching as never before and has taught us so much that we cannot express it in words. Our only desire is to live for our dear Saviour and to give all our strength and time for His service.

And never would Oswald Smith or William Fetler forget the Tuesday morning in Revel at the most northerly tip of Estonia, when Oswald preached on "The Lordship of Christ." There in a great burst of praise the crowd surged to their feet, and with hands lifted to heaven and eyes closed sang "Crown Him Lord of All."

When it was time for Oswald to leave these Russian lands, it was with tears that the Christians bade him good-bye. Oswald himself was too choked with emotion to say a farewell to the crowd on the station platform as they pressed close for a final handclasp, showering him with flowers and gifts for Daisy and the children. It seemed impossible to part. As the train pulled away from the station, they sang, "God be with you till we meet again," and waved handkerchiefs. Oswald waved back, searching face after face in a last glimpse, perhaps forever. Collapsing in tears in his seat, he felt a stab of pain pierce his heart. How he had come to love them! Oswald wrote to Rader:

> When will I visit Europe again? they asked me. Oh, that I could prolong my stay and continue the meetings. God bless these dear, dear people. How my heart has gone out to them. I feel I love the Russian people as I never have loved another; and that I would be willing to forget my mother tongue, say farewell to my native land and spend the rest of my life in their midst.
>
> *Russia, dark Russia — Hark, I hear them day and night,*
> *Moaning and dying, groping still in darkest night,*
> *Weary, tired and hopeless souls for whom the Saviour died,*
> *Can I live in ease and comfort while they are still denied?*
> *Can I let them perish? Oh, I hear their bitter wail —*
> *How can I face them if to help I fail?*

Fetler also reported on the campaign:

> The results of the red-letter season in Gospel Revival have been deep and permanent. Several hundreds of souls were led to accept Jesus Christ as their personal Saviour, and very many were led into a deeper realization of the necessity of being crucified with Christ and filled with the Holy Spirit. We are deeply thankful to Rev. Paul Rader and the Worldwide Christian Couriers for sending to us Rev. Oswald Smith. We all want him to come back again for another mighty soul-saving tour to the midnight lands of Eastern Europe.

TWENTY-SIX

♦♦♦

HE WILL USE YOU YET AGAIN

I have seen the vision and for self I
cannot live;
Life is less than worthless till my all
I give.

OJS

Going on to Paris, Oswald addressed the Russian Christian workers who had gathered from all over France for a conference sponsored by the Worldwide Christian Couriers. He spoke on "The Spirit-filled Life" and much blessing was reported.

Deeply burdened to help these destitute missionaries, Oswald convened a business session where they might fully acquaint him with the special problems they faced ministering in France. It became obvious that the biggest need was financial support and more workers; also, a hall was needed for the large gathering of Russian Christians in Paris. Oswald pledged himself to meet this need.

Responding to the urgent invitation of the Spanish Gospel Mission, Oswald then traveled through the night to Spain. There he was enchanted by the riotous wildflower bloom, the thousands of acres of olive groves, the whitewashed houses all grilled and barred, and the small donkeys with their great bundles of wood and large sacks of grain, clip-clopping along or blindfolded and patiently pacing in a circle, driving the waterwheels which drew up water from deep wells.

Ever curious, he photographed the girls making lace in Almagro; in another village, he saw how wine was made and stored. He visited the great Moorish cathedral in Toledo and the dungeons of the Inquisition. As he drove through the countryside, he tossed tracts from the car which the people eagerly scrambled to retrieve. Workmen on the roads even dropped their shovels to pick up the tracts. And all the while, Oswald's photo collection was growing rapidly.

Since the people did not come in from the fields until sundown, it was a new experience for Oswald to begin a meeting at ten, or even eleven, in the evening. When midnight came, no one wanted to go home. So he would start again for a few more hours. The crowds were not large, but again the response from these hungry hearts was rewarding. "I took to the people and people took to me. If ever God led, He led me to Spain," Oswald said with certainty as he surveyed the desperate need. He later noted that

> the greatest need is a Bible School, where Spanish workers may be quickly trained and sent out. They alone can evangelize their own country; foreigners can never hope to do it. I feel I must undertake the responsibility of this great work. Think of 23 million souls without Christ, with only a handful of missionaries and 45 national workers!

Leaving Madrid, Oswald spent the next five nights on the train, trying both to recover from a severe cold and toothache that had plagued him in Spain and to catch up on his reports. For the last lap of his missionary journey he traveled through to Poland where he was scheduled to hold yet another workers' conference made possible by the Worldwide Christian Couriers.

The hall was much too small, and to Oswald's amazement, probably half the audience was Jewish. What an experience it was — Jews listening eagerly to the message! For three hours they sat drinking in the Word, and seventy-five responded at the first meeting. And how these Hebrew Christians sang Oswald's hymn "Saved!" in Russian and German. For this conference, over 100 missionaries and colporteurs had gathered from various parts of Poland, some walking twenty-five to fifty miles. All of them, including Oswald, slept together on straw in the barns. When Oswald spoke in other cities, the halls there were also crowded out, with hundreds outside listening through the open windows.

Returning finally to Warsaw, Oswald was exultant. In spite of getting drenched to the skin as they jolted along in horse-drawn wagons through the heavy downpour, he could exclaim,

> How good God has been! I have travelled approximately 20,000 miles in fourteen European countries, and have preached 143 times in 114 days. Although I am both physically and mentally worn out, praise God, I am still alive, and all the while He has wonderfully sustained spiritually. I feel I have been lifted to a higher plane than ever before. Oh, how I praise God for victory all along the line. I leave Europe to dedicate myself body, soul and spirit as never before to Him. I feel humbled and unworthy as I think of all He has done for me!

In London, Oswald was elated to find that his reports had been given a prominent place in all the Christian publications there as well as several in America. His vivid, detailed descriptions captured the color and charm of each place visited and made for reading that was more like the *National Geographic* magazine than a dry mission report. Indeed, it was a time for rejoicing.

Oswald chuckled to think of some of the near misses. There was the time at the very beginning of his trip when he had gone to the station in Chicago to pick up his ticket for New York and discovered that in his excitement he had forgotten to renew his clergy pass entitling him to travel discounts. To have to pay full fare during the next six months was unthinkable. Fortunately, he and Daisy had arrived at the station an hour early — "a miracle in itself," Oswald declared. He had rushed over to the office four blocks away, but without a letter to recommend him, had been turned down. Then miraculously the agent had relented and had given Oswald the pass. Racing back to the station, he had grabbed Daisy, rushed down the platform, and boarded the train just as it was pulling out.

Then there was the night in Riga when he had been working feverishly at the printer's, checking the proofs of his books and tracts. Right through the scheduled 6:00 P.M. departure hour he had worked, opting for an 11:55 P.M. train. Shortly after 11:30 he pulled on his coat and headed out the door with Fetler hurrying him on. Almost at the station, he discovered he had forgotten his luggage. The droshky dashed back to the printers, rattling over the stone roads. Fortunately they had not locked up, so Oswald retrieved his bag and sprang aboard the train — again just in the nick of time.

"Tell me not life is vain!" Oswald penned as he sat rejoicing in his lounge chair, looking out over the sun-spattered waves of the blue Atlantic in mid-June of 1929. And he thought of just one year earlier when having arrived home in Toronto from California, he had been plunged into a dark despair. All had seemed lost forever. *Surely I am finished,* he had thought. But now he could exult:

Sing no more that sad refrain —
Look above,
God is love —
He will use you yet again!

OJS

Then as the S.S. *Duchess of York* ploughed through the waves, Oswald began to write an exquisite 1,200-line love ballad about Malcolm, a young Canadian, and his Russian love, Marie, with a setting which swept from Russian snows and prison camps, across the plains of America and through the Canadian Rockies.

As Oswald steamed up the St. Lawrence, ahead in Toronto all was in place for a triumphant homecoming and a great missionary convention; the speakers and singers had already arrived by the time his ship tied up in Montreal. And on the dock to greet Oswald was his beloved Daisy. They had a joyous reunion alone as they journeyed by train to Toronto that night. Oswald felt well; he was rested after nine days at sea, and in spite of his illnesses and strenuous itinerary he had gained twelve pounds.

For two days the family had him to themselves while he organized his slides to show at the convention. In Riga he had 150 of his 200 black-and-white photographs made into colored stereopticon slides, a tedious hand-process. But the results were "simply superb" in Oswald's judgment. And yes, he had brought back a dress for Hope, the most beautiful he could find in all of Europe.

Especially in these days before worldwide travel was commonplace, the crowds jamming Massey Hall found his pictures breathtaking. Then Oswald poured out his heart:

> I have found mission fields worthy of every effort we can make for their evangelization. The waiting multitudes in Europe I can never forget.
>
> With deeper meaning I repeat the words I wrote five years ago:
>
> *"I have seen the vision and for self I cannot live;*
> *Life is less than worthless till my all I give."*

Rader accepted all of his recommendations to the Worldwide Christian Couriers. But these would require a minimum outlay of $3,000 per month for the first year alone. "You'll have to help us raise it," Rader decided.

Thus, after only two weeks at home, Oswald was on the road again, presenting the challenge of Europe's needs to sellout crowds in Chicago, at Lake Harbour Bible Conference, in Minneapolis, Kansas City, Dallas, and the West Coast. Every few weeks he would touch base with Chicago and Toronto, then be off again. Sometimes his good friend Dr. Ralph Hooper accompanied him and held meetings in other parts of the city, sharing in the spiritual counseling. The money poured in — $60,000 in those next few months. The stock market crashed on November 1, 1929, but Oswald, hardly noticing, pressed on until he could report in March 1930:

> When I returned from abroad, the Couriers did not have one single missionary in Europe. Now we are fully supporting 61.
>
> In Spain, God has sent us a Spanish-speaking Dean for the training school for national evangelists.
>
> But we need to open the Bible training school in Riga, and the fifteen Russian evangelists must be supported.
>
> As well, Paris needs a hall for the large Russian meetings there.
>
> We are determined that this great work shall be done without waste, that every cent will count, and that the money will be used as designated.
>
> We are attempting great things for God, in simple childlike faith. God has given us the plan and the program. We are trusting Him, through you, to supply the $20,000.

And the money came in, in spite of the Depression that was paralyzing the North American economy.

TWENTY-SEVEN
♦♦♦
THE CHURCH THAT PUTS MISSIONS FIRST

When a church puts first things first, God moves. OJS

Back home during the long months when Oswald was absent from Toronto — first in Europe and then across the continent reporting on the mission fields — a faithful few were holding prayer meetings, praying Oswald J. Smith back to reopen a great center of evangelism. They had had a taste of that — first during his five-and-a-half years at Christie Street Tabernacle, and then more recently during his four outstanding months in Massey Hall.

Also, burdened with the need to reach the many unchurched, a group of businessmen on their own had rented the 1,200-seat former St. James Square Presbyterian Church at 42 Gerrard Street East in downtown Toronto. (This was one of the many fine buildings left vacant following the merger of most Presbyterian, Methodist, and Congregational churches to form the United Church of Canada in 1925.) These men were bringing in evangelists and special music, but it was a struggle.

Then, in Atlanta one night, God spoke to Oswald and very clearly reassured him that soon it would be time for him to settle down once more and get on with building the center for winning souls and sending out missionaries and funds to the foreign field. The month of March would bring the open door, God "told" him.

So he was not overly surprised to receive a phone call in early March about the work on Gerrard Street East. Would Oswald J. Smith consider taking it over? They had some 500 attending, plus a weekly radio broadcast, but they needed a strong man to build a continuous program. Oswald accepted the challenge.

However, on the first Sunday morning, the treasurer approached him: "Reverend, there is one thing we didn't tell you about this place — we are in debt. There are unpaid bills, and no money in the treasury." Oswald nodded, then turned to go into the pulpit. And as he went, he prayed: "All right Lord, in your Word you promise 'Seek ye first the kingdom of God and all these things shall be added unto you.' For a long time I've been wanting to find out whether that would really work in a practical way. This is my chance to prove it."

Oswald never said a word about the financial needs of the work; he just preached on missions. That evening, instead of his usual evāngelistic message, he again preached on missions, and again made no mention of the debt. Then, he asked the people to come back every night of the week. He brought in a missionary on furlough to help, and each night the congregation got a "dose of missions." The next Sunday Paul Rader was in the pulpit, and Oswald announced that they would hold three services and at each service take up a special offering for missions. The treasurer was stunned.

But the people caught the vision and began to give as they never had given before; souls were saved and the group so awakened that they came in ever-increasing numbers. Within a few weeks, without Oswald having to say hardly a word about local obligations, every bill was paid. From then on, the Peoples Church would not know the meaning of the word *debt,* Oswald vowed. He had confirmed that "when a church puts first things first, God moves."

From the first day, Oswald's flair for generating crowd excitement was evidenced at "The Toronto Gospel Tabernacle." The exciting music once again played a large role, as Eldon B. Lehman led the 100-voice choir and 40-piece orchestra in the lovely contemporary arrangements of such composers as B.D. Ackley, D.B. Towner, George C. Stebbins and Robert Harkness. Many of the lyrics were Oswald's own, for he was continually writing new hymns.

"I knew I could never hold the crowds with my own preaching," Oswald insisted, so he brought in such outstanding speakers as Rader, Anthony Zeoli, Gerald Winrod, Clinton Churchill, and even the more sensational personalities like Mary Agnes Wagner, "The College Girl Evangelist." Although Oswald admitted to not really approving of lady preachers, Mary Agnes with her old-time revival preaching captured the hearts of all. And her featured soloist was the "local songbird, ten-year-old Master Paul Smith" who was popularizing his father's hymn, "There Is Nothing Too Hard for Jesus." Paul never missed a meeting, tagging along at his father's heels everywhere.

The first radio broadcasts were at five o'clock Sunday afternoons over Radio CKNC. Then radio station CKCL asked Oswald if they could carry the morning service. Few church organizations would have anything to do with this new "tool of the devil," but Oswald jumped at the chance to get the message out to even more thousands, at a cost of only fifty dollars for the hour and a half. Finally, *The Back Home Hour,* from 9:30 P.M. to 10:30 P.M. was aired — a program made up mostly of music by the choir and orchestra with just a fifteen-minute message by Oswald. "It's the best variety show on radio!" the station manager enthused.

Soon it seemed that every home in Toronto was listening to Peoples Church broadcasts. Especially on a summer evening, you could walk along the street and hear the same music coming from every house. Oswald found it a great way to promote coming services so that on Sunday nights in particular the church was always jammed, with people from all over the city. Hurrying off the streetcars, they would run along Gerrard Street in hopes of getting a seat.

In order to pack in even more, Oswald started a children's church, and 100 youngsters attended the first night. The first Sunday school picnic was widely publicized in newspaper photos of Oswald baptizing sixty-five new converts in Highland Creek.

TWENTY-EIGHT
♦♦♦
NO ATTACK, NO DEFENSE

What have I to do with questions
That but rob me of my pow'r?
For the letter only killeth
And I dare not waste an hour;
Controversies, criticisms,
Jealousies that gender strife —
I have died to all, and Jesus
Now is reigning in my life.
This, this is now my mission,
To proclaim and make Him known,
Only one absorbing passion:
Christ to live, and Christ alone.

OJS

Now, although Oswald was attracting many unchurched — the lonely, the curious, the misfits who wandered in, got saved, then were fed spiritually, and stayed on to work — some Christians did leave other folds. And for this "sheep stealing," Oswald became the target of the pastor of a large neighboring church. For ten years the man kept writing scathing denouncements in his church paper and sometimes sent agitators into Oswald's meetings.

Oswald refused to reply or to deny the attacks in any way. He considered this preacher "so outstanding, so far above him in so many ways'' that he simply would not attack a man of this calibre. ''Touch not my anointed and do my prophets no harm,'' God had warned. Over the years, Oswald had published some of this man's sermons in the Peoples Church magazine, and continued to do so; Oswald even invited this brother to preach in the Peoples Church pulpit.

''I am firmly on 1 Samuel 24:12,'' Oswald said. ''May 'the Lord judge between me and thee, and the Lord avenge me of thee: but mine hand shall not be upon thee,' '' (KJV). In discussing this situation later with young preachers, he wrote that

> as long as you do not accomplish much, no one will bother you. But just as soon as you commence to become a success, just as soon as people flock to your ministry, there will be those who will be envious of you. All you have to do is to accomplish something that no one else has accomplished, build something that no one else has built, get results that no one else has been getting, become a greater success than those around you, and the most deadly opposition will be yours. There will be jealousy and envy on every side.
>
> And it will probably come from Christian leaders and Christian workers, from the very ones who ought to be standing by you and encouraging you in every possible way. And that is when you will feel like giving up.
>
> But what about Finney? Was he ever criticized? Did he have to face envy and opposition? Yes, he did, and it was almost diabolical. He was slandered on every side, and that by some of the most outstanding leaders of the church of his day. He was always the centre of the storm, in spite of the wonderful success he was having. Dr. Lyman Beecher, one of these leaders, sent Finney a message: ''If you attempt to carry the fire to Boston, I will meet you at the state line and call out all the artillery men and fight you every inch of the way.''
>
> Finney made no reply whatsoever; he simple did what he always did — he went to the woods to be alone with God. There he wrestled in prayer, and God gave him great victory.
>
> Moody and Sankey had the same experience when they went to Great Britain where they were bitterly opposed on every side. Today they are lauded and praised to the skies. The Apostle Paul knew what it was to be opposed; again and again he had an uproar on his hands; everywhere he went he faced opposition, but God delivered him.
>
> And that is the secret — to leave it in God's hands to deliver us. ''God is my defense'' — and what a wonderful defense he is!

Oswald explained the motto he had adopted years ago when first at Dale — No Attack, No Defense:

> I can leave the matter entirely with God. He is able for every emergency. He does not call us to attack others, or to defend ourselves, but to live peaceably with all men, and leave it with God to vindicate us.

While Oswald strived to live peaceably with all people, he did speak out against modernism, atheism, bolshevism, and the teaching of evolution in the schools. His condemnation of Mussolini, for example, provoked a spirited reply from the Italian press. Using the *Peoples Magazine* as his forum, Oswald was not above addressing issues of Christian concern.

Still, it was the personal attacks against his ministry which saddened and distressed him most. How he longed to be free of the heartaches and disappointments of life.

TWENTY-NINE

♦♦♦

SONGS OF A SOUL SET FREE

Take up the broken threads of life;
The lost ideals of other days
Will be reborn amid thy tears
And all thy heart be filled with praise. OJS

That autumn, in his melancholy and sadness, Oswald wrote:

> *When the autumn leaves have turned to gold*
> *And I'm safely sheltered in the fold,*
> *I shall see my Saviour's face,*
> *and extol His wondrous grace,*
> *When the autumn leaves have turned to gold.*

In his hymn "Where Dreams Come True," he reechoed the longing:

> *I'm longing, dear Lord, for that haven*
> *Where we shall be troubled no more;*
> *Like travellers out on the ocean*
> *Who long for the home on the shore.*
>
> *My dreams have been shattered and perished*
> *Beneath the rough waves of life's sea,*
> *And yet in that calm, peaceful slumber,*
> *I'll find their fulfilment in Thee.*

Where my dreams will come true,
Where my dreams will come true,
The joys that I lost in the shadows
Will be found where my dreams come true.

The dreams that had perished almost as soon as they had been born, the plans that had miscarried, had left in him an aching void:

> This past year I have walked before God in sackcloth and ashes as never before! It has been a time of great suffering. I am ashamed, oh, so ashamed. If only I could live my life over again!

But then, God reminded him of the potter and the clay so that with a heart overflowing in gratitude and hope and with tears splashing on the pages, he wrote:

Take up the broken threads of life;
The lost ideals of other days
Will be reborn amid thy tears,
And all thy heart be filled with praise.

Take up the broken threads of life;
The flowers that withered long ago
Will bloom again in God's own time,
And thou wilt say, 'twas better so.

Take up the broken threads of life;
Let God restore the wasted years;
Begin this day to live anew,
And bid farewell to all thy fears.

Finally, he could say that

> there is still hope! God does not cause us to dream dreams, and put within your hearts longings and desires to mock us. If they are born of God, He will make them real. All is not lost. Praise God!

A veritable spate of hymns poured from his pen during this period of his life. In "The Dawning of the Morning" Oswald wrote:

God will meet me in my grief and disappointment
He will banish from my pathway every fear,
For He understands my burden and my heartache,
And He wants to wipe away my falling tear.

I am waiting for the dawning of the morning
When the clouds of doubt and fear will all be gone,
For my Saviour has assured me that the darkness
That has gathered round me cannot last for long.

For dear Chrissie, who was going through deep waters in her personal life, Oswald encouraged her — and his own heart — with the lilting promise:

Happy days will come again,
Dawn will steal across the sky;
Soon the gloom will pass away,
Hope was never born to die.

Happy days will come again,
Light can pierce the darkest night;
God will ne'er forsake His own,
Faith at last will turn to sight.

Happy days will come again,
God will turn your night to day;
Love is bound to triumph yet,
He will wipe all tears away.

Happy days will come again,
Joy and peace will follow pain;
God His own will not deny,
Life can never be in vain.

Happy days will come again,
Though the sky be overcast;
God is caring for His own,
Trouble cannot always last;
For our God is still upon His throne,
Happy days will come again.

When his young sister Ruth cabled home from Peru that her husband had been killed in an automobile accident just as they were preparing to come home on furlough, Oswald sent comfort in his touching poem:

God understands your sorrow,
He sees the falling tear,
And whispers, "I am with thee,"
Then falter not, nor fear.

God understands your heartache,
He knows the bitter pain;
Oh, trust Him in the darkness,
You cannot trust in vain.

God understands your longing,
Your deepest grief He shares;
Then let Him bear your burden,
He understands and cares.

After dedicating his life once more, Oswald sent off the words that B.D. Ackley translated into the magnificent choir number:

Take Thou my voice, O Lord,
I give it gladly
Let it proclaim
to all the world Thy love;
Take Thou my tongue
and may it glorify Thee,
Until at last I sing
Thy praise above.

Take Thou my hands
and let them do Thy bidding,
Use them, dear Lord,
to work for Thee alone;
Take Thou my feet,
and train them for Thy service,
May they be swift to make Thy message known.

Take Thou my heart
and consecrate it wholly,
May it be true,
no matter what betide;
Take Thou my life,
it must be Thine forever,
For I would turn away
from all beside.

Take Thou my love, O Lord,
and consecrate it,
Burn out the dross
and make it all Thine own;
Save me from self
and all of earth's ambitions,

Till self has died
and Thou dost reign,
dost reign alone.

Not long afterward, he received a music manuscript from Ackley asking him to write lyrics for the suggested theme "The Song of the Soul Set Free." Oswald sat down at the piano in his home, and as the melody sang its way into his heart, the verses, including the triumphant chorus, came almost immediately. To Ackley's astonishment, the lyrics soon arrived by return mail:

Fairest of ten thousand, Is Jesus Christ my Saviour,
The Lily of the Valley, The Bright and Morning Star,
He is all my glory and in this heart of mine,
Forevermore I'm singing, A song of love divine.

Once my heart was burdened, But now I am forgiven,
And with a song of gladness, I'm on my way to heaven;
Christ is my Redeemer, My Song of Songs is He,
My Saviour, Lord and Master, To Him my praise shall be.

When He came to save me, He set the joybells ringing,
And now I'm ever singing, For Christ has ransomed me;
Once I lived in darkness The light I could not see,
But now I sing His praises, For He has set me free.

Angels cannot sing it, This song of joy and freedom,
For mortals only know it, The ransomed and the free;
Slaves were they in bondage, And deepest misery,
But now they sing triumphant, Their song of liberty.

'Tis the song of the soul set free,
And its melody is ringing;
'Tis the song of the soul set free,
Joy and peace to me it's bringing,
'Tis the song of the soul set free,
And my heart is ever singing
Hallelujah! Hallelujah!
The song of the soul set free.

The song of the soul set free
Oswald J. Smith
A.H. Ackley
1. Fair - est of ten thou - sand, Is Je - sus Christ my Sav - iour, The lil - y of the val - ley, The bright and morn - ing star.
2. Once my heart was bur - dened, But now I am for - giv - en, And with a song of glad - ness, I'm on my way to heav'n;
3. When He came to save me, He set the joy bells ring - ing, And now I'm ev - er sing - ing, For Christ has ran - somed me;
4. An - gels can - not sing it, This song of joy and free - dom, For mor - tals on - ly know it, The ran - somed and the free;
He is all my glo - ry and in this heart of mine, For - ev - er - more, I'm sing - ing, A song of love di - vine.
Christ is my Re - deem - er, My song of songs is He, My Sav - iour, Lord and Mas - ter, To Him my praise shall be.
Once I lived in dark - ness The light I could not see, But now I sing His prais - es, For He has set me free.
Slaves were they in bond - age, And deep - est mis - er - y, But now they sing tri - um - phant, Their song of lib - er - ty.
Refrain
'Tis the song of the soul set free, set free, And its mel - o - dy is ring - ing; 'Tis the song of the soul set free, set free, Joy and peace to me it's bring - ing, 'Tis the song of the soul set free, set free, And my heart is ev - er sing - ing Hal - le - lu - jah! Hal - le - lu - jah! Hal - le - lu - jah! Hal - le - lu - jah! The song of the soul set free.

Early in this new ministry on Gerrard Street, when his dear friend A.G. Malcolm died, Oswald brokenheartedly penned:

I count him friend who still remains my friend
When I am wrong. And this was true of him.
His loyalty I never can forget,
He did for me what others never did —
Provided for my needs when I was poor
And gave me comforts that I could not buy.
He left his work and helped me in my task —
Was ever friend so kind and true as he?

But Oswald still had his good friend Willis who served as missions treasurer, and in June 1932, they set off together for a firsthand look at some new fields. With the Worldwide Christian Couriers feeling the pinch of the Depression rather severely, more and more the burden of raising funds was falling on Oswald.

THIRTY
♦♦♦
WORLD TRAVELING

It doesn't seem fair that we have concentrated so much on the homeland and forgotten those for whom nothing has been prepared. OJS

Oswald J. Smith's journeys to the then unknown parts of the world infused wonderful zest into his congregation. They insisted they

> were always cake-eaters. When Oswald went away, he made sure the pulpit was filled with the very best preachers and singers. He was never jealous when guest speakers turned out to be better preachers than he was; rather, he delighted in it because Oswald just wanted the best for his people. Then when he came home from the mission fields with up-to-date reports and pictures of action around the world, we felt so privileged to have a man of this stature for our pastor.

The trip with Willis took them to England, France, Spain, Egypt, Palestine, French Somaliland, Ethiopia, India, Ceylon, the Malay Peninsula, and the Dutch East Indies where his dear friend Robert Jaffray was working. In one of the larger cities there, Oswald was asked to hold an evangelistic campaign. Night after night he preached the simple gospel to Buddhists, Muhammadans, even the former headhunters of Borneo. After a few nights, Oswald felt that a sufficient foundation had been laid and so, informed the missionaries that they should be prepared to do personal work since he would be giving an appeal that evening.

The missionaries looked at him with amazement: "You can't give an invitation here. People would lose face."

Dumbfounded, Oswald asked, "How then do you win souls?"

"We just go on preaching and sowing the seed. Finally someone gets convicted and comes to inquire the way of salvation."

"How many come?" Oswald asked.

"Not many."

"Well, I'm going to give an invitation. I've extended invitations in every country in Europe, and everywhere I've gone, men and women have come to the Lord Jesus Christ. If it has worked on those fields, it will work here."

"But Oriental people are different; there would be no response," the missionaries still protested. But Oswald was adamant.

That night when he asked for those who would like to receive the Lord Jesus Christ, some forty individuals promptly stood to their feet, moved to the altar, and fell upon their knees, pouring out their hearts to God and praying aloud. Soon they were standing before Oswald with shining faces, rejoicing in their Savior. Months later, Robert Jaffray reported that the Spirit of revival was still upon them, that they were giving the invitation, and that God was still working in their midst saving souls.

In Sumatra, they hiked through the jungle to be the first messengers of the cross in that area. Oswald wrote home:

> What a thrill! If I were a young man, I would not want to go where others have laboured. I would ask, as Livingstone did, to be sent to new fields, for I would want to be the first to reduce the language to writing, translate portions of the Bible, and give the people the Gospel. I, too, would be a pioneer.
>
> Why waste your life in America or Great Britain? Why settle down to the humdrum of making money? Why not get a vision? You can invest your life in something really worthwhile. You can go where no one else has gone. It doesn't seem fair that we have concentrated so

> much on the homeland and forgotten those for whom nothing has been prepared. What would you do if you should see ten men lifting a log; and if nine were on one end and one on the other; where would you help? Why, on the end where only one was lifting. It is the foreign field that needs help.

When Willis had to return to Canada at the end of eight weeks, Oswald felt devastated. He had had no mail from home and the thought of pressing on for another two or three months was unbearable. "Little did I know what it would cost me in heart anguish to be away," he wrote. "Were it not for His grace I would take the first boat home." As it was, he shortened his itinerary so he could be in Toronto by the end of September. Then he had a cable from Roland Bingham, who was supplying the pulpit of the Peoples Church in Oswald's absence. In his capacity as director of the Sudan Interior Mission, he was requesting Oswald to make another stop in Africa on his way home. "It is a sore blow, but He knows best," Oswald wrote Eldon Lehman, who was in charge of the church back home:

> I thank God from the bottom of my heart for you; never will you know what you have meant to me; there is not a day passes but I pray for you and Mrs. Lehman. I know you will do all you can to comfort and sustain my, shall I say "widow," for she is almost that. I have been gone so long; it is not easy for Daisy. But the "cross is not greater than His grace." Praise God! In His will, all is well. But it will be hard to get me away again!

Looking out across the hills and valleys of Ethiopia, he mused over his favorite phrase in Scripture from the Song of Solomon 2:17: "Until the day break and the shadows flee away" (*KJV*). And in healing power, the words came to him:

> *Like the beauty of a morning sunrise*
> *When the long, dark night has passed away,*
> *Comes the Saviour's presence, as I tarry,*
> *Waiting for the breaking of the day.*

Like the glory of an evening sunset
At the closing of a summer's day,
Comes the Saviour's presence to assure me,
Driving all the clouds of doubt away.

Like the splendor of a glistening dewdrop
When the dawn is breaking in the sky,
Comes the Saviour's presence to my spirit,
Telling me that He Himself is nigh.

Like the fragrance of the rose of Sharon
Blooming on the hillside all alone,
Comes the Saviour's presence, as I murmur,
"Jesus, I am Thine, Thy very own."

Like the lingering shadows in the twilight,
Stretching o'er the valley far away,
Comes the Saviour's presence, as I tarry,
Waiting for the breaking of the day.

Oswald, now forty-one years of age, once more became desperately ill with a strange fever, and collapsed during a trek through the grasslands. Wrestling through the night, he cried out to God: "There is so much yet to do; please spare me, and give me another thirty years to serve you!" God granted his petition, and then some.

Oswald brought home something new from this trip — fifteen rolls of movie film, in addition to the black-and-white stills for magazine reproduction. Shortly before leaving on this tour, Oswald had seen the new 16-mm movie cameras in a shop and thought what a splendid way to make the needs of missions more real to his people. When filming, he always steadied the camera against a tree or propped it on a fence, and thus got some superb shots. The dining room table was taken over for several days while he edited and spliced the 100-foot rolls into 400-foot reels for fifteen minutes of viewing.

Only a few months after this trip Oswald had word that the Chicago bank which held all Worldwide Christian Courier funds had folded and the Chicago Gospel Tabernacle had been forced into bankruptcy. It was a stunning blow to

Oswald. "We must pick up the slack for all those missionaries out in the forefront of the battle," he announced, plunging into a campaign to raise even more mission funds.

The following poems were penned during this period:

THY LOVE, O LORD

Lord, give me grace and help, I pray,
For ev'ry passing hour;
And keep me lest I fall before
The tempter's awful pow'r.

Thou seest all my loneliness,
The hunger of my soul;
The blighted hopes of bygone years,
The dreams of life's lost goal.

O Lord, Thou knowest all my grief,
My disappointed heart;
The sorrows and the cares of life
That make the tear-drops start.

With faith undimmed I turn to Thee,
And 'mid the darkness pray;
For Thou canst see the aching void,
And all the thorn-clad way.

Thy love, O Lord, has never failed,
Tho' dark my night and long;
I turn to Thee my weary eyes
And hope springs forth in song.

DEAL GENTLY, LORD JESUS

Deal gently, Lord Jesus, deal gently, I pray,
And put not Thy servant in judgment away,
But grant me Thy mercy, Thy kindness, Thy grace;
Oh, love me, my Saviour, and show me Thy face.

My heart, it is wounded, and I am opprest,
Oh, heal me, Lord Jesus, and give me Thy rest;
My sins, how they hurt me! O Jesus, my Lord,
Deal gently, I pray Thee, be true to Thy Word.

Oh, do not be angry, rebuke me no more,
But love me, oh, love me, I humbly implore;
Tho' worthy of death, yet, my Saviour, I plead,
Have pity, deal gently, for great is my need.

Tho' much Thou must pardon, I'll love Thee the more,
And weep o'er Thy mercy, Thy nature adore;
I'll live for Thee only, my Saviour, my King,
And all thro' life's journey Thy praises I'll sing.

THE VICTORY

Dear Lord, I hate what Thou dost hate,
I love what Thou dost love;
All my affections and desires
Are set on things above.

Once I was bound by Satan's pow'r,
A slave was I to sin;
Once all my struggles were in vain,
The fight I could not win.

At last, one day, I came to Thee,
And claimed the victory;
My heart was cleansed, Thy blood applied,
Now Thou didst set me free.

Now I can do the things I would
And yield no more to sin;
Now I can love Thee as I ought,
For Thou dost reign within.

THIRTY-ONE

♦♦♦

MY SECOND CHILD HAS FILLED THE VOID

Somehow I feel that all the past has been nothing more than a preparation for the future.
OJS

''Don't you think it's time we had our own building?'' the men of his board began asking. ''Every one of the 1,200 seats is always filled, with people standing.''

''Not until we have at least one-third in cash!'' Oswald insisted. He was determined not to burden the congregation with a debt that he might not be around to help pay off. Nor did he believe in paying interest to mortgage companies with money that could better be sent to the foreign field. And especially since Rader's bankruptcy, there was no way he could be moved from his position: ''I have no right to incur debts and then expect God to come to my aid; He can just as easily give me the money beforehand. 'Owe no man anything' applies to the church too. In my mind, debt is a sin.''

However, in July 1934, he agreed to rent a larger auditorium, the 1,500-seat Central Methodist Church at 100 Bloor Street East. As with Saint James Church, the building had become superfluous after the merger into the United Church.

Then, one evening in late 1936, Oswald and Daisy were having dinner with the W.G. Jaffrays. Oswald and Jaffray, the publisher of Toronto's prestigious morning paper the *Globe and Mail,* had become fast friends over the years ever since Alliance days when Oswald had been a strong supporter and champion of Jaffray's brother Robert, the splendid missionary in Indonesia. Besides supporting him financially, Oswald had visited Robert on the field, always had Robert speak in his church when he was in Toronto, and carried his reports frequently in the Peoples Church magazine. Although the *Globe and Mail* publisher never attended the Peoples Church, he would often ask Oswald to come to the office to have prayer, and the two would get down on their knees together.

This night at dinner, Jaffray asked Oswald about church plans, and Oswald told him they could have the property they were occupying for $65,000. "But not until someone gives us $10,000 will we begin to think about buying," Oswald declared. The next morning the Jaffrays telephoned: "We want to give the first $20,000 toward the purchase of the church." Oswald fairly whooped for joy. Into the church he went, praising God, pacing back and forth scarcely able to believe that God had answered prayer so "exceeding abundantly." When he announced the gift to the congregation — the largest they had ever received — what rejoicing there was! The crowd roared, clapped, and virtually danced with praise and thanksgiving. Within a few months, the purchase was complete, carrying only a small five-year mortgage which was soon paid up, or "burned."

To make even more room, the pipes from the organ were torn out from their place at the rear of the gallery (the whole unit was sold for $40,000 to a Roman Catholic church), and an elevation was fitted with another 150 seats. Still it could not hold the crowds. "Everyone move to the left to make a little room," Oswald would ask. Then people — at least 2,000 of them — would be lining the walls, sitting on the steps of the balcony, jamming the vestibule until Oswald would beg his morning radio listeners not to come to the church. "We've stopped all newspaper advertising because the fire marshall has told us we have too many people in the building. *So please stay at home.* We simply cannot accommodate the crowds,'' he declared before going on to announce the service for that evening.

''And it sounded so exciting you just couldn't stay away,'' those who were young during those days recall. ''Hang the fire marshall,'' they would say. ''Let's beat the crowds.'' And they would be there, sitting in the aisle half an hour before the service began or standing along the back of the balcony, just to get inside before they locked the doors. The place fairly swarmed with young people, especially during the *Back Home Hour* when they congregated at Peoples Church following their own church service. Then when Edwin Orr and Gipsy Smith came to preach, Sunday services had to be moved to Massey Hall once more.

In summers, when other churches geared down, Oswald pulled out all stops, reserving the very best speakers and music artists for then. It would be boiling hot under the gallery with no air-conditioning. Although they did not draw stand-up crowds, the attendance did keep up. Many sat from 6:00 P.M. or 6:15 P.M. right through until the end of the *Back Home Hour* at 10:30 P.M. Not only was Peoples Church a favorite with the workingman, but somehow Oswald made it ''the place to be'' for the young people of Toronto. They congregated there by the hundreds, especially Sunday nights. They came because it was the social thing to do, but they were also blessed and challenged.

At every service, whether Oswald or a guest was preaching, Oswald made sure the way of salvation was presented and an appeal given. Three hundred to five hundred responded each year. As well, hundreds more were saved in ''Radioland'' where Peoples Church was now on forty-six stations from coast to coast.

Looking out over the great congregation one evening, Oswald at last knew in his heart that he had accepted the loss of "his child," the Christie Street Tabernacle, and later wrote:

> *At last in love another dear child God gave*
> *And bid me train him myself alone*
> *His life so precious to save,*
> *And now my heart is happy at last,*
> *And my joy, it overflows,*
> *For my second child has now filled the void —*
> *God understands, yes, God knows.*

> Somehow I feel that all the past has been nothing more than a preparation for the future. There have been so many failures. Today it seems as though God at last has brought me into a haven of rest. The fear, the worry, the defeat is in the past, covered with the Blood. I am living on borrowed time. Every hour belongs to Him. I do not feel that my work is mine anymore. It is all His. I but fit into His plan, His program. My part is to live a holy life as HE indwells, and thus He works. God builds my life; He builds, not I. I am His slave, His bond servant.

The year 1936 was special for Oswald J. Smith in a number of ways. With input from, Dr. Hooper and nurse Louise Kirby, Oswald set up the Missionary Medical Institute in an adjoining building to give prospective missionaries a year's instruction in tropical medicine. (This institute has since become the Missionary Health Institute — International Medical Service of Toronto's North York General Hospital.) Then on May 31, Oswald received his first honorary Doctor of Divinity degree from Asbury College in Wilmore, Kentucky. He was deeply humbled by the experience. "May God make me truly worthy," he said. Then one week later he sailed on the *Queen Mary* for London where he was to preach in Spurgeon's Tabernacle for the remainder of June. It was an awesome, breathtaking experience for the "barefoot boy from Embro," as he so often referred to himself.

And then once more he was off to the Russian mission fields, his first visit in seven years. What a change he found in Latgalia where previously they had mocked him. "The whole population has undergone a transformation as a result of the preaching of the gospel,'' he reported. Seventy-five workers had been trained in the Bible school which he had organized and funded. Every village had been evangelized and at least 6,000 souls had been saved. Ten-thousand Bibles had been distributed, along with 600,000 of his tracts and 46,000 copies of his books.

Said Reverend John C. Kurcit, superintendent of the work:

> It is difficult to describe the blessing that has come to the Russian people through the writings of Dr. Smith, and through the Peoples Church. ''The people which sat in darkness saw a great light'' — this verse most adequately describes the glorious work that had been accomplished under God by the Peoples Church in dark, benighted Latgalia. Dark, indeed, it was when Dr. Smith first visited it nearly ten years ago. Today it is bright with the rays of the Gospel.

Oswald's tour of Latvia closed with meetings in the Salvation Temple in Riga. When the invitation was given, the Spirit of God once again melted hearts, as Oswald reported that

> tears flowed freely; confessions were heard on every side as all prayed together. Time passed unheeded. Higher and higher rose the tide of intercession. It was the sweetest music I have ever heard. Now and then a chorus was sung. Faces bathed in the glory of another world glowed with an earthly light. It was a time of refreshing from the presence of the Lord, a time of revival and blessing. Three and a half hours passed before the meeting closed. Heaven had touched earth and burdened hearts were made glad.

Traveling by train through Rumania with Michael Billester, he was surprised when the train suddenly stopped and they were put off. Declaring that their passports were not in proper order, a policeman directed them into a droshky and escorted them to the police station, with both men protesting hotly to no avail. There it was decided that a mistake had been made and they were freed, although somewhat unnerved.

That night in a crowded little church in Kishinev (formerly Chisinau) again the blessing of the Holy Spirit fell. All hearts were melted and tears flowed copiously; men as well as women sobbed out their confessions to God as prayer rose in a chorus. And thus, at the conclusion of his third visit ended one of the most wonderful series of revival meetings that Oswald had ever held. "God moved Europe in a mighty way!" he marveled. No one before had held campaigns in these Russian lands, and no one since, because very soon the borders were all closed.

After ministering in France, Spain, Germany, Hungary, Poland, Sweden, Czechoslovakia, Bulgaria, Turkey, Greece, Yugoslavia, Austria, Belgium, and Scotland, Oswald sailed for home at the end of three months of revival blessing.

THIRTY-TWO

♦♦♦

FAMILY JOYS

I want you to do something worthwhile with your life. OJS

During his absences from home, Oswald trusted God to take care of his children; he knew they had Daisy and Chrissie to guide them and pray with them. And always everything was all right when he got home. Among the gifts he brought from this trip were Olympic stamps for Glen, necklaces for Hope and his mother, a pearl-and-ruby pendant for Daisy, and more birds for Paul.

Oswald had remained a lover of all creatures great and small. They had had two thoroughbred collies, but they were too hard to care for in the city. Once he brought home the goats he had always hankered for — two kids that bleated and cried so much that son Paul had to stay up with them all night. A beautiful Kashmir cat, a most unfriendly feline, hid away for three days in the big cabinet of the old-fashioned radio. All of these pets had ended up with Uncle Kenneth, who had a farm a few miles east of Toronto.

But when Oswald was preparing for the 1932 trip, a bird dealer who attended the church asked him to buy some African finches for him. Oswald brought him fifty, plus a few for himself, and Kenneth built large six-by-ten-foot cages for the Smith basement. Then from Marseilles, France, Oswald shipped home another 300 finches; in return, the dealer gave Oswald some larger rare birds. Another member of the church with a feed company kept them supplied with bird-seed. Gradually they built up quite a flock and turned the glassed-in porch into an aviary where the birds could fly free. Sometimes Daisy feared their noisy early morning calls would waken the whole neighborhood.

Oswald spent a good deal of time teaching Paul how to feed and care for the birds as well as how to train them to fly; none could talk like Oswald's old pet crow, Tommy, however. (Chrissie got left with most of the cleanup.)

Soon it was Christmas time, and no one was more excited than Oswald. Triumphantly he carried home a carefully selected big spruce tree and set it up in his study for Daisy and Chrissie and the children to decorate. Then, as usual, he would lock the door and the children would beg to see the presents that were piling up under the tree. "Just one glance," he would say, opening the door a crack, then swoosh! closing it again.

On Christmas Eve, all the family would go out delivering presents to Uncle Tom and Aunt Phoebe Findley, to Granma and Grampa Billings, to Daisy's brothers and sisters and Oswald's brothers and sisters who lived in Toronto, making a large, happy family connection. With the children snuggled in bed, both parents would fill stockings and then sit for a few treasured moments by the lighted tree, reminiscing over the blessings of the past year and spinning dreams of what could yet be.

On Christmas morning they would have breakfast before Oswald played Santa Claus and with a great flourish distributed presents to all. And among them would be three big parcels wrapped in brown paper and tied with a piece of string and addressed in Oswald's own large scrawl — for each child a stack of books, never religious, always the classics. For Paul there were the Horatio Alger success books, which would eventually number seventy-five. Oswald started all the children reading early. "I want you to do something worthwhile with your life," he challenged.

Daisy's parents usually joined them for Christmas dinner, with the whole clan including Oswald's parents converging at Oswald and Daisy's for the elaborate buffet which Daisy and Chrissie had been preparing all month.

But the big thing in the lives of the Smith family was the church; their whole world revolved around it. "I step on the gas at 10:30!" Oswald would announce after breakfast Sunday mornings, and he would literally be backing out the driveway as Daisy was shutting the car door. The children were not taken to Sunday school — Oswald saw no need of it for his own children. Primarily he did not want to weary them with too much church. They went to all the services and sat through them, but never junior church.

"Daisy, aren't you coming to the great service this evening?" he would ask. Every new service was the greatest yet, Oswald firmly believed, and he managed to convince everyone around him. Thus the family, especially Paul, attended the mid-week meetings. Paul had been intensely interested in preaching and singing ever since he was the five-year-old "golden-voiced soloist" in California, knowing that one day he himself would be in the ministry. He had come to the altar to give his life to the Lord; Hope and Glen had both confessed Christ as their parents knelt with them at their bedsides.

During the lengthy campaigns Daisy seldom missed a meeting, leaving Chrissie to tuck the children into bed. The only exception was Friday night which she made a special family time when they would all sit around and listen to the *Lux Radio Theatre,* topping off the evening with the elegant treat of a twenty-cent brick of ice cream from the corner store.

Often the children awakened to the gentle sound of their father pacing back and forth in his study as he prayed. They knew he loved them and prayed for them fervently. There was never any doubt of that. And he respected them as individuals. Even though he was away frequently, they felt a great security. When Daisy was wearied by a long series of late nights, Chrissie was there to get the children their breakfast, pray with them, and pack them off to school.

After his "morning watch" — the time he spent with the Lord daily, absolutely without fail, first reading the Word, and then seeking God's face — Oswald would go off to the church, taking half a sandwich for lunch with him. He would be home again by 4:00 for teatime, a ritual with silver tea service and fine bone china teacups. In the living room he would go through the mail that had come in, tossing the opened envelopes onto the carpet in his haste. Then, in preparation for the evening service he would nap until dinner, another formal time. Oswald would carve at the table and Daisy would serve the vegetables. (Roast beef topped off with raspberry or coconut pie was his favorite.) Mealtimes were good family times with eager conversation.

The family altar was always in the evenings. The *Daily Light* was used — the morning portion was read one year and the evening selection the following year. Oswald never missed the family altar no matter who was visiting. He would pull out his Bible when a Bible story was alluded to in the reading, go over it with the children, and then have them act it out. One would be Goliath; one, David; another, Saul; and Oswald would direct the drama. Those were unforgettable nights for the children. When Oswald was away, they took turns praying — almost from the time they could talk.

When it came to discipline, fortunately the children were not defiant; Paul was the only one who went his own way a good deal of the time. "How could you do this to me?" Daisy would cry and send the offender to his room. When Oswald was home, he would deal with the problem, taking the youngster into his study for a "good talking to." He never spanked the children, or even laid a hand on them, for he was terrified that he might lose control over the old bad temper that had possessed him even more than the temper his father had.

("We were controlled by love and respect," Paul just recently explained. "We all appreciated what father was doing, and we were proud of him. We loved and respected our parents and didn't want to hurt them in any way." But Oswald always felt remorse whenever there was a need for correction: "I figured that very seldom was it their fault; generally I was to blame. I didn't pay enough attention to the children; I should have spent more time with them."

"Yet it was an atmosphere of joy and happiness that we grew up in, a wonderful heritage of a Christian home where we were loved," son Glen added.

"Father always brightened up our life, and steered such a straight course," Hope remarked.)

One of the bright spots in Oswald's week was the fifteen-minute *Amos and Andy Radio Show.* Throwing his head back, he would laugh uproariously; he refused to answer the phone when the program was on, and became very upset if Daisy said that she needed him for something. In fact, he was such a devotee that in the days before car radios, if he found himself driving along the road at showtime, he would pull over, go up to the nearest house, and ask the people if they had a radio. If they did, he would ask to come in and listen to "Amos and Andy." He had no problem being invited in when he had the pretty, demure Daisy with him. (He also listened avidly to the heavyweight fights.)

When TV first made its appearance, Oswald was strongly opposed, and wrote an article for the widely circulated *Sunday School Times,* urging Christians not to get involved in any way. So when his Board of Managers presented him with a handsome TV set, he felt sheepish about accepting it, but what could he do? Always an ardent fan of Zane Grey and Sherlock Holmes adventures, Oswald soon found great amusement in TV private-eye dramas and westerns. But the TV went off the moment the program was over, no matter who was in the room.

The Smiths didn't have the usual family vacations because Oswald spent most of the summer months touring the Bible conferences of Canada and the States. In the early Christie Street Tabernacle days, Oswald had rented a cottage on

Toronto Island for the summer, thus getting the children and Daisy away, but close enough that he could join them for brief visits. Later they purchased a cottage on the Kawartha Lakes some ninety miles northeast of Toronto.

When Oswald was not away preaching, he would drive up to that resort area on a Monday. As always, he would have some books with him — Dickens or the poetry of Robert Service or his perennial favorite — Tennyson.

But he spent most of his time with the children. Daisy was not much of a swimmer, so Oswald would take the children out in the boat, teaching them to row and paddle. He also taught them how to swim and handle themselves in the water, as well as how to fish and clean their catch. Daisy had difficulty with her legs, so she would sit on the porch or on the dock and watch while she knitted or worked on her needlepoint. When the children were smaller, she made all their clothes as well as her own.

They had some lovely times together as a family at Elgin House, a fashionable resort in the Muskokas where the owner had built a chapel on the grounds. Whenever Oswald was free, he was invited to hold meetings for the guests. Very often Oswald would take Daisy with him to the summer conferences, leaving Chrissie at the lake with the children, with Daisy's brother Don and his wife, Bonnie, and Granma and Grampa Billings in the cottage next door. Husband and wife would then visit Canadian Keswick and New England Keswick; Maranatha and Gull Lake in Michigan; Winona Lake, Indiana, and Mt. Hermon near San Francisco.

Even when just playing with the family around at the cottage, Oswald was like a racehorse in the starting gate, straining to get on with the race; after only a few days he would kiss his family good-bye and rush back to the church.

Smith ministering in Jamaica.

Top: The great preacher Gipsy Smith, 1908.

Bottom: The newly constructed Peoples Church on Sheppard Avenue.

Smith at age sixty-five in Africa.

Smith and Daisy befriended by koala bears in Australia, 1961.

Top: Laying on the cornerstone of the new Peoples Church, 1962.

Bottom: The Smith family on Daisy and Oswald's Golden Wedding Anniversary, 1967.

Top: Dr. Smith and Dr. Billy Graham at Smith's Diamond Jubilee—sixty years in the ministry, 1968.

Bottom: Smith's books have been translated into many languages.

Smith in the pulpit of the Peoples Church.

THIRTY-THREE
♦♦♦
THE WAYS OF LEADERSHIP

All his strength and energy of body, soul, and mind had to be channeled, contained. . . . Father had this sense of destiny. . . . Paul Smith

Around the church, Oswald Smith ran a tight ship, by any standards. At this point, for every three dollars spent at home, seven went to missions. Only the absolute essentials were attended to. "Forget about painting the church," he told the board. "They need 10,000 Bibles in Borneo." So the elders and deacons would spend nights and Saturdays with soap and buckets scrubbing down the walls of the dingy old auditorium. They did manage to talk a local shop into giving them enough paint to freshen up the nursery and ladies' washrooms.

Oswald worked at a desk jammed into the corner of the general office where he could be a part of the action. When a dentist who had been listening to the service over the radio came down to see the pastor, Oswald took him into the office washroom — the only little cubicle where they could be alone — and there they got down on their knees while Oswald led the man to the Lord.

The staff was kept to a minimum: Eldon Lehman doubled as bookkeeper and two or three stenographers limped along on ancient typewriters. The copier was a museum piece.

Oswald kept a hawk's eye on every expenditure. In the book-room he would weigh a parcel going out, if it needed only three cents postage, instead of four cents, he would steam the extra stamp off. Every cent had to be saved for the mission field. Rarely were letters sent airmail, and it had to be the direst emergency before a long distance call could be place. In the first office on Kendall Avenue, packing boxes served as cupboards; string and wrapping paper from incoming mail were saved for outgoing parcels.

Oswald was just as frugal in his own life, except with Daisy whom he totally trusted to run their household; only in the purchase of larger items would he become involved, if she so requested. He did not allow himself to become caught up in domestic responsibilities. He carried almost no cash — never any bills and only enough change to purchase a newspaper. He hated to spend money in restaurants.

When it came to buying clothes, Daisy found him hopeless. "Why do I need more than two suits, one for every day and one for Sunday?" he insisted. He was reluctant to purchase anything new and mostly got by with hand-me-downs. Once in his younger days when he needed a new overcoat, he put it off until he saw a coat that strongly appealed to him. Rather than plain black, it was grey with a nice trim. He took it home, but for three nights could not sleep for worrying about the purchase. *Will it attract too much attention?* he pondered. Finally he took the coat back, exchanging it for a more modest five-dollar coat. "Worry fled and peace returned; it does not do to go contrary to the voice of conscience," he concluded.

A new pair of shoes was supplied to him each year by a Christian brother who had noticed the big cardboard-covered holes in the soles of Oswald's shoes as he knelt at the altar one night. "What a waste; my old ones aren't worn out yet," Oswald would protest.

"Oswald never wastes a penny," his staff explained. "He doesn't spend money or time like other people — he uses it, puts it to work. He manages everything and everyone around him with an efficiency of movement, an economy of money and time, and a precision that eliminates any spent emotions."

Oswald always had a finely honed sense of timing that kept him one jump ahead of everyone else. He was always the first off a plane and the first to come through the doors at the Union Station. His meetings were started precisely on time, not one minute before the hour or one minute after, and they always concluded on time — with radio, this was a necessity. He kept tight control of the service; the chairs were placed on the platform close to the pulpit so that not one second would be lost between the prayer and the special music. As one person finished his part, the next person on the program would be close at hand, ready to speak into the microphone. If a person was taking more than his allotted time perhaps with a long testimony, Oswald did not hesitate to cut him short, usually gracefully. But he never cut off a preacher.

Oswald streamlined the communion service so that the entire congregation could be served in just twelve minutes with no sense of hurry, only great efficiency. He explained, "I wanted everyone to be able to stay for communion and that wouldn't happen if we went overly long. The roast in the oven at home might be burned!"

Things were done immediately. Receipts for gifts had to go out that week. Magazine copy had to be ready well ahead of time. Nothing was held over to clutter his mind — he handled a piece of mail only once, dictating replies to correspondence as it came in. Then he expected his secretary to have the letter ready for signing the next day. Bills had to be paid promptly. "Owe no man anything," he drummed into his staff. By the end of the week, everything had to be done so they could start Monday with a clean slate.

Oswald was patient and sensitive toward his helpers. To a secretary who was looking weary, he would suggest in his soft-spoken way, "You've worked long enough; you'd better knock off and start fresh in the morning." His workers knew he prayed for them constantly. When they were ill, he showed his concern with letters and gifts. One secretary after three years commented, "I have learned many lessons in the happy fellowship of this office; I count it a rare privilege to have been associated with one of God's choicest saints."

They knew they had his unquestioned loyalty. Slander was never tolerated in the Peoples Church — "Slander is the devil's work; don't you do it for him," Oswald would blast. However, when there was a proven problem that had to be dealt with, he would talk to the party involved. If the problem persisted to the detriment of the work, he would gently ask for the person's resignation, always managing to rebuke with such love that friendship was maintained.

Oswald maintained that

> the whole point is to restore such a one to full fellowship. The Christian may be backslidden, but the Holy Spirit never leaves us. We are baptized by the Spirit into the Body of Christ when we are saved. We can lose His power by sin and failure. A flame can be quenched and put out, but the Person of the Holy Spirit cannot be put out of our lives. However, you can yield to an unclean spirit if you want to, and so be influenced and controlled to a certain extent.

In the early days of the ministry, there were a few cases of casting out demons from believers who had drifted away; the elders had joined in prayer for their deliverance. But exorcism was something Oswald was reluctant to deal with. He made the observation that

> too often the state following is worse than before. The person has to have a sincere desire to be rid of the unclean spirit or there is not much point in dealing with him. We have avoided this as much as possible, concentrating on God and His mighty power. We kept our people occupied with the miracle of the crowds coming, of souls being saved, the missionary money coming in week by week, and the work going ahead. That is the way you build a work.

Oswald also kept up a large correspondence with friends from boyhood and Bible college days, former professors, and music arrangers — new friends he had met on recent travels. He was much loved in both his and Daisy's families where he noted birthdays and special events with cards and letters or poems of congratulations and encouragement. "Oswald's pen must be dipped in some golden love-stream," one friend responded.

His prayer list was long, for he prayed at least daily for his brothers and sisters — his entire family. The elders and officers in the church, too, were daily brought before the "Throne of God" in prayer; in sickness or special trial they would have phone calls, visits, and letters from their pastor.

At times Oswald was preoccupied, seemingly remote and aloof, passing people without recognizing them. At social gatherings he was impatient with small talk and would clam up, excusing himself as soon as possible. There were times when he was charged with being unsociable, yet there were young people's parties he attended, entering into all the games with great glee. Put with any seven- or eight-year-old child, he would chat happily until it was time for him to leave. The children who came to prayer meetings always got a hug and a special greeting from Oswald.

And this was one reason when he was on tour that he always requested to be put up in a private home — he hoped to be with children and to have company. He could not stand the loneliness of an empty hotel room night after night. Oswald desperately needed to have people around him. He couldn't bear to be alone except in prayer.

Recently his son Paul explained:

> Some said Father was absentminded; I say he was single-minded. All his strength and energy of body, soul, and mind had to be channeled, contained. Particularly with the restrictions that were imposed by his frail body, there could be no lavishing on the peripheries. All had to go by the board. Father had this sense of destiny — "I am here for a purpose" — and this enabled him to go through the tough places. He had this sense of destiny from the word go; he knew from boyhood that it was important that he keep records and pictures.

THIRTY-FOUR
♦♦♦
PROSPERITY FOR THE CHURCH

. . . *A man's heart goes where his money goes.* OJS

Oswald always insisted that a church should be prosperous:

> God's will is clearly set forth regarding material blessing: "Beloved, I wish above all things that thou mayest prosper and be in health, even as thy soul prospereth" 3 John v. 2. The three go hand in hand, spiritual, physical and material prosperity. That is God's highest will.

He believed that there were two master keys that would unlock prosperity for any congregation. First, *the church that puts missions first would be blessed* — he had proved that abundantly. Second, he insisted that

> *evangelism is the secret of material as well as spiritual blessing* in the local church; that if the evangelistic campaign is a spiritual blessing to the church, it will also be a financial blessing. The two cannot be divorced.

And time after time, Oswald proved this. The Christie Street Tabernacle and the Peoples Church had both been built on evangelism, and every campaign had left money in the treasury. These top-ranked preachers and musicians were always paid a flat, prearranged fee and were accommodated in private one-dollar-fifty-cents-a-night guest homes or a quiet, but decent, hotel nearby.

> Unless there is financial blessing, there is mismanagement somewhere. The pastor who labours to train workers, and who, without any extra remuneration toils and plans for the campaign, should surely see to it that the campaign leaves the church better off financially as well as spiritually.
>
> Whether on the foreign field or in an evangelistic campaign at home, propagating the gospel and winning souls is the business of the church. Seeking the lost, praying for the lost, giving to save the lost, singing to save the lost, preaching to save the lost, reaching the unreached with the gospel, telling the untold the sweet, old, old story of the Saviour's love is our obligation on earth. Only as the church fulfills her obligation does she justify her existence.
>
> And the church that does these things will be blessed materially, physically, and spiritually.

Oswald never lost sight of the simple goals he had set for his ideal church while he was still a seminary student:

1. To reach the unsaved for Christ
2. To make the prayer meeting a live service
3. To turn Christians from worldliness to spirituality
4. To build a large, enthusiastic Sunday school
5. To develop a strong missionary church
6. To increase church attendance
7. To put spiritual men in every service.

Oswald Smith kept his church organization simple. "I cannot find any scriptural authority for democratic church government," he insisted. "Personally it is not for me." Thus he had set up a Board of Managers and appointed twelve members to deal with the business affairs. (His old friend Willis was vice-president.) Next he had appointed seventy-five elders to do the "spiritual work" of the church — serving communion, dealing with souls, leading them into a deeper walk, visiting the new converts in their homes, and visiting the sick. Lastly, nine deacons were appointed to handle the offerings. It was his greatest desire that all the elders be on their knees in the special prayer meeting at 10:15 each

Sunday morning and in the Personal Workers' prayer meeting at 6:00 Sunday evening and also in the Half-Night of Prayer the first Friday of each month. The ushers were always drawn from the elders, not only to put them on display, but more importantly to have responsible, mature men meeting the public and being on the lookout for those in need.

But how did he make sure these were "spiritual men" who believed in what he was doing? There was no way he wanted a repetition of the problems with church boards that he had experienced in earlier pastorates. Oswald developed a formula that was transparently simple:

> As well as the scriptural requirements for elders and deacons, I look for men who are putting the spiritual work of the church first, who are men of prayer in every sense of the word; they never miss a prayer meeting; they're anxious to see souls saved. I watch them for months; I look for men who have no use for the world or worldly pleasures [although Oswald never preached against shows, dancing, et cetera].
>
> Then, they must back up this concern with constant giving. I know a man's heart goes where his money goes. If they have a true heart for God's work, they will see that a good portion of their money goes to God's work.
>
> By this and this alone we must judge all spirituality, because if a man is truly spiritual, if he is a real Bible student, if his doctrines are Scriptural, he will want to carry out our Lord's last orders — "Go ye into all the world and preach the gospel to every creature." A truly spiritual man will put world evangelism first; and he will give liberally to missions. Otherwise, all our Bible knowledge, all our doctrinal standards are nothing but make-believe.
>
> Thus I discovered that if a man attended the services faithfully, including the prayer services, and gave regularly, if he showed a keen interest in souls and missions, I could generally count on him to back our purposes; he was a pretty safe man to put in office.

The men Oswald gathered around him were no "rubber stamps"; some were presidents and managers of large corporations. Perhaps more than anything else, it was his integrity that attracted his supporters. "The church books are always open to anyone, and it's certain that the money goes where it's supposed to," conceded Canada's sharpest religious critic, Gordon Sinclair. Senior board members agreed:

> As well as OJ's total integrity, we were impressed by his tremendous organizational skills, his attention to detail, his incredible sense of timing, his single-minded dedication, and lack of self-seeking. He was totally dependable — if he said he'd meet you at noon, he'd be there, ahead of time. He never kept anyone waiting. He was a man of his word. But most of all, the obvious blessing of the Lord was upon his ministry. Souls were saved at every service. There was an excitement. Our whole family was ministered to, and we were challenged and stretched by the missionary vision.

Oswald had no assistant with whom he shared the pulpit; however, his good friend Dr. Ralph Hooper was still listed as associate pastor, along with Dr. Peter Wiseman, the Reverend F. Dickie, and the Reverend A. Sims, a Theodist minister who had joined forces with him at Christie Street. These men had no administrative duties and no pay except for the usual honorarium when they preached. In Oswald's absence, some would sit on the platform, although the song leader usually led the service. Some conducted weddings and funerals. Oswald's deaconess since Dale days was still with him — Miss Alice Porter — as was his faithful prayer warrior George Stenton, who had retired from his job reading gas meters and now served as unpaid "Visiting Minister," along with Dr. Robert Watt, former president of Livingstone Press. Oswald had to restrict his own pastoral visiting to his elders and the very ill.

Once the church was established, the Smiths lived in relative comfort, although he rarely took more than $5,500 in salary from the church in addition to car and telephone expenses and life insurance premiums. But he did receive love offerings from other churches where he preached. He was entitled to keep these for himself — quite apart from the many thousands of dollars he raised for overseas aid and brought back to the Peoples Missionary Society.

Indeed it was a big and flourishing operation that Oswald J. Smith was supervising. Besides the large church family, there were the mission in the slum areas, the ministry to the Jews, and the Missionary Medical Institute. The Russian Gospel Training Institute was still in the planning stages. There was the Bible school at the church each Monday night with more than 200 of their own young people enrolled in accredited courses. *The Peoples Magazine* Oswald edited himself, each month gathering or writing the articles and doing the layout. (Actually he pinned the cut galleys in place.) His books and hymns were constantly being translated and reprinted. Always there were campaigns in the offing both at home and away from the church. Above all, there were the scores of missionaries whom Peoples Church was supporting. Consequently, Oswald was a "world-watcher," carefully reading the newspapers and at least fifteen periodicals and listening to the radio news for anything that might affect his mission program (or his prophetic ministry.) He was constantly encouraging both the setting up of Bible schools to train nationals and the equipping of missionaries with printing presses to get out Scripture portions and hymnbooks. This vast world family was carried in his heart.

THIRTY-FIVE
♦♦♦
THE FAITH PROMISE CHALLENGE

LET US BRING BACK THE KING

We will bring Him back, the King
And His praises gladly sing;
We will tell to all around
What a Saviour we have found.
And He'll come, He'll come again
Come o'er all the earth to reign.

He is longing for His bride,
For He wants her by His side;
But He still must stay away
Until we His word obey;
And the Gospel of God's grace
Has been heard by all our race.

Thus we'll bring Him back, the King,
Jesus Christ, of Whom we sing
And He'll reign on David's throne
In a splendour all His own.
Let us then with hearts aflame
Sound the glories of His name.

OJS

In a brief, uncluttered statement of faith, Oswald set out the beliefs of the Peoples Church:

> We believe in an unmutilated Bible; salvation through the blood of Christ; entire separation from the world; a Spirit-filled life for Chris-

> tian service; victory over all known sin through the indwelling Christ; rugged consecration to sacrificial service; practical faith in the sufficiency of Christ for spiritual, temporal and physical needs; the purifying hope of the Lord's return; and a burning missionary zeal for the bringing back of the King through world evangelization.

"To bring back the King through world evangelization" — that was Oswald J. Smith's burning, driving passion. Single-mindedly, wholeheartedly, the entire ministry of the church was geared to this. *"The ministry of the church is missions,"* he would repeat again and again. The high point came each year in the four-week Annual Missionary Convention, announced by a banner hung right across Bloor Street.

And here Oswald was in his glory. Hundreds of feet of banners draped the balcony of the church and blazed across the choir loft, bearing his favorite slogans:

> *Why should anyone hear the gospel twice before everyone has heard it once?*
>
> *If you cannot go, you must send a substitute!*
>
> *The light that shines the farthest shines the brightest nearest home!*
>
> *You can't beat God at giving; give and it shall be given unto you; God is no man's debtor!*

One paper described the event:

> With all the excitement of a circus ringmaster, Oswald Smith stages two shows daily, featuring colorful, native music groups and costumed missionaries.

Each session included slides or movies. In the Exhibit Room behind the main auditorium, missionaries were on hand to talk with prospective candidates, and displayed such wonders as twenty-two-foot python skins from the Amazon jungles, South African drums, and witch doctors' masks. A refreshment booth was set up so that visitors would not have to go out to eat, and musicians strolled through the crowd singing and playing. "At our church we have hot dogs and Indians," one youngster bragged.

More than ever, Oswald's heart cry was for those who had never heard the name of Jesus Christ, who were still without all the blessings that follow the transforming power of His gospel. *If he could not go, he must send others* — within Oswald Smith this was a flame that refused to be snuffed out. And so he set about kindling a missionary fire in the hearts of all hearers, preaching as a "dying man to dying men," challenging young people to give their lives to carry the gospel to those still "in heathen darkness." And each time he gave the appeal, from all over the audience dozens would stream down the aisles to offer themselves for service.

As Oswald had always visualized, raising support for missions was not left to any one organization within the church. Rather, in the Peoples Church is was the prime duty of each individual — from the tots in the primary department through the college-and-careers, to the filing clerks and millionaires, the housewives and retired seniors. Oswald challenged them all to decide on a "faith promise," the amount they felt God would put into their hands to give to missions, quite apart from, and beyond, their regular Sunday offering. (He never mentioned tithing.) Then he urged people to trust God to supply this amount — even if they could not see a way in their budget — and then to get ready to praise Him for the miracle as each month they would watch God provide! No reminders were ever sent out, and miraculously, each year more than the amount promised came in.

Now, when Rader's Worldwide Christian Couriers organization had folded, Oswald had been left without a vehicle to carry the funds and recruits to the foreign field. He had been faced with the decision of how best to handle this, and for a short time had administered the funds directly himself. But then he decided this was unnecessary duplication, that it would be more satisfactory to work with the faith missions who were already established on the field. On the basis of the "faith promises" received, Peoples Church would commit itself to share in the support of workers around the world.

Oswald decided that partial support was preferable to total support because in this way their people could have more "windows on the world." From the missionary's standpoint, his base would be broadened to provide more prayer support as well.

Each year the challenge was to see how much they could pledge beyond the previous year's commitment. In the meetings when the offering was being taken, pledges were handed to the ushers as they moved up and down the aisles. At the adding machines, a bank of volunteers totaled the amounts. Occasionally a radio listener would telephone a pledge. These would be handed to Oswald to announce: "One hundred dollars, $100, sixty dollars, $120. . . . Ah, here is one we'll keep for dessert," he would chuckle as he received a larger amount. On the platform, a huge thermometer registered the totals. Up, up the red marker inched each night, closer to the goal.

On the final night the suspense was almost unbearable as "dessert" after "dessert" was read off. There would be a hymn while the grand total was added up. And then dramatically, Oswald would announce the "faith promise" offering for the coming year.

"Praise God!" would burst from every heart, and as the thermometer's red marker shot past the previous year's total to a new height of giving, the congregation would stand to its feet as the choir led in a mighty "Hallelujah Chorus." It was as if the entire church had heard "The Cry of the Lost":

I've heard of a land far away
Where millions in darkness are dying,
And they sadly moan as they pass alone
Through years of endless sighing.
"Oh! we're lost! we're lost, and at awful cost,
For we heard not the Story old
Of a Saviour's love and a Home above,
A shelter within the fold."

I see them in anguish and tears
Unable to stifle their moaning;
But in vain they plead, not a soul gives heed,
Nor hearkens to their groaning.
Yet, they'll stand at last when their life is past,
And they'll tell as they leave the throne
That since no one came in the Saviour's name,
They suffered and died alone.

Enough that the Master I love,
In sorrow and pain has been calling;
That He bids me bear of their woe my share,
For lo, the night is falling.
And they seek for light in their hopeless plight,
For the Light that comes from above;
So I gladly go, leaving all below,
To tell them of Jesus' love.

OJS

THIRTY-SIX
♦♦♦
TO THE CANNIBALS AND HEADHUNTERS

There's an urge upon my spirit
That compels my feet to go. OJS

As Oswald was planning the 1938 Missionary Convention, that old restlessness began to stir in him; the smoldering fires began to flame once more. "Oh, God, how can I remain at home when so many still have not heard?" he cried as he paced the floor night after night. In the pulpit, with eyes burning with a consuming passion, he pleaded with his people:

> "Why must we continue to reach out?" you ask. "Souls are being saved here by the scores. Why not concentrate here, and evangelize our own country?"
>
> I answer. . . . Why did David Livingstone leave for Africa before everyone in Scotland had become a Christian? Why did William Carey go to India and leave so many of his own countrymen in darkness? Why did Judson go to Burma before winning the last American to Christ? Why did the Apostle Paul leave Palestine and journey to Europe before he had evangelized his own country? Why?
>
> *Because it was God's plan.* Every tribe and tongue must hear. The field is the world, not one section of it, but all of it. "God so loved the world." Not a part of it, but all of it. *When God thinks, He thinks in terms of a world. You and I must get a world vision if we are to have God's vision.*

Do you remember when the Lord Jesus fed the 5,000, He had them sit down row on row? Then do you remember how He took the loaves and fishes and blessed them and broke them and gave them to His disciples? And do you remember how the disciples started at one end of the front row and went right along that front row giving everyone a helping? Then do you recall how they turned right around and started back along that front row again, asking everyone to take a second helping? No—a thousand times—no! Had they done that the people in the back rows would have been rising up and protesting, "Come back here. Give us a helping. We are starving. It isn't right; it isn't fair. Why should those people in the front row have a second helping before we have had a first?" There are countless millions in those back rows famishing for the Bread of Life. We must train those in the front rows to share what they have with the back rows, to reach them with the Gospel. "Unto the uttermost part of the earth" was His final command. How dare we disobey?

The front rows, the home work, will never lack. Let those of us who have seen God's vision, who have heard God's call, let us bend every effort to send out the Gospel to *all* the world for *this is the one and only task that Jesus left for His Church to do.* If we withhold the Gospel, "his blood will I require at thine hand," will apply to us.

If the King is to reign, we must finish the task. He is counting on us. How long are we going to keep Him waiting? Let us lay everything else aside and concentrate on this one great objective, the completion of the evangelization of the world in our own generation. *This, and this alone is the most important work of the hour!*

"Oh, God, send me out that I might send others!" was Oswald's prayer as he began to plan an extensive trip to Australia and New Zealand; enroute, he would visit the islands of the South Pacific, the notorious headhunter and cannibal country.

And this time there would be no need to face all those months alone. Daisy could come with him; there had not always been money, but this time he had enough.

"Daisy, just think of those long leisurely days at sea, the coral reefs, and the palm trees, the white sand beaches of Fiji and Samoa, the marvels of Australia and New Zealand. How wonderful it will be! There is so much I want to show you!" Oswald enthused.

But to his astonishment and dismay, Daisy was disinterested: "You never wanted me with you before, and I'm not going now. The children still need me."

"But that's ridiculous," Oswald argued. "I always wanted you with me, but we had agreed that your part was to stay with the children when they were little."

Now with Glen twenty-one and entering medical school at the University of Toronto and with Hope eighteen and Paul almost seventeen, Oswald thought they were old enough to be left. And they would not exactly be on their own—not with Chrissie to run the household and both sets of grandparents always close by. But all his protests were in vain. He and Daisy quarreled, and Oswald left, feeling deeply hurt, thinking that Daisy was putting the children ahead of him.

"I never minded our quarrels because it was such fun making up," Daisy later confessed. But with Oswald halfway to Honolulu, making up was not so easy, and an exchange of bitter letters did not help. Other times when they quarreled, Daisy would go away for a few days or a pall of silence would descend between the two of them until Oswald could stand it no longer and say, "I must have peace! I can't stand this, Daisy. We must talk."

"Yet, with two such strong personalities, we are bound to disagree often," Daisy rationalized. "Oh, how could I let you go so far away without me? When I think of how frail you are, it makes me tremble. My darling, you know I would go anywhere with you if there were no children. I feel I did the right thing to stay home in spite of my loneliness. The children are our responsibility until they are off our hands. We mustn't be selfish."

After twenty-one days at sea, Oswald arrived in Sydney to begin country-wide inter-church campaigns arranged by a group called "Campaigners for Christ." These men reported that they were impressed immediately with Dr. Smith's burning enthusiasm, his attention to details, his powers of concentration, and thoroughness of method." They had booked him to speak in churches and town halls, to civic luncheons and student groups, with several radio interviews. Again it was a very strenuous itinerary.

Such crowds had not been seen since the days of the Torrey and the Chapman revivals. In every place but one, people were turned away. The press described Oswald as a

> slightly built Canadian with a quiet personality. This forty-nine-year-old's power lies not in his gift of oratory; but in his loyalty to the Word of God and his obvious close communion with the Lord Jesus Christ. This man, like Enoch of old, literally walks with God.

They were referring to the address he had given to the clergy of that city. Oswald had unusual rapport with the many ministers' groups he addressed, thanks to his having been pastor of a large city church for twenty-three years, rather than a "professional" evangelist. Word of the phenomenal success of his Peoples Church had preceded him.

He told his fellow ministers about his "morning watch," how for over thirty years he had not knelt for prayer but paced back and forth, and prayed aloud—a sure cure for falling asleep, he had found. "A pastor's power for service will rise or fall in direct proportion to how faithfully he spends this time alone with God," he declared.

Many of the clergy were astonished when Oswald explained that the Peoples Church had no women's missionary auxiliary: "Because if the main work of the church is missions, is it right to hand that work, in effect, over to a small group of women?" Just before he left Canada, the Peoples Church had pledged $46,000 to partially support 135 missionaries working in 20 fields. "The more a church gives for work abroad, the more it receives for its own needs. We put missions first and God has added all the rest," Oswald said with authority as he challenged the ministers to take up the task of world evangelism and missions.

"Dr. Oswald J. Smith's gospel addresses were extremely simple, but delivered with an intense force which stamped reality upon all his utterances," his hosts reported.

At the end of eight weeks, over 1,000 people came forward seeking salvation, and hundreds of young people volunteered for foreign service.

And then, sailing from the north of Australia, Oswald set out for the Coral Islands of his boyhood adventure stories. He traveled for seven days with Dr. Norman Deck, and Australian dentist, to the Solomon Islands where they boarded the sailing schooner of Deck's brother, Northcote, a medical missionary under the Plymouth Brethren.

The brothers lived on this very comfortable launch as they ministered to these former cannibals and headhunters. The food was good and the water safely boiled; thus Oswald could relax and completely enjoy the idyllic days of cruising among these lush, South Sea tropical islands.

Some of the villages they visited were totally Christian, thanks to Deck's preaching. Oswald was delighted to see the Bible school where scores of native preachers were being trained to take the gospel to those who had not yet heard it. Most of the women wore grass skirts only. The fact that the younger women were often totally naked provided a challenge to Oswald's photographic skill to shoot at such an angle that he would not have to do a great deal of editing.

He enjoyed preaching to these open, responsive people, always speaking from his *King James* Bible held aloft in his left hand. Dr. Deck interpreted as they stood together in the clearing among the little thatched-roof huts, sometimes throughout the day or at night by the light of reed torches. Oswald found their singing mellow and musical. Sometimes they used their own haunting, minor-key melodies and at other times the more familiar hymns of Fanny Crosby with native words.

Back home in Canada, up at the lake as she waited alone night after night for her partying young people, Daisy was having second thoughts: "I've given my whole life to the children. . . . Sometimes I wonder if it pays." Then she got out all of Oswald's old love letters and began to read them through. The children came home and went off to bed. Still

Daisy read on. Finally, as the pale of dawn was streaking the horizon, Daisy, with tears washing down her face, began to write:

> Oh, my darling, where has time gone? I wish I could get back these last twenty years and live them over. How different it would be. Why could it not have been as we planned when we love each other so much?
>
> I'm afraid I have given too much time to the children instead of to you. But they seemed so delicate and required so much care.
>
> You have been a wonderful Daddy, providing them with so much, and living such an example before them. You never question my judgement, especially with the children, and darling, I thank you. I appreciate your faith in me.
>
> You were always so kind to me in the things that mattered most. I was never as strong as some women but you never asked me to do hard work. Yet being sick and miserable made me irritable and cross so often when I should not have been. Please pray that the Lord will heal my old worn-out body so that I may be to you a true helpmate.
>
> You have been a wonderful husband and lover, always remembering anniversaries with pretty roses and gifts. You have been such a success as a preacher and leader and a Christian—how proud I am of you. To think God gave me such a man for my own. I am glad you are my husband, even if I do not have you as much as other women have theirs. With you, my darling, half-time is better than all the time with any other. I love you too much, with a love that hurts my very soul.
>
> But I have given you pain, and you are so sensitive. Can you forgive me? It's not too late, is it?

And then the first week in September, Daisy received a cable from Australia: OSWALD SMITH SERIOUSLY ILL IN HOSPITAL. Daisy was stricken:

> My world has stood still since I got the message. Every star went out of the heavens, even the sun ceased to shine. Oh, my darling, you are everything to me. After the wonderful meetings you have had, no wonder the devil would like to kill you. But, oh, it cannot be yet for a while. I have had you so little.

After leaving the Solomons for Fiji and Samoa, Oswald had become deathly ill with extremely high fever. He had been rushed to a hospital in Australia and there it was diagnosed that he had a form of malaria. Soon he was on the ship bound once more for America. In Los Angeles, to his amazement Daisy was waiting for him.

"Daisy, my dear, dear Daisy!" he exclaimed. "What a mistake it was for me to go to the Solomon Islands. I should have come straight home to you when I finished in Australia. Will you forgive me?" He had been gone almost seven months. This time they had five days to themselves on the train traveling across the continent to Toronto.

What a joyous welcome awaited Oswald. He was astonished. Such a fuss had been made about his mysterious illness—the papers had been full of it. Strangers had stopped Daisy and the children on the street to inquire about him. Everyone in the church seemed to be living in a daze. Then when word came to the Wednesday prayer meeting that Oswald had recovered, everyone stood and sang the Doxology—"Praise God from Whom all blessings flow. . . ."

Oswald's movies of the "savages in the islands of the South Pacific" were so sensational that the church across the street had to be rented to accommodate the crowds that began gathering at 5:00 P.M. for the 8:00 service. He would show his films in one church, then dash over to the other where Eldon Lehman had kept the people singing until Oswald arrived. In recognition of his extensive travels, a few months later Oswald was made a Fellow of the Royal Geographical Society of London, England.

THIRTY-SEVEN

♦♦♦

"THE MODERN MOODY"

You must get your priorities straight. . . . OJS

As his fiftieth birthday approached, Oswald gave himself to heart preparation for the "momentous day":

> What a long, long road it has been, and oh, so many twists and turns. The years have not been perfect years. There have been many failures, heartaches and disappointments. The spirit has been willing, but the flesh often-times weak.
>
> I feel but thirty, and look but little more. I have preached 5,400 sermons and completed five world tours; I have written scores of books, hundreds of poems, hymns and gospel songs.
>
> It has taken God fifty years to train me. Oh, that He might now use me. I place myself utterly at His disposal. There is still much land to be possessed. There are other peaks to be scaled. Oh, that I had 100 years yet to work out all that is within me!

Then on his fiftieth birthday—November 8, 1939—he wrote:

> *Life is so brief; man's days on earth so few,*
> *He scarce has learned to live when he must die.*
> *If only he like those of ancient days*
> *Could count his life by centuries, and know*
> *That after he had lived a hundred years*

And learned the art of living, he might then
Look forward to long periods of time
In which to give expression to the strange
Pulsations of his heart and mind—ah, then,
This life would be worthwhile, 'twould not be vain.

But is it vain? Are we not told of yet
Another age in which the man that dies
An hundred years, is but a child; where God
Will conquer death and men at last will live
To finish here on earth the work begun?

More than ever he was in demand as a speaker across the country for both evangelistic and prophetic ministry. "The modern Moody!" they billed him. For every campaign he accepted, he turned down at least a dozen others. Every invitation was spread out before the Lord, asking for direction whether it should be a yes or a no. Certainly Oswald loved preaching and holding meetings; however, he hated the loneliness and separation from his family, and frequently was unwell when away from home. "I certainly never went on these tours for pleasure," Oswald insisted. "But I was never meant to be tied to one church, one pulpit. This was my work. I felt a compulsion on my life from God, so I would go."

The "cake eaters" at home thrived on a diet of such greats as John R. Rice, Vance Havner, Dr. Walter L. Wilson, and Harry Ironside, pastor of the great Moody Church in Chicago. Oswald finally managed to secure Gipsy Smith for his pulpit. When just a lad teaching the Indians in British Columbia, Oswald had written home to his mother, urging her to attend the meetings Gipsy would be holding in Toronto and to send him any clippings. "Although once a common gypsy in a gypsy wagon, he has become the world's greatest evangelist; I would give a lot to hear him," young Oswald had written. When Gipsy finally came to the Peoples Church in May 1940, it seemed that the whole city wanted to hear Gipsy Smith. Many of the services had to be moved to Massey Hall. Oswald and Gipsy became lifetime friends.

Later, when Jackie Burris came to town, the crowds packed out Peoples, then Massey Hall, and finally had to move into Maple Leaf Gardens with an estimated 11,000 attending. It was the first time that a religious meeting had been held in the famous hockey arena.

Oswald had continued to bring in the top musicians of the day. Among the favorites were Charlotte Copeland and Fred Zarfas, who decided to be married, and Oswald had the honor of performing the ceremony. The Peoples Church was absolutely jammed. Looking out at the crowds, Oswald turned to the groom: "Isn't it too bad we can't take up a collection!"

During those times when Oswald was away on his own, he felt secure in the knowledge that Daisy would be at every service, and thus provide a listening post on the various guests. Keenly sensitive to the congregation's response, she reported it with vivid detail. Choosing to keep a low profile, she had developed a fine women's Bible class, which was her main ministry around the church. But more frequently now, she accompanied Oswald on his trips.

Also of invaluable assistance around the church was Dr. P. W. Philpott, formerly pastor of the Moody Church and the Church of the Open Door in Los Angeles where Oswald had often preached for him. Although considerably older than Oswald, they had become fast friends. Philpott was an outstanding preacher, in fact, "Canada's greatest living preacher," Oswald would say; he provided a stabilizing force around Peoples Church in Oswald's absence.

In all probability, the ministry that gave Oswald the greatest joy was to share with other congregations the secret of how he had built the greatest missionary program of any single church in Christendom and to help them become thriving "missions first" churches too. He was unorthodox when it came to raising funds for missions. When the plates were going around a church, he was known to raise both hands and cry out: "Wait a minute! I think I hear too much silver going in the offering plates. Ushers, we're going to start again!"

Yet, the pastor at Philpott Tabernacle in Hamilton reported that "even the critical went away amazed and rejoicing as Dr. Smith led the people in a time of 'hilarious giving' that brought in $10,000 the first day." And an editorial in *The Christian* magazine pointed out that

> Dr. Smith employs no extraneous and doubtful methods in raising funds. Financial needs and objectives are openly and precisely stated, but the appeal is always for direct, systematic, and proportionate giving, as enjoined in the Scriptures. No inducements of any kind are offered except the assurance of divine blessing on cheerful and sacrificial giving for the glory of God above.

The Roman Catholic press also took a close look at Oswald's fund-raising:

> We find it difficult to believe that one Protestant church in Toronto could give more than all the Catholic churches in Ontario and Western Canada. The brutal truth is that they are not all millionaires, just plain Protestant people whose enthusiasm for foreign missions has been fired by a zealous pastor. We must catch some of our Protestant neighbours' enthusiasm.

In 1940, Oswald was invited to Boston's prestigious Park Street Congregational Church to conduct the first missionary convention in its 135-year history. For six years he returned to challenge them with his "faith promise" offering plan; during those six years their mission giving went from $3,200 to $58,000 annually (and today as of 1981 was $600,000).

The same story could be repeated hundreds of times across Canada and the USA, in large and smaller congregations, sometimes with Oswald visiting, sometimes with the ministers traveling to the Peoples Church to see for themselves. Such was the Reverend Homer Kandel, minister of a struggling church in a small town in Ohio:

> When we had no missionary program of any kind and less than 100 people, I drove to Toronto and Dr. Smith helped me plan our first convention. That year our first Faith Promise Offering was $16,000. During the next fourteen years we raised $1.5 million for world mis-

> sions. At the same time we moved into a new church building with 300 attending; and we have more young people training for full-time service than ever before.
>
> Another blessing is that at least fifty churches have come to us to find out how to start a missionary program; thus hundreds of thousands of dollars have been raised for the cause of world evangelization, and all because Oswald Smith took time to help a very small church in an unheard-of place.

Sometimes the challenge came indirectly, as it did to the Methodist pastor in Greenville, Illinois, when a member of his congregation lent him a copy of *Passion for Souls* by O.J. Smith: "I had read but a few chapters until my soul was literally aflame with a completely new vision of world evangelism. Along with it came a crushing sense of guilt!—Guilt that I and my church could have been so criminally asleep for so long." This pastor began to preach missions, and "God sent His Holy Spirit upon the congregation in mighty revealing and convicting power. In a great altar service, the congregation went down before God in deep penitence." Thus the people began to give to missions, and within two years, the general finances of the church were in better condition than ever before.

Even on the foreign field, missionaries who had attended the Peoples Church annual missionary conventions began to challenge the national churches to have "faith promise" offerings. Stirring up others to pray, to give, and to go—this was Oswald's great mission, and the program was snowballing worldwide.

During this time, Oswald had several bouts with malaria; when he was ministering in Jamaica, he came down with a particularly severe case. The Jamaican doctor took one look at him: "Dr. Smith, I'm going to knock this out of you once and for all." Oswald has never found out what was in the shot he received; he only knows that it nearly killed him and that when he came back from wild fever and delirium, he was cured. Permanently. (There has been no recurrence since then.)

Cuba, Jamaica, Mexico, Haiti, Alaska (in Alaska his companions thought Oswald would starve to death because he simply refused to pay the high prices for food)—Oswald was flying to appointments now and consequently could pack in a tighter itinerary. But there was also less time to write—no 1,200-line poems, no book chapters in flight. Still he managed to fit in some writing.

For instance, one day he stopped in Philadelphia to go over some hymns with B.D. Ackley. Homer Rodeheaver walked into the studio where they were working and exclaimed, "I've just heard Harry Rimmer preach a powerful sermon on the resurrection of Lazarus, depicting how all was so dark, and *then Jesus came!* I've written this tune." Rodeheaver played it, adding, "I'm looking for someone to write the words."

"I'll do it," Oswald volunteered and hurried back to his room at the China Inland Mission headquarters. Quickly he dashed off the lyrics, and Rodeheaver at once began using the song to conclude every meeting. Soon Oswald's poem was known around the world:

When Jesus comes the tempter's power is broken;
When Jesus comes the tears are wiped away.
He takes the gloom and fills the life with glory,
For all is changed when Jesus comes to stay.

A little later, B.D. Ackley wrote Oswald, asking for something on the resurrection with no mention of Easter so it could be used year round. Oswald dug out a poem he had written years earlier, did some revising, and the resulting collaboration was one of the most powerful hymns of all time—"He Rose Triumphantly":

He rose triumphantly, In pow'r and majesty,
The Savior rose no more to die;
O let us now proclaim The glory of His name,
And tell to all, He lives today.

He rose triumphantly
Oswald J. Smith
B.D. Ackley
1. Our bless - ed Lord was slain, (was slain,) The Christ who came to reign, (to reign,) And in a grave He lay, To wait the com - ing day.
2. They sor - rowed when He died, (He died,) Nor sought their tears to hide, (to hide,) But soon their bit - ter pain Was turned to joy a - gain.
3. The stone was rolled a - way, (a - way,) For Christ was raised that day, (that day,) And now He lives a - bove To man - i - fest His love.
Refrain
He rose tri - um - phant - ly, In pow'r and maj - es - ty, The Sav - iour rose no more to die; O let us now pro - claim The glo - ry of His name, And tell to all, He lives to - day.

Then Jesus came

Homer Rodeheaver was deeply moved and wrote to Oswald:

> Your wonderful poem inspired Mr. Ackley to do his very best work, and I believe "He Rose Triumphantly" will live throughout the ages, and will give many thousands a new inspiration and a new vision of what the resurrection means to the world.
>
> God has peculiarly endowed you with a gift of putting into practical, readily poetic form these great gospel song messages which flow from your own great heart, and all of us who love gospel songs are deeply indebted to you. During these latter years, no one has made a greater contribution than you; all of your poems are good.
>
> You have no idea what a joy it is to work with you. I wish I had more of your fine faith and splendid spirit. You've certainly done a magnificent job!

Actually, Oswald always considered it little short of a miracle that he had been introduced to Ackley, the main writer for the Rodeheaver Company and the most outstanding sacred composer of the day. He felt grateful that BD, and later his brother AH, had shown an inclination to work with him. Of Oswald's 1,000 hymns, 200 had music by Ackley, and these began to appear in American hymnals just as soon as Ackley had written the music.

In the midst of this activity, Oswald had taken time to accompany son Paul as he set out to enroll at Bob Jones University in Cleveland, Tennessee. ("Father didn't just bring us into the world and then dump us," Paul recently explained.) They journeyed down by train, and Oswald helped Paul settle into his room, then spoke in chapel before returning home.

Oswald kept up a regular correspondence with Paul, and was delighted when his eighteen-year-old son began going out weekends to preach to the hill people in the moonshine country of Tennessee. Instead of traveling over the mountains by mule as Oswald had done, Paul managed to rent a Model A Ford from a fellow student.

However, because of the war, Paul, who was of draft age, had to leave the States and enroll in a Canadian university which offered military training. The only school that combined this with seminary studies and which would recognize his American credits was Union College on Canada's West Coast. The president was a member of the old school of Methodists, and had preached in the Peoples Church pulpit "with all the spiritual fervour and enthusiasm of John Wesley," Oswald recalled. The school seemed a good choice, totally reliable and trustworthy.

But reading between the lines of Paul's letters from Vancouver, bit by bit Oswald sensed that Paul was losing interest in attending church, and seemed to be growing cold and indifferent. And then one day there was a letter: "Dad, very frankly I find I am not believing the things you have taught me to believe." By the time Paul had completed his theology studies under liberal professors, he had lost his faith entirely.

When he came home, Oswald as always put his arms around him and kissed him, saying "Paul, oh, Paul, it is so good to have you home!" They talked; Paul was not argumentative, just very sad. He had lost his vision, turning away from all he had believed and preached.

For months Paul just drifted aimlessly. Oswald and Daisy simply loved him. Once Oswald took him along as song leader for a campaign, hoping that being back in an evangelical atmosphere would turn the tide. But Paul accepted a long-term student pastorate with a liberal church. It all seemed so hopeless.

These were agonizing days and nights for Oswald and Daisy. Hour after hour they cried to God to bring Paul back, to set him on fire to preach the gospel again. Many nights Oswald prayed the whole night through, seeking God's forgiveness for their having sent Paul to the wrong school:

> We had given each child to the Lord when they were born; I had prayed for Paul every day of his life, that God would make him a man after His own heart. I was sure he would come back. But oh, the sorrow, the regret for what I had put him through!

For Oswald it was a time of deep soul-searching before God:

> There has been so much failure. I feel that I am the weakest of the weak. Again and again I have bemoaned the corruption and pollution in my heart and loathed myself before God. Life is passing so fast, and I have accomplished so little. I am so tired of my own efforts and long to see a manifestation of God's power.

Finally the day came when they knew Paul was back. It had been a gentle returning as Paul sorted through the options and finally decided yes, he would trust, he would believe. Jesus must be virgin born; the alternative was unthinkable. And He must be risen; there was no denying the fact. And He must be God. God's Word must be true. All of it.

Once more Paul began preaching with fire and great blessing. Then one day he brought home Anita Lawson, a lovely soprano soloist whom he had decided to make his wife. After Paul and Anita's marriage, Oswald and Daisy were delighted when the young couple joined them for an evangelistic swing through the British Isles where Anita's singing and Paul's trombone solos blessed thousands.

Oswald always took it for granted that Paul would succeed him at the church, so it was a day of "deep satisfaction" when Paul finally was installed as assistant pastor in 1952.

"Paul, you must get your order of priorities straight: God must come first, the work second, and the family third. Otherwise, you'll never make it," the older Smith admonished.

THIRTY-EIGHT

♦♦♦

COME WITH YOUR HEARTACHE

I believe the only way we can evangelize the world in our generation is with the printed page. OJS

Now back in 1944 a young evangelist had come to Toronto; Oswald had had him speak to their young people's group and had not been overly impressed. Still, they had kept in touch. Then in 1948 Oswald found himself with this same young man, now an evangelist with Youth for Christ, riding on a little train through the mountains of Switzerland headed for YFC's first conference on evangelism, the Beatenberg Conference.

"I'm going to be speaking to some young people's groups here, and I've never used an interpreter. Tell me how you do it," the eager young evangelist asked Oswald.

"It's not hard," replied Oswald. "The trick is to talk fast in short, simple sentences; then collect your thoughts while the interpreter is translating; then talk fast again, and so on." Oswald gladly shared many valuable lessons as they journeyed.

During this Beatenburg Conference, Oswald did a good deal of the preaching, ministering on missions and the "deeper life,"stirring the young workers to evangelize with more fervor. Among those listening were the Palermos, Torry

Johnson, Bob Cook, and Oswald's young friend Billy Graham.

But even as they discussed world evangelism, Oswald secretly and sadly held the opinion that when Billy Sunday and Gipsy Smith had left the scene, the days of great evangelistic campaigns had finished forever.

Then to his utter amazement, the very next year one of the greatest evangelists in world history burst on the scene. It happened in Hollywood, California. Billy Graham was conducting meetings when suddenly, and quite unexpectedly, the power of God fell on the audience, causing hundreds to stream to the altar to accept Christ. That became the first major Billy Graham Crusade. In the weeks that followed, God's special anointing on this young man's ministry would become obvious to the whole world.

Oswald was tremendously excited to hear about this, and flew down to rejoice with Billy in this great wave of blessing. For the next several years, he always tried to spend a few days at each crusade, encouraging Billy and praying with him. They developed a warm correspondence and mutual caring.

Among the converts at that first major crusade in Hollywood were several members of the movie colony; they began meeting for fellowship and Bible study. In 1952 when the group decided to have a family retreat at *Forest Home* (Tim Spencer's cabin), Oswald J. Smith—who had never darkened a movie-theater door—was suggested as the speaker "who could bring them something from the Lord." He accepted, and this opened up a whole new chapter in his life. The group immediately took to heart this conservative Canadian with his dry British wit, and Daisy's wonderful sense of humor delighted them as she fussed over her husband, making him tea and being sure he got his rest.

One evening at Forest Home, the country-and-western singer Redd Harper was among the group sitting around on the floor of the cabin. "Got any new songs?" they asked him, so Harper pulled out his guitar and sang one he had just written called "Quiet Time."

"Would you sing that in tomorrow morning's session? I'm speaking on 'The Morning Watch' and it would fit in perfectly," Oswald requested.

A few nights later, he and Harper met again at a meeting in Stuart Hamblin's home. Again Harper sang and said a word; then Oswald spoke. When he gave the invitation, several responded. Stuart took them into a bedroom and Oswald followed, dealing with them there as they knelt around the bed.

Not long afterwards, Harper received a letter with some verses from Oswald, asking if he could set them to music. Redd knelt down and prayed, "Well, Lord, if you want to be sweet enough to send me music for these lovely words, I'm available." Thus, "Come with Your Heartache" was born, a song that George Beverly Shea picked up immediately and began to sing regularly over Billy Graham's "Hour of Decision" and in crusade meetings.

Another day in Pennsylvania, Harper saw a little plaque on the wall of a pastor's office: PERHAPS TODAY! The thought burned itself into his soul. *Sounds like a song,* he was thinking, and then suddenly he knew that God wanted Dr. Smith to write the words. Harper dashed off a note with the suggestion. That was Tuesday.

On Thursday he got a letter written by Oswald in a motel in San Diego where he was staying, with three verses and a chorus. Impossible! "This timing is miraculous," Harper's pastor friend said. "The Lord must know we need that song right now; let's pray, Redd, that the Lord will give you the right melody." The next morning Harper had it, and "Perhaps Today" was sung at the Sunday services with great power, as it has been sung ever since. Harper then recorded twelve songs that Oswald and he had collaborated on — it was one of the very first stereo LP albums ever pressed.

When Harper discovered that Oswald was not getting a cent in royalties from the hundreds of gospel songs that had been published, he arranged for Oswald to become a member of ASCAP (American Society of Composers, Authors, and

Publishers), and this membership has poured thousands of dollars into Oswald's beloved missions.

On one of his trips to California, Oswald worked with Redd Harper, who had gone into the ministry largely through the influence of Oswald's books. They joined hands for a series of eight all-day radio missionary conferences to raise support for World Literature Crusade. Harper sang and played the songs they had collaborated on, Lorin Whitney was at the organ, and Lee Childs sang solos. Between songs, Oswald answered questions on world evangelism from listeners — he had become a champion of Jack McAllister and the Every Home Crusade, which made available, free for the asking, gospel portions and tracts to thousands of missionaries around the world.

It pleased Oswald that the literature was printed in the country of distribution and thus was more acceptable to the nationals. He told listeners that

> millions are learning to read and Every Home Crusade works first in countries where literacy is highest. I believe the only way we can evangelize the world in our generation is with the printed page. The Christian workers are in place, but they are saying, "Give us the tools and we will finish the job." Christians are spending 96¢ of every dollar here at home, and only 4¢ for overseas missions. I urge all Christians with a missionary vision to get their money overseas. We can never send out sufficient missionaries, but we can complete the task of getting the gospel of Jesus Christ to the whole world by means of the printed page. "Faith comes by hearing, and hearing by the Word of God," whether it is the spoken Word or the written Word.

With this stirring appeal they raised $97,000, enough to deliver gospel messages to 85 million souls. The format was repeated a few times throughout the Southwest.

Oswald spent a good deal of time with the founder, Jack McAllister, especially after World Literature Crusade undertook to translate several of Oswald's books into many other languages. McAllister regarded Oswald as one of his very special friends, the man who had the greatest influence on his own life. He signed his letters to Oswald: "Your son in the faith."

THIRTY-NINE
♦♦♦
FIRE IN SOUTH AFRICA

You can produce only what you yourself are. OJS

Best of all were Oswald's frequent trips abroad, and usually Daisy accompanied him now. "My darling, you are dearer than in the days of old," Oswald told his wife in a passionate love poem celebrating their fortieth wedding anniversary.

They took several trips together to Great Britain and Europe. In 1955, Oswald, who was now sixty-six years of age, but had no thought of being put out to the retirement pasture, set off with his sixty-five-year-old sweetheart for a whirlwind tour of South Africa. That land would be stirred as never before. From the first night when Oswald had stepped off the plane after a long, tedious flight, he preached with fire and conviction.

"God has turned our city upside down," Reverend Glyn Tudor of Cape Town noted. "Brief though Dr. Smith's visit was, he left behind a different city from that to which he came."

The *Weekend Supplement of Die Burger* carried the story:

> Dr. Oswald J. Smith, who is regarded as the greatest Evangelist-Missionary of his time, was unknown to most people in South Africa when he started his Union-wide campaign in Pretoria. But it very

> soon became known that a most extraordinary man had arrived in South Africa. The number of people that went to listen to his messages increased nightly. In every town the churches and halls were ultimately too small to accommodate the large numbers, and hundreds were turned away.

The newspapers asked:

> Who is this man who is drawing such unheard-of crowds to religious gatherings? And what is the message he brings that the people flock in their thousands to hear him?

Who and what indeed! Oswald had an unostentatious presentation. He always dressed conservatively, preaching in the robes befitting a Presbyterian minister.

One church leader remarked:

> But have you heard Oswald Smith preach? Have you felt the prophetic fire, the apostolic fervour of his messages? An electric current of life runs through them; they go straight to the point. Trained by years of speaking with an interpreter, Smith uses short, pithy sentences that smash like sledge-hammer blows against the heart. There's a powerful simplicity, an incisive directness, a sincerity and unmistakable authority as he preaches the Word of God. Every child could understand his messages, and yet no adult could hear them indifferently. When he speaks, you have the impression he is speaking to you alone.

Oswald spoke first to the ministers and Christian workers (some had traveled almost one thousand miles), challenging them to a deeper walk with Christ. "You can produce only what you yourself are," he charged. "A carnal pastor produces carnal people. A missionary-minded pastor produces a missionary-minded congregation." His books had preceded him, and hundreds more were bought: *The Victorious Life, The Man God Uses, Passion for Souls.*

He spoke to the English, the Afrikaaners, and the black Africans. He addressed special gatherings of business people, high school and university students, and missionary trainees, while Daisy addressed several large gatherings of women.

The evening sessions packed out the largest churches in each city. In Capetown, the closing meeting was held in the football stadium with six thousand people.

Oswald preached to the unsaved, with hundreds coming forward. He preached to those wanting victory over sin in their life, and hundreds more filled the altars weeping. The closing message of each city's campaign was the challenge of missions: "The supreme task of the Church today is to obey the simple command of our Lord and 'Go and tell all men.' If you cannot go, you must send a substitute," Oswald demanded. Then they sang

> *Give of thy sons to bear the message glorious,*
> *Give of thy wealth to speed them on their way;*
> *Pour out thy soul in prayer for them victorious,*
> *And all thou spendest Jesus will repay.*

while hundreds of young people came forward, volunteering their lives to the task of world evangelism. Oswald challenged the parents to stand with them, pledging to give full support. And then he taught these African congregations how to take up a "faith promise" offering. To give their sons and daughters, to give themselves to prayer, and then to give of their wealth — in most cases these were totally new concepts, obligations that simply never had dawned on them before.

Said Reverend John F. Wooderson, pastor of the Durban Tabernacle:

> We suddenly realized we were right on the edge of an enormous mission field. As we listened to God's servant, we determined that an annual missionary convention would become an essential part of our church's programme, that we would begin to evangelize those on our very doorstep.
>
> But the greatest miracle was to witness the harmony and unity, the "wonderful spirit of oneness" that had been achieved amongst the believers, especially where the religious life had been divided into two main racial groups, with "no dealings between the Jews and the Samaritans." But God has used His servant Dr. Smith to at last bring the two groups together.

Thus reported Baptist pastor Dr. Arthur B. Arnott.

Others spoke of Oswald's gracious humility, how easy he was to work with, how grateful for even the smallest service or favor rendered him. "We have much reason to bless God for all Oswald Smith has meant to us. *He is a giant of a man.* We can regard Dr. and Mrs. Smith as God's choicest gifts to South Africa," they concluded.

Oswald had highly satisfactory meetings with several missionaries the Peoples Church was supporting; then he and Daisy managed to steal away to Kruger National Park. To the photographer and animal lover in Oswald, this proved an unparalleled treat. While filming a family of baboons, he looked up to see a big male with head cocked in curiosity scarcely three feet from the whirring camera. Oswald photographed zebras, gazelles, giraffes, hippopotamuses, wildebeests (gnu), and finally a pride of five lions and ten cubs right on the road, encircling their car. What choice big game for an exultant Oswald to "capture" and bring home to his people!

Returning to Canada, Oswald barely had time to sort out his films and pack a smaller bag when he was on the road again, this time holding missionary conventions throughout the United States. In Tulsa, Oklahoma, he raised $20,000 for missions; in Louisville, Kentucky, at the Church of the Open Door, the missionary offering was $16,000; at Calvary Temple in Denver, Colorado, the "faith promise" totaled $70,000. In all, he helped raise $126,000 for missions in those few months. That summer on a swing through Western Canada, he helped churches there raise another $43,000.

What other challenges would Oswald face or had he already had enough?

FORTY

♦♦♦

THERE IS JOY IN SERVING JESUS— IN SOUTH AMERICA

The gospel is dynamite *and I want to leave it wherever I go, so that. . . there will be an explosion and someone will be saved!* OJS

In September 1957, Oswald and Daisy headed south for what would become "the greatest united evangelistic campaign in the history of South America," again with the aim of stirring up the national churches to do more for missions themselves, and then to lead souls to Christ and Christians into a victorious walk. Twenty-five denominations cooperated in this first inter-church crusade, with one- to three-week campaigns held in the eight large cities of Argentina, Brazil, Uruguay, Paraguay, Chile, and Peru. Even though the Christians had been praying for months, their faith had not prepared them for the crowds that poured into churches, theaters, tents, and stadiums. In Buenos Aires, attendance was 15,000 on opening night, and swelled to 27,000 by the closing meeting, making it the largest religious gathering in that city's history. In addition, many meetings were televised and shown across the land, reaching multiplied more thousands.

"Perhaps the success of Dr. Smith's preaching lay in his delightful simplicity and the strong personality that backed his clear and plain words," wrote Dr. Martin Durksen, president of the Executive Committee for Buenos Aires.

"It didn't take the *porteños* five minutes to realize that this frail, white-haired preacher with erect bearing and piercing eyes was filled with a passion for their souls' welfare; a man obsessed and possessed with one thing—to get every lost soul in the building to Christ," wrote Phil Saint (brother of the martyred Nate Saint), who presented an illuminated chalk drawing each night, the only entertainment of the program. The choir music was thrilling; and then as 20,000 voices sang the theme song of the campaign,"Gozo hay, si, en servir a Cristo!"—Oswald's own great hymn "There Is Joy in Serving Jesus"—Oswald felt his heart would burst with praise and thanksgiving.

As soon as the appeal was given, businessmen, housewives, students, children, an old ragged beggar with wrinkled face half hidden in a dirty, matted beard—all pushed their way down the crowded aisles by the hundreds upon hundreds. Oswald was totally amazed at the response. They came without coaxing—in all, 4,500 for salvation; another 6,000 for victory over sin, while 1,700 young people dedicated their lives to God's service. These names were given to local churches for follow-up.

His good friend, Jack McAllister, founder and director of World Literature Crusade, had come along at his own expense, and was a tremendous help to Oswald. Jack took most of the daytime meetings, thus letting the sixty-eight-year-old Oswald rest his voice, and also did a fine job of promoting Oswald's books, four of which had been translated into Portuguese and Spanish. Before leaving Toronto, Oswald had taken up a special $11,000 offering for literature for South America so that these books could be sold at cost. He had also brought along thousands of gospel leaflets, always insisting that the printed page could accomplish more than the spoken message. "The gospel is *dynamite* and I want to leave it wherever I go, so that every now and again there will be an explosion and someone will be saved!" Oswald would say.

The beloved Michael Billester of the Russian Gospel Association, with whom Oswald had made his last visit to Europe's Russian people, had planned his visit to South America's Russians to coincide with Oswald's campaign. Consequently, on Oswald's first Sunday in Buenos Aires, he was thrilled to find himself preaching to a large Russian congregation, many of whom had been saved under his ministry in Poland twenty-five and thirty years earlier. Now they were leaders among the Russian Christian community of South America. In Russian, they lustily sang Oswald's favorite hymn, "Saved!" A large missionary offering was taken that morning to be used to translate *Passion for Souls* into Russian.

But no collections were taken at crusade meetings. Supporters had already covered campaign costs, and Oswald had paid for his and Daisy's transportation. Sometimes they were accommodated in the homes of Christians. But when Oswald was left on his own, he always looked for the cheapest hotel accommodation. And although Oswald was not bothered, the fastidious Daisy was nearly eaten up by the fleas that infested these third-rate quarters. She suffered a great deal and was covered by flea bites; still she always emerged looking absolutely immaculate—a perfect model of quiet, matronly good taste. Somehow she managed not to scratch as she addressed the many large groups of ladies where "she won all hearts with her beautiful smile and tenderness."

Oswald, too, always appeared unflappable. Once, just as the service was drawing to a close in one place, the whole platform suddenly collapsed under the weight of the large choir and platform guests. It simply dropped to the ground about four feet, and everyone tumbled amid shouts and confusion. Oswald was scheduled to autograph books, so he just gathered himself up and oblivious to the commotion surging around him, took his place at a table and got to work. Fortunately, no one was seriously hurt.

All in all, the three-and-a-half month campaign was significant in many ways. "The greatest miracle was not in seeing the large multitudes attend the meeting, but the harmony and understanding co-operation established among all the churches supporting the campaign.'' Martin Durksen pointed out.

''Oswald Smith has stirred us up to the great missionary opportunity all around us,'' said another. One of the most respected national leaders in South America—Dr. Jose Borges dos Santos, president of the Supreme Council of the Presbyterian Church in Brazil—was profoundly shaken by Oswald's ministry on missions, and so enthused that he immediately devised a plan for the support of at least two missionaries. And just as in South Africa, it was the infusion of this dynamic and vision into the national churches which made Oswald rejoice. Night after night, weeping young people and older people, the rich and the poor, made their way to the altar. But most importantly, the national church was set aflame.

Said one Christian worker:

> He woke us up! Many of us had read his books and caught something of his evangelistic zeal and missionary vision. But then to see with our own eyes what God can do through a life wholly consecrated to Him—it was a heaven-sent lesson in masterful preaching, a special refresher course for those of us engaged in evangelizing.

''I believe that this history-making campaign will be used of God to strike fire in the hearts of evangelicals all over the continent, marking a new era of soulwinning and revival. *A new day has dawned for South America!*'' concluded Fletcher Andersen of the Methodist Church in Rosario, Argentina.

Oswald himself reported:

> But oh, the need for more great soul-stirring evangelistic campaigns to reach the cities of South America. For years we've been sending missionaries to the jungle when we should have been sending evangelists to the cities. You seldom hear what is happening in the country; but what happens in the city is known everywhere. The Apostle Paul always headed for the great cities, the centres of population, knowing that if he could reach them, the country also would be

reached. He generally had an uproar. It is seldom that anything is accomplished until there is an uproar. People must start talking about the Gospel. That was what happened in our campaigns.

We need evangelism on the foreign field. We must capture the cities for God! So much to do and so little time! God help us to do more than we have ever done before to get out the message and bring back the King!

FORTY-ONE
♦♦♦
PASSING THE MANTLE

Don't let your people get bored. OJS

When Oswald and Daisy arrived back in Toronto, they were enthusiastic as they shared their trip with Paul. Oswald told his son:

> This is such exciting, blessed work, Paul. I'm hardly missed around the church now that you have everything under control so well. You really are doing the job of senior pastor—let's give you the title, and that will free me totally to visit and raise money for the foreign fields around the world. I could stay on as missionary pastor to oversee the giving and the convention; you take charge of everything else. After all, I'll soon be seventy, and you are nearly thirty-seven; it's time you had full charge.

And so it was agreed.

But as Oswald was preparing the agenda for the next board meeting, he had a letter from Paul:

> Father, it will never work. Don't give in your resignation; give them mine instead. To leave you with the missionary convention is to leave you with the heart of the church. So long as you are connected in any way with the church, you will always be regarded as the senior pastor. I would just be holding the ropes until the "real pastor" returns. I'm just "young Paul" to most of the elders, and that is what I will always be. So I'm leaving to go into full-time evangelism.

> You have done a fabulous job of founding and running the Peoples Church, and I agree with Billy Graham that you are undoubtedly the most remarkable man I have ever known. I stand back and watch in abject and mute amazement. I will never be the man you have been.
>
> It's hard to express what a son feels for a great father. You've done so much for me that to begin to enumerate would be impossible, and any kind of thank-you would be almost sacriligious. I want you to know that I am very proud of you as a great man, and I love you very much as a father.

Oswald reread the letter and shrugged ruefully. It was a hard thing that he was asking of Paul. If he were young, he would not want to build on another man's work; he would want to make it on his own. Yet he was asking Paul to set aside those aspirations and follow in his father's footsteps.

Oswald knew a little of how difficult it was to fill another man's shoes—he certainly had had a tough time at Dale. There had been those who had told him to his face that he would never be man enough for the job; they were just waiting for the "real pastor" to come home from overseas. To that board, Oswald had just seemed a raw youngster incapable of managing a large established church.

And Oswald knew of the times when he would have given anything to take back a resignation. He slipped Paul's letter into his desk drawer and made no comment to anyone.

When Paul returned from the campaign he had been holding, he read over the board meeting minutes and saw that no resignation had been recorded. Oswald managed to avoid any conversation about the matter, and Paul slipped back into his usual routine. Almost imperceptibly, Oswald began shifting responsibilities and tasks over to Paul, easing him into one decision after another.

Then one day Oswald spoke to Paul:

> Paul, I see what you mean about the crowds beginning to slack off. All that you have been saying is true: there are no empty pews yet, but the people are no longer packed in tight. They rarely are standing around the back or sitting in the aisles any more. So many have moved to the suburbs, as you have pointed out. If they drive back downtown, there is no place to park here. It's not like the old days

> when everyone used to come by streetcar. I've decided you are right—the time has come to relocate.
>
> But that is a task I feel too old to undertake, whereas you are just coming into your prime. You are the one who must head it up, choose the new location, design and build the new complex, bring in the people. Will you do it?

Paul jumped at the chance, knowing that his "father's footsteps were just too big for anyone to fit into. But if it were a totally different program, I could see there could be a way."

Thus, on the first Sunday in 1959, a full year after he had turned down the job, Paul Brainerd Smith was inducted as pastor of the Peoples Church. "I have only one piece of advice, Paul," the older statesman offered. *"Don't let your people get bored.* A pastor should never overexpose himself. Your people should hear other voices, better voices than your own. And remember, it takes all kinds of bait to catch all kinds of fish."

Immediately Paul called a board meeting and proposed that the elders seek a new site closer to the heart of the growing metropolis. And hopefully, with the rapid escalation of downtown real-estate values and with good planning, a new church could be built debt free.

"And, Father, you must have a proper office." So Oswald found himself ensconced in a spacious area off the upper Sunday school hall. And he hated it all alone up there, much too far away from the bustle and action of the ground floor general office. *But I'm here very little,* he had to concede as he shoved some books and his Bible in a bag and headed with Daisy for the airport.

Soon after Paul's induction, Oswald and Daisy toured the British Isles, Iceland, Norway, Finland, and Sweden, where again halls were packed. One tent held 3,000 and still hundreds sat outside. Prayerfully, heartily in Swedish, they repeatedly sang Oswald's hymn, "With Thy Spirit Fill Me." In the fall of the same year, the Smiths ministered in Hong Kong, Hawaii, and Japan where Oswald was keynote speaker for the "100th Anniversary of Christian Missions."

He was introduced as "the pastor of the most missionary-minded church since the days of the apostles."

The next year—1960—he was back in Japan and also preached in Alaska. Nineteen sixty-one brought Hawaii, Fiji, Australia, and New Zealand; 1962, Iceland. Everywhere his books had preceded him.

Then on October 28, 1962, the Smiths were home to celebrate the opening of the fine new Peoples Church: a 2,100-seat facility with Oswald's favorite fan-shaped auditorium, located away from the former business core, but near the intersection that marked the center of Metro-Toronto's sprawling urban growth, and close to thruway and subway service. The giving that year was still in proportion: "$53,000 on ourselves, $318,000 for missions!" Paul and his father could rejoice. With little active responsibility in the church, Oswald cut his $5,500 salary back to $3,000 and took off again.

His itinerary was as follows:

1963: England, Ireland, Wales
1965: Trinidad and Barbados
1968: Honolulu, the Fiji Islands, and Australia

On the Australia trip Daisy could not come along because of illness, but Oswald had Gordon Hamilton, a young baritone soloist from the church, with him. Gordon had sung "Then Jesus Came" in the morning service one Sunday in June and afterward Oswald had spoken to him. "What are you doing in August?" he asked.

"I'm leading your choir while your music director is on vacation," Gordon had replied.

"That can be looked after. I want you to come to Australia with me." Gordon left in a daze. Later Oswald called to let him know the arrangements. "Our plane leaves at 6:30 P.M. Be sure to be early," Oswald admonished.

Gordon had to drive in from out of town and thought he would have time to spare when he arrived at the airport at

4:30. But Oswald was already there; "Here you are, right on time!" he beamed. Oswald settled into his seat where he read and dozed most of the time, chatting only occasionally. Gordon felt a twinge of conscience as he enjoyed the in-flight movie while Oswald studied a devotional book. This was Oswald's nineteenth world tour.

In Australia they were often billetted in the same home, and right after breakfast Oswald would excuse himself. Gordon would hear him pacing back and forth in prayer for the rest of the morning: "He must have walked miles." After lunch there was no sight-seeing for Oswald; he rested and took care of himself so that halfway through the six weeks, when Gordon was ready to collapse with exhaustion, Oswald was "just steaming right along." Meetings and more meetings and TV interviews.

It was bitterly cold in the South Australian winter, and people brought blankets to the stadiums. The campaign planners were concerned for this frail-looking seventy-nine-year-old; he was so thin and pale, reporters thought, that he "must have one foot in the grave." A heater was placed close by him on the platform, the only heater in the whole building. Oswald wore a warm sweater under his suit and seemed oblivious to the shivering all around him. The "fire in his bones" blazed out in every sentence. Newspapers reported:

> Let him open his mouth to speak and the outward frailty vanishes. Smith becomes a man of robust spirit, bursting with life and energy, a man on fire. The flame of his zeal reaches you, then your neighbour, and presently the entire congregation is engulfed in a spiritual conflagration.

As at other times, auditoriums were packed out and hundreds turned away. Congregations were challenged to new giving. Over two thousand individuals were counseled.

Gordon discovered that some people did not appreciate Oswald's tendency to talk about himself and what he had accomplished. They thought him somewhat proud, but the more Gordon got to know him, the more humble he found him to be:

> He wasn't bragging about what Oswald Smith had done, but rather, it was his total amazement about what the Lord had been able to do through this weak, unworthy, unfitted country boy. He was continually surprised by God's greatness and goodness to him.

During those six weeks when they were together almost all of their waking hours, Gordon developed a tremendous respect for this "warm, often comical, very human" companion. "Oswald Smith is truly a man of God," Gordon summed up simply.

And then they flew home to what Oswald described as the greatest honor ever bestowed upon him or the Peoples Church—the arrival of Billy Graham in Toronto personally to help celebrate Oswald's sixtieth anniversary in the Christian ministry. Graham summed up the life of Oswald J. Smith:

> No other man that I know has the drive, determination, or the singleness of mind to serve God. Oswald Smith has been a legend in his time. He stands tall in Canada and the nations of the earth. My whole life and my ministry have been touched and directed by Oswald J. Smith. I want to do the same as he has done as long as I have breath.

There had been many honors for Oswald over the years, beginning with the first honorary degree of Doctor of Divinity from Asbury College in 1936. This had been followed by a Doctor of Literature from Bob Jones College in Greenville, South Carolina; then a Doctor of Laws, in 1946 from Houghton College in Houghton, New York. In addition to his membership in the Royal Geographical Society, Oswald had been made a member of the Eugene Fields Society of Authors in St. Louis, Missouri, in 1940; a member of the Royal Society of Literature of the United Kingdom in 1952; then a member of the American Society of Composers, Authors, and Publishers in New York, in 1956; followed by an Outstanding Community Service Award from his own Burrough of North York.

In 1958, the "golden jubilee" of his ministry was celebrated with a great meeting in the 6,000-seat Varsity Arena. "But mother is not with me and my heart is broken. I've suffered until I am sick," Oswald mourned, for Maud Laidley Smith had gone to be with her Lord just two weeks earlier.

Then in 1965, the Evangelical Fellowship of Canada was formed with Oswald as first president. "I am trying to keep out of the limelight, to walk in the shadows with God; and yet He honors me! God deals with me far better than I deserve," Oswald marveled in his diary.

FORTY-TWO

♦♦♦

TILL THE DAY BREAK AND THE SHADOWS FLEE AWAY

O God, my Lord, for eighty years I've lived
'Mid peace and strife;
Afflictions sore I've known, and battles great
Have filled my life.

But still in Thee I'll trust as in the past,
O Saviour mine,
For long ago Thy grace discovered me
And made me Thine.

OJS

As he approached his seventy-eighth birthday, Oswald resigned from the post of Minister of Missions, turning the convention and full missionary duties over to Paul:

> I believe I can now leave the entire work in your hands since God has given you vision, gifts, and talents under the anointing of the Holy Spirit to carry it on. He has more than fulfilled my dreams and expectations, and my heart is filled with gratitude to Him for all He has done.

Responded Paul:

> Father made it so easy for me; he didn't leave, he just moved over. We didn't often sit down and discuss what should be done or how to do it — we just did things, and there was a tremendous 'gut' sense of unity.

Each day Oswald still went into the office for a few hours to attend to the mail and work on new translations and printings of his books and tracts, which went out by the millions each year. There was more time for the family now, and Christmas was more special than ever with grandchildren around. After Daisy's elegant buffet, they dressed up and put on skits.

Paul's daughters, Jann and Jill, recall the fun of watching Oswald's movies of the family. ("I loved to visit Grandfather," Jann recently said.) As a very tiny tot, she had sat on his lap while he explained the way of salvation:

"Poppa, when I die, how long will it be till I'm with Jesus?" she had asked. Oswald did not answer, but blinked his eyes.

"Poppa!" You didn't answer me!" little Jann demanded. He just blinked again. "Poppa!" the frustrated child protested.

"Didn't you see what I did?" Oswald gently asked.

"Yes, you blinked your eyes."

"And that is how long it takes after you die until you'll be with Jesus," Grandfather Oswald explained.

Each of the children received a letter from him on birthdays, sometimes signed simply *Oswald.* Said Jann and Jill:

> We always knew he prayed for us every day by name, and we were terribly proud of him. The church was a big part of our life. When we were little, "playing church" was the favorite game of all the grandchildren. We knew that for Grandad and Father, the church was their whole life. But we got to share in it. Lots of children have busy fathers, but they don't get to share in their world at all. We did.

Oswald and Daisy also had some lovely times of going back to the old places. He preached at Severn Bridge again, at Bellwoods, and then in his parish in South Chicago. "I knew God would open that pulpit to me once more!" he praised. He still made time to write poetry:

> *We must go on, the night is fast approaching,*
> *The past is gone, we cannot change it now;*
> *We weep, we pray, and yet forget we cannot,*
> *O God, forgive, as at Thy throne we bow.*

We must go on, although our tears are falling,
For all our work on earth will soon be o'er;
Our prayers, our toils will some day be rewarded,
And we shall dwell with Thee for evermore.

We must go on, the future still awaits us,
The present, too, is ours to live for Thee;
Our past, dear Lord, oh, help us to forget it,
And by Thy pow'r, come now and set us free.

(1968)

O Lord, I long to do Thy will
To walk with Thee each day;
For I have often missed the path
And turned to my own way.

Tho floods of sorrow overwhelm
My soul from day to day,
Yet will I put my trust in Thee,
And let Thee have Thy way.

So many things would claim my time,
But they are not for me;
Thy will alone must be my goal—
I yield, dear Lord, to Thee.

(August 1969)

ONE LIVING FLAME

When I remember all the winding roads
That lead to man's eternal destiny;
The joys and sorrows of the thorn-clad path,
Amid the storm clouds and the sunshine bright,
I wonder why I doubted and despaired
And why I ofttimes murmured and complained.

Then I considered how I loved and lost
And how I faced the silence of the tomb,
And how amid the tangles of my life
I trembled on the brink of dark despair;
And wondered if the night would ever pass
And I would rise to tread the heights again.

When I behold the happiness of love,
The love that ever satisfies the heart,
Where two dissolve in one and never more
Desire alone the joys that both may share;
Or drink the cup that God himself ordained
To reach the summit to man's greatest bliss.

Then joy is pain and pain is lost in joy
And life becomes God's will forevermore;
For then I turn from all I hope to have
And fix my gaze upon His matchless face;
Until at last for me to live is Christ
And living find in death eternal gain.

When this I know, then what can earth impart,
Or this dark world bequeath to mortal man?
A moment here and then, in endless time,
A life at last where all is clear and plain,
And broken hearts are healed forevermore
Within the centre of God's will and plan.

Then I recalled the dreams than cannot die,
The fires that burn forever in my soul
Like some volcanic force that must erupt
And pour its passion in one living flame
Of holiness and sanctified desire,
By God ordained long years before the Fall.

Where now is hope, the hope that burns undimmed?
Where now is faith, the faith that knows no doubt?
Where now is love, the love that cannot die?
Where now but in the heart that dwells in God
And finds its hidden springs within His will,
For there man's satisfaction is complete.

(Tokyo, 1970)

The Christian and Missionary Alliance also paid tribute to him with a beautiful plaque at one of their Annual Council meetings. Oswald could scarcely believe the glowing words he was hearing! "Now it is all over. How I praise God He has overruled! I have been fully vindicated, but I had to live to be over eighty before it happened."

There were trips to Embro (his childhood place) where he had preached in the church. A plaque was unveiled in honor of the native son who had "travelled extensively, written 36 books which have had six million copies printed in 125 languages, and composed 1,200 hymns." Oswald had kept in touch with friends from school days all through the years.

Now there was more time for visiting friends, although their number was beginning to dwindle. He had buried Mrs.

Morrow and Eldon Lehman. Hooper was gone, as was Alice Porter, his faithful deaconess, and finally Chrissie French, the much beloved companion of the whole Smith family and Oswald's great prayer warrior. Oswald wrote that

> *although our tears are falling*
> *We must go on, the future still awaits us,*
> *The present too is ours to live for Thee. . . .*

Both Oswald's and Daisy's parents had also left them. Daisy's dear mother, her close companion over the years, had been laid out in the Smith living room before the funeral service. Oswald's parents had lived with them for the last ten years of their lives; Oswald had had the great joy of hearing his aged father, Benjamin Smith, just before his death, make a clear confession of his trust in the blood of Jesus Christ to cleanse him from his sins and fit him for heaven.

And now Daisy was not well. In her eightieth year she had made her ninth and last world trip with Oswald — this time to Norway, Sweden, and Denmark — and had spoken to many women's meetings with great blessing as always. "I still feel young!" Oswald rejoiced, but Daisy had had several major surgeries. Following an operation for cataracts in June 1970, she never seemed to be well again. Repeated falls resulted in a fractured arm and two fractured hips, forcing her to lead the life of a chronic invalid. Glen, now a doctor in Vancouver, was gravely concerned, but there seemed little even he could do.

In April 1972, while everyone had gone off for the great final service of the annual missionary conference, Norma Cooper, Daisy's friend from South Africa days, stayed home with her. But midway through the service, Paul was startled to see his mother being assisted into the church. This was Daisy's forty-fourth missionary convention, and she could not stay away. The whole church applauded Daisy, who had been absent for so long; then they all praised God together for a missionary offering totalling $532,207.

During the next few months Daisy became weaker. Oswald would come home from the office and lie down on the bed beside her to talk about the day and read any interesting papers to her. Sometimes he would have his meals on a tray with her in the bedroom. On October 24, Oswald sat by her bedside for family worship. He read and prayed; then Daisy spoke, "Now I am ready to go." Two days later she slipped into unconsciousness.

On the eve of November 1, 1972, Oswald knelt and prayed by the bedside with Daisy as had been their habit through the years together; then tenderly he embraced the unconscious form and placed a gentle kiss on her forehead. "Goodnight, my dear, dear Daisy," he whispered and went to sleep in the next room, leaving a special nurse on duty. At 3:30 A.M. the nurse aroused Oswald: "She's gone." Gently, in her sleep, Daisy had slipped away into the presence of the Lord she had loved and served so truly.

It was almost more than Oswald could bear to lose his wife of fifty-six years, and he began to sink into a nervous depression, going through the motions of mechanical living. "Oh, what a sad heart. Only God knows . . ." he wrote mournfully. Christmas came and with it excruciating longing and loneliness: "Daisy was always the life our Christmas." He went down to visit her grave: "Oh, God, it is so dark. How am I to go on?"

Somehow Oswald managed to assist Paul in the first of their weekly telecasts beginning in January 1973. With his daughter, Hope, Oswald went off to Florida to fulfill his engagements. (In recent years, he and Daisy had spent much time together at Trinity College, Southern Keswick, and Bibletown.) By summer of 1973, he returned to his full schedule and preached for two months in the western provinces. "Almost all of next year is booked. Praise God, He has not put me on the shelf," Oswald recorded.

During the following winter, Oswald seemed to feel the loss of Daisy even more acutely:

> What a treasure she was, what an untold help in my worldwide missionary work. Everyday for 56 years when I left the house, I kissed her good-bye, and again when I returned. How I thank God for her

> even though my heart is heavy. Oh, how I wish I had done more for her. Now it is too late.

A case of flu turned into pneumonia with complications, and for several weeks Oswald barely held on. Once, he struggled out of bed and checked his drawers to be sure all was in order for his homecall. Then he bounced back again, and that summer preached his twelve-thousandth sermon at Canadian Keswick. He spent many happy hours organizing his 10,000 feet of 16-mm film. Prostate gland surgery and two surgeries for facial skin cancer set him back slightly.

But there was still so much to do. His books were being printed and sent into communist lands. "A soul is won to Christ for every fourteen cents invested in gospel literature overseas," Oswald championed. Almost every mail brought letters telling of souls behind the Iron Curtain coming to Christ through the reading of Oswald's books and tracts. Pastors were using his book *The Man God Uses,* with each chapter a lesson for their secret gatherings. "When we studied the chapter about going and telling others, witnessing to people who did not know Jesus Christ, we had a revival among the believers!" one group reported with joy. Oswald was still traveling constantly across the States and Canada while Paul had taken over the international trips.

The ministry of the Peoples Church had expanded rapidly in the new setting. With 2,000 enrolled, the Sunday school had grown to be one of Canada's largest; a dayschool with 650 students was operating, as well as a 200-acre ranch camp. The missionary conventions were bringing more nationals into the pulpit, and in 1976 the offering went over $1 million. A yearly one-day telethon appeal for relief for some particularly needy area of the world such as Bangladesh, Upper Volta, or Haiti, brought in another $100,000. The "Living Christmas Tree," featuring all the choirs and orchestras of the church, began drawing audiences of over fifteen thousand each year. Paul had proved to be an unusually successful TV pastor, and hundreds of letters were coming in each week; a team of eight associates now worked closely with him. The minister of music since 1960—David Williams—was a brilliant composer, and collaborated with Oswald on some new hymns.

In 1977, at age eighty-seven, Oswald received an honorary Doctor of Humanities from the California School of Theology. He recorded in his diary:

> How good God is! But Daisy was not here to see it. Five years have passed since she went home to be with Christ. I miss her more than ever. How I love her. I want to go as soon as He wills it. God give me grace!

September 1978 brought another grand celebration marking the fiftieth anniversary of the Peoples Church. Bill Davis, the premier of the Province of Ontario, delivered greetings to the eighty-eight-year-old founder, now snowy-haired, but with eyes still twinkling bright blue. Said Premier Davis: "Through its many spheres of service, the Peoples Church has contributed to the moral and spiritual welfare of our nation; and through its mission projects it has become one of the best-known churches in the world."

In April 1979, the *Reader's Digest* of Canada presented Oswald and Paul with leatherbound copies of the article carried in that month's issue: "Peoples—Canada's Show-Biz Church." Stated the article:

> At times when other churches are reconciling themselves to smaller congregations, Peoples is a religious phenomenon. With 2,600 worshippers on Sunday morning plus another 180,000 watching by television, almost certainly this is Canada's largest congregation. It has probably given more money to world missions, for both preaching and relief ministries, than any other congregation in the world.
>
> "A great church built on the priority of missions," says The Billy Graham Association which places Peoples first in its list of the world's great congregations.

That summer Billy Graham came to Toronto for a crusade, and each night Oswald was on the platform, encouraging and backing Billy with his presence and prayers as he had done through the years. After the great 1,000-voice choir had sung

"The Song of the Soul Set Free," Graham paid special tribute to his old friend:

> Oswald Smith is one of the greatest song writers of the century. He is one of the greatest preachers of any century. I've never before met a man who has been preaching for seventy years and is still going strong. Oswald Smith is one of the greatest missionary statesmen of any century. I want Dr. Smith to stand and I want us to give him a tremendous welcome.

It was a thrilling tribute to a man in his ninetieth year.

FORTY-THREE
♦♦♦
THE FIRE STILL BURNS

Then I recalled. . .
The fires that burn forever in the soul. . . . OJS

Oswald had been enjoying relatively good health, but when he reached his ninety-first birthday in 1980, life seemed to change for him. Quite inexplicably, he felt that his life was over, his work done; others would have to take it up.

Yet at the 1981 missionary conference this man who had raised more money for missions than any living man was able to preach twice and was on hand to join with Paul in announcing the grand total of the "faith promise" offering—more than $1.3 million for the support of some 242 missionaries and 222 nationals. That made a total of $17 million for missions from the Peoples Church.

On Father's Day he had preached for almost an hour to a crowd of 1,800 to 2,000 seated at Kennedy Road Tabernacle in Brampton, Ontario. When he gave the invitation, fifteen came forward to give their hearts to Christ.

Each Sunday on the televised service, Oswald still led in the invocation. "Now turn with me if you will in your hymnbooks to number ____," he would say. Paul would have given him the number just before going onto the platform, but Oswald carried no notes to remind him.

In Paul's absence, he conducted communion, taking his stand behind the communion table with shoulders somewhat stooped, a step somewhat faltering, and a voice that quavered when he began to read the Scriptures. But when he prayed, the voice was as strong as that of any young man. Quietly the elders went about their duties, serving communion to the congregation of about two thousand in less than ten minutes and being served themselves in another few minutes with the choir singing "Blest Be the Tie that Binds"—all in twelve minutes flat so as not to interfere with any other service, just as Oswald had stipulated years before.

On his ninety-second birthday he entertained family and friends who had gathered with the singing of an old favorite, "My Bluebell." Other years he has sent them into gales of laughter with a spirited rendition of his own special "Midnight Gallop" in which he raced up and down the piano keyboard at a terrific clip in wildly syncopated octaves.

At present, Oswald spends most days quietly at home where the same rigid schedule must be adhered to as always. Meals must be precisely on time. The closet is just as bare as ever, although the Sunday suit and everyday suit have been augmented by a white silk jacket for summer Sundays or Florida engagements. A few shirts and ties, two pairs of shoes, his slippers, a bathrobe, and a topcoat complete his wardrobe.

Eagerly he awaits the arrival of the mail each day as it is brought over from the church. (He voluntarily gave up his driver's license at age eighty-six.) With a dictaphone beside him, he opens the mail, dictating a response as he reads. To magazines seeking permission to reprint some of his writings he responds: "Do not hesitate to use anything that might be a blessing. Please send me a copy." And each mail brings a variety of magazines carrying something of his.

To the young brain-damaged veteran who constantly writes him, Oswald dictates a letter of warm encouragement and signs it: "My kindest regards, ever your friend, Oswald. P.S. You may call me anytime." When the young man's family decided he was bothering Dr. Smith too much, sometimes telephoning five times a week, they ordered the young veteran to stop. With that, he threatened to commit suicide. "Oswald Smith is the only person in this whole world who cares about me," he tried to explain.

When Oswald learned of this, he gave orders to his own protective household: "No matter what, let me speak to this young man." (His daughter, Hope, who is now alone since her children have grown, lives with Oswald, along with Ann Cook, the cherished housekeeper of many years.)

Oswald beams with pleasure as he reads greetings from family and friends far and wide:

> We love you very dearly, more for what you are than for the many great things you have done as an ambassador of the Lord Jesus Christ.

It always comes as a surprise to him that people remember him, love him, care about him. Jack McAllister wrote him:

> Oswald, I want you to know that there will never be a time in your life when I do not go on remembering you. I have prayed for you by name each day.

Requests still come from pastors across Canada and the States for help in establishing a church missionary program. He corresponds with those who are involved in the translation of his books and continually receives reports from overseas of the blessings that his tracts, books, and hymns have brought. From Africa:

> You should hear the girls hilling sweet potatoes singing in Ngambai the song you and Redd Harper wrote "I'm Singing for my Lord." The Christians love it. The whole of Moundou is ringing with it!

From South America:

> When I read your book *Passion for Souls,* I knew I must leave my work and train for the ministry.

From South Africa, Dr. John F. Wooderson, pastor of Durban Tabernacle, reports on that church's outreach, born out of Oswald Smith's visit:

> As we listened to your challenge, we realized that we are right on the edge of an enormous mission field. We set a goal for "faith promise" giving, and to the praise and glory of God's name, we exceeded our goal by more than 100%. But the greatest achievement was that numbers of people began to prove the unfailing faithfulness of God in enabling them to keep their "faith promise" to Him and each year as they promised more to missions, their faith rose, and what followed in the spread of the gospel was something in which they had a tangible part.
>
> In the province of Natal and Zululand, thousands of Zulus came to know the Lord as their Saviour as a result of our being able to support numbers of preachers of their own tribe. We were able to build 27 churches in that area. Far and wide, in other parts of South Africa, churches were built and missionaries helped with support.
>
> We have built a larger place of worship, but no money was diverted from giving to missions. We put missions first, trusting God to take care of building costs. And He has—the whole complex is paid for.
>
> The impetus and pattern for all this came to us through the ministry of God's choice servant—you, Dr. O. J. Smith.

There's a letter from a mission leader:

> First of all, I want to thank God for the influence you have had on me personally. It seems that wherever I have gone throughout Africa, everyone engaged in foreign missionary effort knows, honors, respects and reveres the name of Dr. Oswald J. Smith. In America, everywhere I go, missionary programs have been set up and organized similar to the one you instituted in Toronto.
>
> You have lifted men and women from all walks of life and made your name immortal in the cause of missions around the world. We pray for you, talk about you and admire you. Only eternity will reveal to all the value of your earnest burning zeal in the cause of Jesus Christ.

Oswald is interrupted by the phone ringing. It's a national pastor passing through Toronto, and he just had to call to say how he was thanking God for Dr. Smith's ministry. Oswald gives thousands of his books to pastors in the Third World (even paying the postage) and they, in turn, sell them for a few cents' profit. Thus he carries on a large correspondence with these Third World pastors.

The bank statement is in, and must be checked. He keeps his accounts meticulously, paying bills immediately. Paul comes by, and over a cup of tea they discuss the problems of the church, now with a staff of eighty-nine including teachers for the dayschool and a total church budget of $3.4 million. "I'm out of step with all this," Oswald admits. "It's all so different from what a handful of us accomplished from that one small office on Bloor Street."

Oswald has increasing physical problems. It distresses him that he can no longer walk for his "morning watch." Right after breakfast which is served to him in bed, he spends the remainder of the morning reading his Bible, always with a pen beside him as he reads. Then in intercessory prayer, he cries out to God for total purity, for forgiveness for any thought not from God. He brings before the Lord all the children and grandchildren and great-grandchildren, the long list of other family and friends, and the burdens and needs of the church and great mission family. "He loses all track of time, and after his daily meeting with God, his face shines with holy light," those around him say.

Yet the old merry twinkle is there as he teases the granddaughter he is to marry (he has performed marriage ceremonies for more than six hundred couples). Or as he triumphantly pulls out two bothersome teeth with kitchen pliers before being discovered by the women-folk who fuss about, horrified at the blood spattering the washroom mirror.

He still delights to reread the lifetime favorites: *The Last of the Mohicans* and *The Deerslayer* by James Fenimore Cooper; *The Adventures of Sherlock Holmes;* Sir Walter Scott's *Ivanhoe; Treasure Island* and *Black Beauty;* Dumas' *The Count of Monte Cristo* and *The Scarlet Pimpernel;* Victor Hugo's *The Hunchback of Notre Dame;* Sabatini's *Sea Hawk* and Robert Service's poems.

"Would you change your life if you had it to live over?" He ponders the question before replying:

> As David Brainerd said, "I would not have spent my life otherwise for the whole world."
>
> Yes, there are things I would do differently; there are mistakes and regrets. I regret that I was so judgmental as a younger man, and that I left Daisy so soon after the baby was born. I should have found more time to spend with the children, but there always seemed to be so many pressing matters, and Daisy and Chrissie seemed to be managing so well; then before I knew it they had grown and were leaving home.
>
> I never should have gone to Manitoba College; I never should have left the Alliance so hastily; I should not have accepted that pastorate in Los Angeles.
>
> Praise God there are more victories in my life now, and not the same battles that I used to fight. There never was a problem with pride because there were never enough results to make me proud or to glory in. Of course I am still aware of sin in my life, because the more clearly we see God's holiness, the clearer our own sinfulness becomes. The longer I live, the more unworthy I feel. The wonder of God's love becomes more overwhelming with the passing years. More than ever, "the love of Christ is all my plea." Gideon's army were tired, but they still kept chasing the enemy. I'm tired now, but praise God I'm still chasing the enemy.
>
> *The greatest need of Christians, the greatest need of the church has not changed. More than ever today we need the Unction of the Holy Spirit. When the Holy Spirit first came on the apostles, there was boldness, and power, conviction and conversion. The people came gladly; they continued stedfastly; they praised God, suffered persecution, and they prayed. When the Holy Spirit takes control in a church, there will be blessing and unity and power. Souls will be saved. The gospel will go out. There will be a spiritual work. Perennial revival is only possible where there is continuous brokenness of heart.*
>
> *And the glory of that vision will be with me to the end. . . .*

Now it's the last Sunday in 1981, and after an absence of almost three months due to illness, Oswald J. Smith walks onto the platform of the Peoples Church to a standing ovation. When Paul calls on him to preach, he stands to his feet with some hesitation, straightens his shoulders, walks to the podium, and places his handwritten notes on it. He looks trim and fit in the neat navy blue pin-striped suit; scars of repeated skin cancer surgery mark the still handsome, albeit hawklike face. With that same twinkling smile, he greets his people, wondering how many pulpits that morning are occupied by a preacher in his ninety-third year!

And then he announces his message for the morning: "I want to speak on 'saving faith,' and I want to make it so simple that everyone present can understand." With scarcely a glance at the handwritten notes he has placed on the podium (and not wearing any glasses), Oswald leans into the microphone as he has done so many thousands of times before. Any trace of hesitation quickly vanishes as he speaks in a voice gathering strength and with simple directness lays out the way of salvation:

> There are three steps to saving faith: First you must *hear;* that is why we send missionaries to the foreign field. Then you must *believe* that "God so loved the world that He gave His only Son."
>
> I turned in my dictionary to find the meaning of the word *believe* and discovered the definition: "to consent with the mind." There was no word about the heart. But "consenting with the mind" will not save anyone. I've traveled all over France, Spain, Italy—in fact, in every country of Europe except three, many, many times; and there I find tens of thousands of people who believe that Jesus died; yet they are not saved. They are living the same life they've always lived, committing the same sins they've always indulged in. They have consented with their mind; they are giving intellectual assent to the truth. But they have not passed out of death into life.
>
> In the Old Testament you find the word *trust* 152 times. But the New Testament translators discarded the word *trust,* substituting *believe* instead. Yet we must "trust" the Lord Jesus Christ as our own personal Savior if we are to be saved. In the *New English Bible* I looked up Acts 16:31 and found they had translated it "Put your trust in the Lord Jesus Christ and you will be saved." That is the way the original read. All my life I believed the Bible, every word in the Bible. But it was not until I was sixteen years of age that I knelt in Massey Hall and trusted the Lord Jesus Christ, and passed out of death into life.
>
> What does it mean to *trust?* Trust implies committal. The best illustration is the marriage ceremony where a young woman puts herself into the hands of the man by her side, trusting him to look after her for the rest of her life; the young man will provide the home, the food for the table, the clothes she will need—all the rest of her life. She is putting her trust in him completely when she commits herself to his care and keeping.

> You can believe as much as you want, but not until you put your trust in Jesus Christ will you know that your sins have been forgiven.
>
> Trust demands action. Here is a chair; I may believe that if I sit on that chair I will rest. But I will not experience that rest until I sit down on it, trust myself to the chair. Not until you put your trust in the Lord Jesus Christ will you be saved. . . .

For only fifteen minutes he preaches. Then Paul steps forward and asks if there are those who want to put their trust in the Lord Jesus Christ right now, and all over the auditorium hands are lifted by the dozens. The choir sings "Just As I Am," and the seekers and personal workers stream forward to line the altar. Oswald offers a prayer of dedication and thanksgiving, leading them to the foot of the Cross from where they can rise in newness of life and go on their way rejoicing.

Young converts and old friends crowd around to shake his hand. The clasp is still strong, the eyes clear and sparkling with warmth and affection. He talks of the new compendium of his five best-selling books, and this "man God has used" is excited that they will live on to give out the message long after he has passed on.

But until then, says Oswald Smith:

> *The land before me waits to be possessed.*
> *I take it still by faith,*
> *By faith I onward go. Unsatisfied,*
> *I thirst, nor can I rest. Still voices call*
> *As in my youth and I must ever climb,*
> *Must scale the highest peaks and conquer yet,*
> *Or else must die!*
>
> *Ah, then, away with ease!*
> *Let me press on*
> *Until He calls Who called me long ago.*

For Oswald Jeffrey Smith, the man who put missions first, there is a fire that yet burns—a fire in his bones—and a heart that yet agonizes for a dying world.

At age forty-nine, Oswald wrote: "Someday you will hear that Oswald Smith is dead. Don't you believe it. At that moment I will be more alive than ever, for I have an indestructible life!"

There is no death, the Christian cannot perish,
God's Word is true, Eternal Life is mine;
I once was dead, but now I'll live forever,
For I am saved by Christ, my Lord divine!

There is no death, Oh, Glory! Hallelujah!
The Son of God has suffered in my place,
He took my death that I might live forever,
And He has saved me by His sovereign grace.

EPILOGUE
by Douglas Percy

Coming into a hotel in Chicago one day, I saw Mrs. Oswald J. Smith sitting in a corner of the lobby. Surprised, I asked where her husband was. "He's up in our room praying, and he walks while he prays. There isn't room for me then, so I leave him to pray alone."

Walking while praying — the phrasing is apt, as surely these two aspects of spiritual life must go together. In Oswald Smith we saw a man of the Word and of prayer, one whom God could trust with a great and worldwide task. There must be hundreds of missionaries now serving on the mission field of the world, and more hundreds on the home field who have received vision, encouragement, and challenge from Dr. Smith.

We doubt if we will ever see his like again. Such single-hearted purpose and devotion to the Lord Jesus Christ are the unusual today. Such passion for a world that is lost, without God and without hope, is the exception, rather than the rule. Such imagination and daring for the cause of Christ too often is tempered by a conservative, security-conscious attitude on the part of Christian people today. We who know and love Jesus Christ should pause and thank God for such a man as Oswald J. Smith.

But we should also remember that when a task is laid down, another must pick it up. In the words of the great hymn lies the challenge: *"Who follows in his train?"*

Have you heard the Master's call?
Will you go, forsaking all?
Millions still in sin and shame,
Ne'er have heard the Saviour's name.
Some may give, and some may pray,
But for you He calls today;
Will you answer,
"Here am I?"

OJS

APPENDIX

♦♦♦

THE MAN GOD USES

A Vital Message for Christian Workers.
By Oswald J. Smith

I HAVE been trying to think during these past days of the qualities that will enable God to use men in Christian service; and so far as I can discover there are at least eight that are essential. Moreover, I am absolutely convinced that any man who is willing to pay the price may be used of God regardless of talents and gifts. Not perhaps to the extent of some, but certainly to the full limit of his capacity, and if not the fault is his.

Now, it may cost a good deal. God does not always reveal the whole price at once. But when we reach the place where we are so desperately in earnest about it that we are willing to make any sacrifice, then it is that God can begin to use us.

Well I do remember how I walked up and down my room in prayer exclaiming: "Oh, God, use me, use me, no matter what the cost! Gladly will I pay any price if only I may be used of Thee." Are you willing to pay the price?

1. *The man God uses is the man who has but one great purpose in life.* A divided heart can never bring complete satisfaction. The man of mingled interests will seldom make a success of anything. If he would succeed in business he must give the major portion of his time and the best of his thought to his business. It is the man who divides his time between the office and the gambling table who fails. If his affections are divided between his wife and another woman married life is bound to end in disaster. No young man would be satisfied unless he held the supreme place in the heart of the woman whom he would make his wife.

The very same is true of the man who would be used of God, only to a far greater degree. The work alone must claim his whole attention. He has no room for other things. Paul was a man of "one thing." "This one thing I do,'' he exclaims. That was the secret of his success. He had a great surging passion to make known the Gospel, and he gave himself day and night to his work. And in writing to Timothy he urged him to "be diligent in these things; give thyself wholly to them."

The trouble is that men are interested in too many things today to be used of God. I have known college students whose interests were so divided between their studies and girl friends that their lives made no impression whatever. And let me say that no young man can be mightily used of God who is continually spending his evenings, his time and thought in the society of women.

I know of ministers who are in business on the side. Their whole time is not given to their one great work. Before I entered the ministry I purchased a vacant lot for speculative purposes, but after my ordination I sold it as quickly as possible that I might be perfectly free to give my whole thought to my work.

I am not urging that you have no other interests in life. There are duties to which you are bound to give your attention. What I do insist upon is that you make them as few as possible, and above all that you consider them as secondary, thus putting God and His work first and looking upon it as your one great purpose in life.

2. *The man God uses is the man who by God's grace has removed every hindrance from his life.* Now then, you don't need to tell me what it is that hinders God from using you. God knows and you know. You must get right with Him. It may be only a weight or it may be a definite sin, possibly your besetting sin. Perhaps it is impurity in thought, word or deed. Possibly it is pride, jealousy, malice, covetousness, unbelief, or self in one form or another. It may be tobacco. But whatever it is it must be removed before God can use you. Remember it was Achan who caused Israel to fail. Is there an Achan in your heart, a shelf behind the door, a sin that no one sees but God? People think you are what you appear to be, but do they really know you as you are? Dare you withdraw the veil and let them see all? (Isa. 59:1,2).

3. *The man God uses is the man who has placed himself absolutely at God's disposal.* Some of us act as though we were afraid of God, afraid to let Him have full sway. God says, "If any man willeth to do His will." What could the potter do if the clay refused to yield? What could the doctor do if the patient refused to trust? Of what value are insubordinate soldiers?

Well, then, are you yielded? Have you said an eternal "Yes" to God and an eternal "No" to self? Are you dedicated? Have you surrendered all? Has your will been laid down and have you accepted His for your life? Will you go where He wants you to go, and be what He wants you to be? Are you able to sing every verse of Frances Ridley Havergal's great consecration hymn, "Take My Life?" Do you mean it? And can you say with all your heart:

Here Lord, I give myself to Thee,
Friends and time and earthly store;
Soul and body Thine to be—
Wholly Thine for evermore.

4. *The man God uses is the man who has learned how to prevail in prayer.* The men who have been greatly used of God have all been mighty in prayer. As you read their biographies, you discover that the spirit of prayer predominates. Jacob exclaims: "I will not let Thee go except Thou bless me," and hears God say: "Thou hast striven with God and with men and hast prevailed." Jesus in the midst of the greatest activity and opportunity for service withdraws from the multitude and seeks a solitary place in which to pray, sometimes spending whole nights alone with His Father, praying with such anguish of spirit that His sweat turns to blood. And this is the story of every man who has been used of God. Are you willing to pay the price?

You may be marvellously gifted and equipped for the service of God, but if you have not learned how to prevail in prayer, you can never expect God's blessing on your labors. Let me urge upon each one the necessity of withdrawing to the secret place to pray the prevailing prayer, the prayer that affects its objects. We must pray through and get the answer. Oh, for a return to the prayer-life of such men as Bramwell, Oxtoby, Carvasso, John Smith and Finney!

5. *The man God uses is the man who is a student of the Word.* God's Word is your weapon. If you doubt its strength what power can you have in wielding it? It is your only source of information. When the Word of God becomes your meat and drink, your daily study and a very part of yourself, then, and not until then, will you be able to use it as He intends. Do you believe that the text you proclaim is the living, inspired Word of God? And are you confident that it will never return void? God cannot use a man who doubts His Word.

6. *The man God uses is the man who has a vital, living message for a lost world.* You are looking forward to the foreign field. Well, what are you going to tell them? Have you a message? Why are you going?

If your mission is merely one of Social Service, Education, Political Reform, you had better leave it to the social service expert, the school teacher, the doctor and the reformer. If it is to substitute western civilization along with the Christian religion for heathenism, better leave it to government agencies with their systems of uplift and reform.

Ah, no! there is only one message great enough to take us from our homes of comfort, carry us across the seas, and set us down in the midst of persecution, ridicule, sacrifice and loneliness, and that is the message that "Christ died for our sins," the message that "God so loved the world that

He gave His only begotten Son, that whosoever believeth in Him should not perish but have everlasting life," the message of the Cross. Nothing less will suffice. "Go *ye* and preach the Gospel." The rest is the business of the state.

But what message have you for the homeland? Why are you entering the ministry? If it is merely to entertain, you had better turn your work over to the theatres for they can do it better than you can. If it is to educate the people by reading religious essays, better advise them to study Carlyle, Emerson, Browning, and Shakespeare. It will cut down expenses and save them the necessity of coming out in bad weather. Besides they can cultivate a taste for poetry in clubs held for that purpose. Or if it is simply to charm them by the beauty of oratory or great musical compositions, the chautauqua and concert hall will answer better.

Oh, my brother, you have a far greater work than this. The highest, most glorious, and most important of all Callings is yours. The others have their individual vocations but yours embraces all, for you deal with all classes and conditions. Nor have you any time for argument or controversy. Yours is a Message that God has commissioned you to deliver, a Message of life and death, and He will hold you responsible for your stewardship. Oh, that you might realize the greatness of your task!

We are not in the pulpit to please and entertain, nor are we to parade ourselves. "The minstrel who sings before you to show his skill will be praised for his wit, rhymes and voice, but the courier who hurries in breathless, to bring you a message, will be forgotten in the message he brings." Oh, brethren, what do men think of us? Do they say: "What a great sermon!" or "What a great Christ! What a wonderful Saviour!"

Remember we are to represent Jesus, and that means that we must be dead in earnest, for to some our message will mean death, to others Life. Then let us preach as though we mean what we say. A great actor one time explained the difference between actors and ministers by saying: "You clergymen talk about real things as though they were unreal, while we actors talk about unreal things as though they were real."

Listen, men! If you are firmly convinced that "all have sinned," that men are lost, and that Jesus Christ is the only one who can save them, and you go forth to proclaim that message, then I bid you God-speed; and let me tell you, your ministry will be glorious.

Oh, then, let me ask you again: Have you a message that the Holy Spirit honors? Does He convict of sin when you preach? Are souls saved and believers edified? Are you proclaiming man-made sermons or God-given messages? For if your message is born of the Holy Ghost you need never be ashamed. Thousands have flocked to hear it all down the centuries, and thousands will do the same again. Audiences have been held spellbound by the simple Gospel Message, and it still grips. No need to fear. Go forth then and speak, confident of His power.

7. *The man God uses is the man of Faith, who expects results.* The great trouble with the majority of us is that we don't expect anything to happen. We do not look for results. We are content to go on in the same old humdrum way, and if a soul in anguish should cry out: "What must I do to be saved?" we would be dumbfounded.

Now, I want to say that I have never yet been content to see things go on in the usual quiet way. Unless something happened I felt I had failed. I have always expected the extraordinary, nor have I been disappointed.

You remember that young preacher who came to Mr. Spurgeon discouraged because he was not seeing results.

"Why, you don't mean to tell me," exclaimed Spurgeon, "that you expect results every time *you* preach, do you?"

"Well, no," responded the young man, somewhat taken aback.

"Then that is why you don't get them" was the pointed reply.

I notice that when men play football they do not kick the ball at random, but they endeavor to drive it into the goal, and so with hockey. And thank God, we too can have a goal.

I never saw a race where men ran this way and that, all over the field. They had an object in view, and they ran toward a certain point. And we too are in a race, but a race, thank God, for souls.

When a lawyer pleads a case, he does not merely entertain. He is there for a verdict. And, praise God, we are out for a verdict. Nor should we be satisfied without one.

In a shooting match every man fires at a mark. Have we a mark, and do we take aim?

In the days of the Great War recruiting meetings were held, not to entertain, but to secure recruits. Apart from this result the meeting was in vain. Are we looking for recruits for our King, and do we expect some to respond? Let us have faith for definite results.

8. *The man God uses is the man who works in the Anointing of the Holy Spirit.* "Tarry ye at Jerusalem until ye be endued with power from on High." They tarried. "Ye shall receive power when the Holy Ghost is come upon you, and ye shall be my witnesses." And the thought of witnessing without that power never entered their minds.

Read the biographies of God's men and you will discover that each one sought and obtained Enduement of Power from on High. One sermon preached in the Anointing is worth a thousand in the energy of the flesh.

This then, is *the man God uses.* He has but one purpose in life. Every hindrance has been removed. He places himself absolutely at God's disposal. He has learned how to prevail in prayer. He is a student of the Word. He has a vital, living Message for a lost world. He expects results. And he works in the Anointing of the Holy Spirit. Oh, my brethren, let us see to it that we have these eight qualifications in order that God may use us to the fullest possible extent. Then will our Ministry be glorious indeed.

[illegible]EVE

I proclaim the great Evangel,
I proclaim it full and free
God has promised to supply man's every need.
I proclaim complete provision,
I proclaim it from His Word
God has offered life that now is life indeed.

I believe the supernatural,
I believe God intervenes
In the lives of those who trust Him here below.
I believe the Name of Jesus,
I believe the prayer of faith
Will accomplish signs and wonders as I go.

I believe that He is able—
I believe that Jesus saves.
Oh, the joy of knowing One who lives today.
I believe that He is willing,
I believe without a doubt
That He's still the same as when He went away.

I have seen Him save the sinner,
I have seen Him heal the sick,
Fill believers with His Spirit from above.
I have seen Him cast out demons,
I have seen Him calm the storm,
For He still delights to manifest His love.

I accept Him as my Saviour,
I accept Him as my Lord,
He is still the great Physician as of yore.
I accept the Holy Spirit,
I accept the Word of God,
And I'll preach a full salvation evermore.

I am watching for His Coming,
I am watching day by day;
Oh, the joy of that glad meeting in the sky!
I am watching for the Bridegroom,
I am watching for my Lord,
For His Coming now I know is drawing nigh.

Reverend Oswald J. Smith

From *The Prophet,* May–June, 1924. Used by permission.